Intimacy and Spectacle

CONTESTATIONS

*A series edited by*

WILLIAM E. CONNOLLY

A complete list of titles in the series appears at the end of the book.

# Intimacy and Spectacle

*Liberal Theory as Political Education*

Stephen L. Esquith

*Cornell University Press*

Ithaca and London

First published 1994 by Cornell University Press.


Printed in the United States of America
⊖ The paper in this book meets the minimum requirements of the American National Standard for Information Sciences—Permanence of Paper for Printed Library Materials, ANSI Z39.48-1984.


Library of Congress Cataloging-in-Publication Data

Esquith, Stephen L. (Stephen Lawrence), b. 1949
    Intimacy and spectacle : liberal theory as political education /
Stephen L. Esquith.
        p.    cm. — (Contestations)
    Includes bibliographical references (p.      ) and index.
    ISBN 0-8014-2989-7
    1. Liberalism—History.   2. Political socialization—History   3. Political participation—
History.   4. Power (Social sciences)—History   5. Democracy—History   I. Title
II. Series
JC574.E78   1994
320.5′1—dc20                                                          94-16159

*For Chris, Sam, and Sunny*

And what activity the desire of power inspires! What toils it sustains! How it sharpens the perceptions and stores the memory with facts.
—Ralph Waldo Emerson, "Education"

The connections of the ear with vital and out-going thought and emotion are immensely closer and more varied than those of the eye. Vision is a spectator; hearing is a participator.
—John Dewey, *The Public and Its Problems*

# Contents

# Preface

My interpretation of liberal theory has two aspects. The first is critical: liberal theory, I argue, has played an active but neglected role in the making of liberal citizens into clients and consumers and the evolution of power into expert authority in liberal societies. The second goal is more prospective. Through an Emersonian reading of power, I describe how political theory in this context can disrupt both the intimacy of professional-client relations and the consumption of grand political spectacles, so that power and citizenship can be understood in more democratic terms. I want to explain the workings of liberal theory *as* political education and then suggest a more democratic alternative.

It is a pleasure to thank several teachers, friends, and colleagues for their help over the course of this project. Rusty Simonds encouraged my earliest interests in political theory during the late 1960s; those interests still have an important place in this book. More than anyone else, Sheldon Wolin, through his interpretation of political theory in *Politics and Vision* and by his own example, has taught me to take the relation between political theory and political education to heart. My interest in political education began with a dissertation done under his direction. His comments and suggestions on this manuscript were, as always, invaluable.

As the editor of *Political Theory*, Tracy Strong helped me bring some of the basic themes of this book into focus in my "Political Theory and Political Education," which appeared in the issue of May 1992. Martin Benjamin, Roger Meiners, and Dick Peterson, my colleagues at Michigan State University, commented on parts of the manuscript. It is much improved thanks to them.

Without Bill Connolly's detailed comments the book simply would not have reached completion. I could not have asked for a more generous and critical editor. Roger Haydon of Cornell University Press made several helpful suggestions as the manuscript took final form; thanks to him, the main idea is more distinct. Alice Bennett's copyediting cleared away much of the dead wood; thanks to her, many of the specific arguments are clearer. I am also grateful to Teresa Jesionowski of Cornell University Press and Jim Isaak for their help preparing the final draft. Michigan State University has provided regular research support and a classroom in which to test the idea that political theory and political education belong together. To the university and its students I owe a deep debt of gratitude.

STEPHEN L. ESQUITH

*East Lansing, Michigan*

Intimacy and Spectacle

# Introduction

In his 1987 performance before the congressional committee investigating the Iran-contra affair, Oliver North comforted his audience at the same time that he dazzled and shocked them. The climax came when he explained his failure to ask National Security Adviser John Poindexter why he had not discussed with the president raising money for the Nicaraguan contras and selling arms to Iran in return for the release of United States hostages.

> First of all, I am not in the habit of questioning my superiors. If he deemed it not to be necessary to ask the President, I saluted smartly and charged up the hill. . . .
>
> I don't believe that what we did even under those circumstances is wrong or illegal. I told you I thought it was a good idea to begin with. I still think it was a good idea, counsel.

Then, when asked why the president had dismissed him if what he was doing was such a good idea, North stole the show:

> Let me just make one thing very clear, counsel. This lieutenant colonel is not going to challenge a decision of the Commander in Chief for whom I still work, and I am proud to work for that Commander in Chief, and if the Commander in Chief tells this lieutenant colonel to go stand in the corner and sit on his head, I will do so. And if the Commander in Chief decides to dismiss me from the NSC staff, this lieutenant colonel will proudly salute and say, "thank you for the opportunity to have served," and go, and I am not going to criticize his decision no matter how he relieves me, sir.[1]

1 Quoted in Theodore Draper, *A Very Thin Line: The Iran-Contra Affairs* (New York: Hill and Wang, 1991), pp. 549–50.

1

North's heroic posturing transformed a question about Reagan's decision to fire him into a question about professional duty. Here was North, the very model of a professional soldier, ready to give his life in battle for the commander in chief, and the Democratic Congress was trying to trip him up. The image proved irresistible.

Politics in contemporary liberal societies is punctuated by intimate spectacles. In the United States, the most familiar are televised debates and hearings. In watching the army-McCarthy hearings, the Kennedy-Nixon debates, Watergate, and the Iran-contra affair, viewers feel that candidates and witnesses are confiding in them as they shape public policies. When spectacles fail to materialize, they are often simulated: experts testify on cue about the effects of capital punishment, the dangers of genetic engineering, the limits of free speech, and other hard choices that professionals and their clients face or about the delicate balances that public policymakers must achieve.

These intimate spectacles condense the normal course of political events, in which personal contact with professionals who can suggest and legitimate political grievances alternates with the consumption of public programs designed by experts. What makes the North case unusual is the way it combines the intimacy of clientism and the spectacle of consumerism, which ordinarily are more loosely intertwined.

The siting of a new toxic waste dump, for example, can trigger intimate contacts between clients and professionals as well as public spectacles featuring community activists, scientific experts, and government officials. As clients, parents consult family doctors about the effects toxic wastes might have on their children, and business owners ask their lawyers for advice on liability. Meanwhile, activists publicize past illegal dumping, file lawsuits, and mobilize grassroots protests; scientists testify about the risks to life and limb; and government officials make amends or defend their records. Intimacy and spectacle seldom crystallize around an individual personality. Instead, there is a complex pattern of clientism and consumerism, the social practices that constitute expert authority.

This pattern of intimacy and spectacle sets the pace and tone of the politics of policymaking in liberal society. Citizens are not necessarily rendered completely passive by the pronouncements of expert officials or the personal care of professionals. As clients, they can seek out second opinions and file malpractice suits; as consumers, they can organize effective boycotts and public education campaigns. Often they do not resist in these ways, but this is not the issue — at least not the issue I want to examine. What is important to me are the orientations toward power and citizenship that clientism and consumerism presuppose and the way these orientations have arisen.

What has happened in environmental policymaking also has occurred when public elementary schools have been closed, halfway houses for disabled persons opened, and abortion clinics picketed. Power ebbs and flows in liberal societies as citizens respond to the advice of professionals and the presentations of experts and advocates, sometimes on a grand scale as in the Iran-contra affair, but more often in local events where the guarded trust of clients in professionals and the skeptical consumption of symbols and values sustain and sometimes inflame one another.

Take *The City of Cleburne, Texas v. Cleburne Living Center, Inc.*, decided by the United States Supreme Court on July 1, 1985, and described by Martha Minow.

> The city of Cleburne, Texas, refused to grant a building permit for a residential group home for mentally retarded people. A city zoning ordinance required a special permit for the construction of "hospitals for the insane or feeble minded, or alcoholic or drug addicts, or penal or corrections institutions." To receive a permit, an applicant had to obtain "the signatures of the property owners within two hundred feet of the property to be used." When the Cleburne Living Center sought such signatures, neighboring property owners objected to the proposed construction and thereby prevented the applicants from building their home.[2]

Professing concern for the health and safety of the residents of the proposed group home as well as that of other residents of the area, "neighboring property owners" tried to protect their own property values, which they saw as threatened. Lawyers and advocates for the home argued that the history of treatment of the mentally retarded in the United States warranted "heightened" judicial scrutiny of alleged discrimination. Property owners argued for a more "reasonable" approach: local government should be allowed to make distinctions between persons to protect the well-being of the community.

This constitutional dispute over the meaning of the equal protection guarantee, Minow correctly notes, was really about the power to label other people as different. In this case the advocates for the Cleburne Living Center held the view that all persons deserve an opportunity to live independently. Independence, however, does not mean isolation. Mentally retarded adults are no different from other adults: they need a community within which to develop their own identities. But the property owners saw an important difference between the community they belonged to, in which their identities depended on everyone's maintaining property

---

[2] Martha Minow, *Making All the Difference: Inclusion, Exclusion, and American Law* (Ithaca: Cornell University Press, 1990), p. 102.

values, and the group home, which would perform a similar function for retarded adults. The majority of justices on the Supreme Court accepted the property owners' labels but held that in this case the dangers cited were not peculiar to group homes for the retarded. Therefore there was no reasonable basis for denying a permit to this group while allowing other risky groups to build.[3]

Just beneath this narrow holding lies the characteristic modern liberal orientation toward citizenship and power. Citizens in this case are defined in terms of their classification by professional experts (mentally retarded), their status as consumers (property owners), and their own counterinterpretations of the prerogatives attached to these roles. Similarly, the power that experts (doctors, lawyers, and professional advocates) exercise depends on their representation of the history of past discrimination, the meaning of mental retardation, projected fluctuations in the housing market, and citizens' ability to protect their rights as clients and advance their consumer interests in court. The *Cleburne* case illustrates how political conflicts in liberal societies revolve around the constitution of expert authority by clients, consumers, and professionals in and outside government, whether or not they end up in court.

How have citizens in liberal societies acquired this orientation toward power and this understanding of themselves as cautious clients or skeptical consumers? It has been a gradual process that cannot be attributed to manipulation or greed. These political roles depend on a certain practical reasoning acquired through a political education, to which liberal theories themselves have made essential contributions.

Much of liberalism's stature as an enduring achievement of the Enlightenment has been due to its appreciation of the political importance of education, but liberal theorists still have not recognized their own significance as political educators. When we read liberal theory *as* political education, we can understand the evolution of political power into expert authority and the making of liberal citizens into clients and consumers as integral parts of the history of liberalism, not as distortions of liberal ideals.

This reading of liberal theory also casts a new, critical light on the tenuous relation between liberalism and democracy. Expert authority, clientism, and consumerism dominate politics in liberal societies. Public spaces in which democratic citizens can examine where these social practices are taking them have been crowded out by specialized policymaking arenas for experts, clients, and consumers and overshadowed by spectacular political images. Liberal theory's methods of deliberation and the political orien-

[3] 473 U.S. 445-46.

tations they foster have contributed to this weakening of democratic life.

At the same time, liberal theory as political education suggests a way of moving beyond this antagonism between liberalism and democracy. When we center political education within both liberal theory and democratic politics, we no longer have to think of democracy as primarily a system of majority rule that threatens individual liberties. The remedy for the politics of policymaking is not more (or less) participation for citizens as they are—that is, as experts, clients, and consumers—but a more democratic political education that enables them to understand liberal society's forms of political power and recognize the limits of its modes of citizenship. The intersection of democracy and liberalism is to be understood not in terms of an institutional compromise between majority rule and minority rights, but rather in terms of a new orientation toward power that is poised enough to contest expert authority and hear the voices that the politics of policymaking domesticates.

My thesis, then, is that over the past century the liberal tradition has been a powerful form of political education in mixed corporatist and pluralist political economies, especially the United States and Great Britain.[4] This is true despite the partisan assaults on liberal ideology, the erosion of liberal social programs, and the selective deregulation of major industries at the national level during the Reagan and Thatcher years. Precisely because the social practices of liberal societies have become more contested and liberal regulative principles more controversial, the methods of philosophical reasoning developed by liberal theorists have had to play a more active mediating role. More specifically, these methods have expanded and revised the speech genres of policy analysis and professional ethics, and this accounts for liberal theory's continued importance as political education.

The argument for this thesis is divided into three parts: theory, tradition, and critique.

Part 1 of the book presents the main features of liberal theory *as* political education. In addition I suggest a conception of democratic political education that serves as the basis for my later critique of liberal theory and as the starting point for an alternative democratic theory.

In chapter 1 I briefly define the key terms of the argument. Some (*power* and *citizenship*) are familiar, and I alert readers to the various usages they have in my argument. Other terms (*social practices*, *speech genres*, and *philo-*

---

[4] Compare Andrew Shonfield, *Modern Capitalism: The Changing Balance of Public and Private Power* (Oxford: Oxford University Press, 1965) and Charles S. Maier, *Recasting Bourgeois Europe: Stabilization in France, Germany, and Italy in the Decade after World War I* (Princeton: Princeton University Press, 1975).

*sophical mediation*) have special meanings. In chapter 2, using these terms, I distinguish between a political theory *of* political education and political theory *as* political education and between the traditional and the modern problems of liberal political education. Humanistic corporatism, I argue, is the general structure within which the modern problem of liberal political education—teaching clients and consumers how to trust in expert authority—has appeared and modern liberal theory as political education has operated as a mediating philosophical method. With these distinctions in hand, I introduce another kind of political orientation, the orientation of the reader. I argue that how one reads political theory depends on an orienting metaphor toward it, and that some orienting metaphors are more sensitive than others to the notion of political theory as political education. The liberal orientation toward power and citizenship has been reinforced by an orientation toward liberal theory that ignores its power to mediate the conflicts of clientism and consumerism.

"Moral philosophy," John Rawls believes, "is Socratic."[5] In chapter 3 I examine the humanistic methods of modern liberal theorists, especially their methods of Socratic dialogue, in order to explain the idea of liberal theory as political education more fully. I use the example of the college classroom to illustrate how humanistic methods of modern liberal theory have prompted citizens to trust expert authority within certain broad limits. Then, anticipating my concluding discussion of democratic theory as political education, I contrast these methods of practical reasoning with what I argue is a democratic method that is more concerned about its own relation to power and also more critical of citizenship in a mixed corporatist and pluralist society.

Part 2 is a detailed interpretation of the tradition of liberal theory as political education. In chapter 4 I review the contrasting political theories of Thomas Hobbes and Immanuel Kant as mediating forms of political education. Although neither Hobbes nor Kant is noted for a theory of political education, I argue that each sensed that political theory could function within the authoritative speech genres of liberal society to resolve certain conflicts and orient citizens toward particular forms of power. Kant was more successful but much less forthcoming than Hobbes in trying to develop a method of practical reasoning with this kind of power, and some of the Socratic elements in his theory anticipate Mill and Rawls. Hobbes's work has hardly been forgotten, but its importance for modern decision theory points up its limitations as a mediating philosophical method.

---

[5] John Rawls, *A Theory of Justice* (Cambridge: Harvard University Press, 1971), p. 49.

In chapters 5 and 6 I turn to the work of John Stuart Mill and John Rawls. The *Autobiography* plays a leading role in my interpretation of Mill. It symbolizes and also contributes to the exemplary character of his theorizing. Mill represents his own progress from Socratic engagement to Platonic maturity as the development of an exemplary political individual capable of telling the difference between Good and Evil, and inspiring others to do the same. In his 1867 inaugural address at the University of St. Andrews, Mill closed by telling his audience that the "ultimate end" of their studies was to make them "more effective combatants in the great fight which never ceases to rage between Good and Evil."[6] The message has not been forgotten. Rawls's Socratic method of practical reasoning is more disembodied but equally important in the context of the mixed corporatist society of the late twentieth century. Rawls has incorporated elements of Kantian casuistry and Mill's emphasis on personal identification into an abstract method of practical reasoning. This method sets wide limits on the exercise of expert authority within mixed corporatist societies by teaching citizens how to compose "internal dialogues" of their own among a finite set of domesticated inner voices.

Part 3 expands the criticism of liberal theory as political education and provides a fuller statement of a democratic alternative to liberal theory as it has actually developed within humanistic corporatism.

In chapter 7 I offer an allegorical description of the modern shopping mall to criticize the exemplary images that liberal theory has highlighted. This allegory parallels my earlier interpretation of the college classroom as a typical policymaking arena in which trusting voices are produced. Together these two settings suggest why liberal theory as political education has failed to engender the character needed to judge either the sights or the sounds of the politics of policymaking from a democratic perspective. Where can we turn for help? In chapter 8 I argue that Ralph Waldo Emerson is one resource for democratic theory.

Liberal theory has rested on an Emersonian interpretation of the conscientious theorist that values sight as the primary faculty for political judgment and artificially confines political dialogue to dialects that depreciate the experiences of those who are consigned to the risk pools in a politics of policymaking. A new democratic theory centered on the task of political education can rely on a different Emerson: the synesthetic Emerson who encourages citizens to stay in touch with one another so that

---

[6] John Stuart Mill, "Inaugural Address Delivered to the University of St. Andrews," in *The Collected Works of John Stuart Mill*, ed. John M. Robson (Toronto: University of Toronto Press, 1963–91), 21:256.

they can hear their own voices more clearly and thus keep their balance.[7] Like Emerson's "sturdy lad" who "feels no shame in not studying a profession" and who "teams it, farms it, peddles, keeps a school, preaches, edits a newspaper, goes to Congress, buys a township," today's democratic citizen must also be "like a cat [that] always falls on his feet."[8] Emersonian democratic theory would teach citizens how to read what Emerson describes as the compensatory and circular laws of power and how to listen sensitively to the accents of others so as to hear and judge the power in their own voices. This is what I mean by democratic political poise. If the language we use to compose ourselves for democratic politics does not address the dynamics of power and the unfamiliar accents of others, we are likely to overstate the dangers or benefits of power and demonize those who do not speak in a domesticated political voice.[9]

The challenge for democratic theory as political education today is to find a way to transpose this conception of poise. How will democratic citizens learn to control expert authority and restore their faith in the liberal virtues of tolerance and reasonableness in discussion? Chapter 8 closes with four contemporary examples of this Emersonian political character, its limitations, and its relation to these liberal virtues. The first case involves the relationship between a lawyer and her client; the second is the example I began with, the Iran-contra affair. These cases illustrate how, through an Emersonian reading of power, democratic citizens can put clientism's promised intimacy and consumerism's imagined pleasures into a more critical perspective. The last two examples briefly suggest how liberal moral virtues might benefit from a democratic Emersonian education in power.

This is certainly not the only challenge facing democratic theory. The democratic reform of economic institutions, the decentralization of gov-

---

[7] I do not mean to imply that Emerson himself experienced synesthesia. My figurative use of synesthesia does not presuppose that there is an explanation for it that is not reducible to either semantic confusion or neuropathology. See Richard E. Cytowic, *Synesthesia: A Union of the Senses* (New York: Springer-Verlag, 1989), for one such explanation.

[8] Ralph Waldo Emerson, "Self-Reliance," in *Essays: First Series*, in *Complete Works of Ralph Waldo Emerson*, 2d ed., ed. Joel Myerson (New York: AMS Press, 1979), 2:76.

[9] On the dominance of visual metaphors in Western philosophy in general, see Michael Levin, ed., *Modernity and the Hegemony of Vision* (Berkeley and Los Angeles: University of California Press, 1993), and Martin Jay, *Downcast Eyes: The Denigration of Vision in Twentieth-Century French Thought* (Berkeley and Los Angeles: University of California Press, 1993). A democratic theory more sensitive to the dynamics of political education and its shortcomings in modern liberal society would not simply substitute listening for seeing. A democratic political education obviously requires a mixture of both. But, I will argue, in order to appreciate and criticize liberal theory as political education, we have to listen to the voices it has favored as well as recognize the images it has more self-consciously highlighted.

ernment bureaucracies, and the development of new vehicles for mobilizing citizen participation outside the existing party systems are the most obvious tasks for democratic theorists to address. But to accomplish these tasks democratically, citizens must also learn how they have grown accustomed to thinking about politics as clients, consumers, and professionals. Simply expanding the reach of liberal citizens as they are will not be enough to make these concrete institutional changes.

PART I

THEORY

CHAPTER ONE

# Terms of the Argument

Power and citizenship are the focal points for this critical interpretation
of liberal theory as political education. What makes individuals in a liberal society citizens is their shared practical orientation toward power:
where they think power comes from, what they think they can and should
do with it and about it, and finally what they actually do together based on
these beliefs. Modern liberal theory has been an education in power, and
its presence as such has been largely overlooked within liberal societies.

After distinguishing the various usages of power and citizenship that my
argument depends on, I contrast classical liberal theorists' understandings
of political education with the less searching views of political education of
modern nineteenth- and twentieth-century liberal theorists. Then, in the
last section, I show the relationship between my own approach to political theory and similar theoretical projects. I compare the way I use the
term *social practices* with the ways Rawls and Foucault use it; I explain my
appropriation of Bakhtin's notion of speech genres; and I explain how liberal philosophical methods of practical reasoning bridge the gap between
theory and practice.

## Power and Citizenship

I use the term *power* to refer to five political phenomena. Other forms
of power exist, of course, but I am interested in political power only, and
only within liberal societies.[1] Once I have identified these forms of power,

[1] When I use the term *power*, as in the power of the state or the power of public opinion, I
include both the resources of the agent and the contextual constraints that make it possible
for the agent to use those resources effectively. See Thomas E. Wartenberg, *The Forms of
Power: From Domination to Transformation* (Philadelphia: Temple University Press, 1990).

I will sketch their relation to different modes of citizenship. None of this is true by definition. These terms introduce the argument, and their promises have to be redeemed later.

*State power* is the power of the government and its agents or unofficial surrogates to carry out protective, regulative, and administrative functions. State power can be very extensive, as it is when the state is largely responsible for social welfare and a large national security system. Or it can be a more limited instrument of protection. Both Lockean liberals and most Marxists have argued that this is the dominant form of political power in liberal societies. They disagree only about whose interests, needs, and desires it serves.

*Public opinion* is a more diffuse form of instrumental political power. It is sometimes broadly identified with dominant social customs and prevailing popular values. At other times it refers more narrowly to political attitudes and beliefs that have been measured using survey research techniques. The power of public opinion is the power of the majority and of those who represent majority opinions to impose their values and social customs on others, with varying degrees of cooperation, acquiescence, and resistance. Public opinion can be a tyranny to individuals who directly dissent from it, but for most citizens in liberal society the hegemony of public opinion is not experienced so acutely.

*Organized interest groups* have the power to represent themselves effectively within the electoral political process. They use their financial resources, organizing skills, and marketing and advertising techniques to sway public opinion and influence, if not to temporarily control, state power. This process is described by twentieth-century liberal theorists as pluralist bargaining, but it can be traced back to Locke's famous *Letter on Toleration*. Some organized interest groups can influence state power outside electoral politics as well, but their power within the policymaking process depends on another form of power—expert authority.

The power of *expert authorities* who work as government officials and professionals derives from what they know (and are thought to know) and where they sit. Although some experts, such as pollsters and public opinion analysts, exercise power as interpreters of state power, public opinion, and interest group activities in electoral politics, most are involved in a more complex set of relationships based on the trust of clients and consumers outside electoral politics. This is the power of expert authorities to mediate among a restricted group of highly disciplined interest groups and government agencies in the formulation and implementation of complex public policies. This activity is often called neocorporatism, in contrast to pluralist politics. It ranges from the management of natural and human resources to the disposal of toxic wastes.

Finally, *political theories* themselves have played an important role in the constitution and exercise of political power in liberal societies. My thesis that liberal theory has operated as a form of political education is an attempt to emphasize this neglected dimension of power. Theory is not a polemical instrument that can be used like state power to serve specific interests; nor is it reducible to rhetoric on a par with public opinion, even though some liberal intellectuals write polemically and make rhetorical speeches. The methods of practical reason that give liberal theory's utterances their accents and overtones are not reducible to either polemical barbs or flashes of rhetorical wit. They are peculiar to these particular theoretical utterances. The power of liberal theory has been the power to define certain modes of citizenship by orienting individuals toward power, including its own, through methods of practical reason.

What, then, are the primary modes of citizenship in liberal society?[2] The most familiar is the *private citizen.* Private citizens are episodic voters and even more episodic participants in public life who separate public power from private happiness and see the former as a necessary but never sufficient means to the latter. Private citizens think of power in terms of conflicts between the state on one side and private interest groups on the other. During periods of heightened political activity, private citizens also fear that the power of public opinion as well as the state might become a threat to individual rights, especially rights to privacy and property.

Citizens in liberal society also think of themselves as clients of official experts or professionals involved in providing public goods and services, or they think of themselves as consumers of these goods and services. *Political clients and consumers* are oriented toward neocorporatist or mixed corporatist forms of power, and the goods and services they value derive their political significance in several ways. They can, for example, be political because they are publicly subsidized, directly provided by government, or simply necessary for informed access to political institutions and practices. Clientism and consumerism are social practices that cut across the public/private distinction that defines political space for private citizens.

The term *Socratic citizens* refers to one aspect of the complex and ambivalent orientation of liberal theorists toward power. Socratic citizens have a heightened and peculiar ambivalence toward state power, interest group politics, and public opinion. Unlike private citizens, Socratic citizens feel a strong responsibility for liberal society as a whole but an even stronger moral obligation to certain ethical values, including moral dialogue and tolerance for individual conscience. At the same time as they

[2] Like power, citizenship can be analyzed in more abstract terms than I have used here. For a useful summary, see Will Kymlicka and Wayne Norman, "Return of the Citizen: A Survey of Recent Work on Citizenship Theory," *Ethics* 104 (January 1994): 352–81.

have a deep respect for self-rule, they have a firm belief that genuine experts should be trusted. The Socratic citizen is a model for skeptical private citizens and in other respects is a mediator between experts, clients, and consumers.

In one sense the term *Emersonian citizens* refers to another aspect of the political identity of those members of liberal society who exercise theoretical power. Emersonian citizens are more hostile to official political life than are Socratic citizens and more independent of other citizens. Self-reliant Emersonian citizens approach power through personal experience and believe that individual moral judgment must be based on a clear, unobstructed view of the present and fashioned out of a pristine natural language. Unlike Socratic citizens, Emersonian citizens are apt to deny the existence of their own theoretical power. They believe their vision is free of the corrupting influences of power. Liberal political theorists are a blend of these Socratic and Emersonian modes of citizenship.

Finally, as liberal societies have matured over the past two centuries, all four types of citizens described above arguably can be considered *democratic citizens*. They have certain rights as free and equal citizens and certain minimum obligations that we associate with political self-rule. But I will use the term in a more restricted sense to refer to citizens capable of understanding the interconnections between the various forms of power in liberal society and committed to transforming power so that citizens in general have more control over it than they do under the current mixed system of pluralism and corporatism, no matter how humane. Democratic citizens are not full-time, public-spirited participants. It is their orientation toward power, not their optimism or the amount of time they spend together, that sets them apart from other citizens in liberal society. In this sense, I argue, democratic citizens are also Emersonian, but not the way liberal citizens are.

Lined up in a row, these key words are lifeless. They have to be understood in the context of a tradition in liberal theory that places power at the center of a citizen's education and then in the context of liberal politics, which depends on citizens' having that education in power.

## Political Education in the Liberal Tradition

Political traditions in the modern world are necessarily a product of purposeful, self-conscious reconstruction. Liberalism is no exception; it too relies on a reconstruction of the past and a vision of the future to achieve its ends and maintain its legitimacy. The purpose that will guide my reconstruction of liberal theory as political education is the need to reorient liberal citizens toward power so they think of it as something they produce and take responsibility for rather than something whose products they skeptically consume or someone whose authority they guardedly trust.

The relation of liberal theory to an education in power begins with Thomas Hobbes. Notorious for his mechanistic view of power,[3] Hobbes realized that power comes in many forms, from reputation and eloquence to science, and that they cannot all be reduced to the causes and effects of matter in motion. This is especially true of political power. The "greatest of human powers, is that which is compounded of the powers of most men, united by consent, in one person, natural, or civil, that has use of all their powers depending on his will; such as is the power of a commonwealth."[4] It is this awesome political power, as Hobbes liked to say, that liberal citizens must consent to if they are to preserve their freedom and security. And consent, even in Hobbes's world, is more than a matter of two bodies colliding.

Hobbes knew that arranging for the acceptance of political power was not going to be easy. When feeling themselves "in the precincts of battle," Hobbes argued, "men" will seek to band together (*Leviathan*, p. 88). On the other hand, their passions for competitive economic advantage, reputation, and an equally natural distrust ("diffidence") of one another will drive them apart (p. 112). Politics seems to offer no solution to this deep-seated problem. And so Hobbes, like later liberal theorists, sought an education for politics prior to and outside the precincts of battle. If liberal citizens can learn to act rationally based on those apolitical passions that "incline" them toward peace ("fear of death; desire of such things as are necessary to commodious living; and a hope by their industry to obtain them"), they will be more likely to trust one another (p. 116). Hobbes thought that with the right "prospective glasses, namely moral and civil science," to counteract their "notable multiplying glasses, that is their passions and self-love" (p. 170), "the children of pride" would know enough to submit to "the King of the Proud" Leviathan state, thereby allaying each other's fears (p. 307). Once equipped, they would be able to protect themselves from their own "perpetual and restless desire of power after power that ceaseth only in death" (pp. 85–86).

The problem with Hobbes is that his conception of power-packed, power-hungry individuals makes his rationalist solution to the problem of political education implausible. Prospective glasses are not enough to curb the habits of Hobbesian "man." Hobbes suspected as much himself and struggled with other approaches to political education, from command-

---

[3] Thomas Hobbes, *De corpore*, in *The English Works of Thomas Hobbes*, ed. William Molesworth, 11 vols. (London: J. Bohn, 1839–45), 1:120–21. (Hereafter cited as *EW.*)

[4] Thomas Hobbes, *Leviathan*, in *EW*, 3:74.

ments to introspection, with equally limited success before succumbing to an illiberal authoritarianism.

John Locke took the liberal parts of Hobbes's argument two steps further. First, he shifted the focus of liberal theory away from the power of individuals onto the power of the state. Instead of asking how liberal citizens can learn to trust each other enough to erect such a sovereign, Locke suggested that the real problem for citizens, who already enjoy some degree of social peace and who are not as volatile and hard-driving as Hobbes assumed, is how far they should trust the government. Locke argued that it was reasonable for them to trust in those who hold political power, despite all the dangers and uncertainties, as long as power was divided so that officeholders would not be able to judge their own cases. He believed that this kind of qualified trust neither could nor should be avoided if citizens want to have a say in political life.[5]

The second innovation in Locke's account of political education is his focus on the "mastery" of desires, not just their proper channeling. In *Some Thoughts concerning Education*, Locke wrote that "the Principle of all Vertue and Excellency lies in a Power of denying our selves the Satisfaction of our own Desires, where Reason does not authorize them."[6] Citizens are not at the mercy of their passions, and so political education can be "principling." Reason can override the passions, not just scout and spy for them as Hobbes thought.[7] Although all citizens, rich and poor, can benefit from this kind of education in "mastery," the main task of political education in a liberal society is to educate those entrusted with the power of the state. But they have to understand its particular abuses and temptations. Locke's conception of political education as the mastery of desire is modeled on his general theory of education, but it is not a method for cultivating democratic citizenship. It is a program for "enlightened paternalism."[8]

While Locke narrowed and shifted the focus of political education, he remained convinced that its object must be power. Jean-Jacques Rousseau shared this fundamental belief that political education is an education in power, but unlike Locke, Rousseau wanted to extend political education to all citizens and grant them a share in power. Rather than seducing or cor-

[5] See, for example, John Locke, *Two Treatises of Government*, ed. Peter Laslett (New York: New American Library, 1965), II, secs. 142, 171, pp. 409, 428. Also John Dunn, " 'Trust' in the Politics of John Locke," in his *Rethinking Modern Political Theory* (Cambridge: Cambridge University Press, 1985).

[6] Quoted in Peter A. Schouls, *Reasoned Freedom: John Locke and Enlightenment* (Ithaca: Cornell University Press, 1992), p. 207.

[7] Hobbes, *Leviathan*, p. 61.

[8] Gordon S. Wood, *The Radicalism of the American Revolution* (New York: Vintage Books, 1991), p. 149.

rupting them, national power would unite them. "It is," Rousseau argued in *The Government of Poland*, "education that you must count on to shape the soul of the citizens in a national pattern and so to direct their opinions, their likes, and dislikes that they shall be patriotic by inclination, passionately, of necessity."[9] Rousseau's conception of political education, as this statement reveals, does not uncouple power and desire. Through participation in a rich political culture, citizens master their individual desires for the sake of love for their country.

Unwilling to accept Hobbes's reductionist conception of persons as volatile matter in motion or Rousseau's romantic view of participation in the constitution of national forms of power, Immanuel Kant set a new tone for modern liberal theory. He accepted Locke's view of the need to organize state power correctly, but he believed that beyond this task liberal citizens had no need for an education in power. Kant's famous remark that the "problem of organizing a state, however hard it may seem, can be solved even for a race of devils, if only they are intelligent," though hyperbole, has attracted liberal theorists ever since without fully convincing them.[10] As long as the basic institutions of society do not make it too difficult for citizens capable of rational and informed decisions to trust those in power enough so they can carry on with the rest of their lives, a broadly based political education is unnecessary. Subsequent liberal theorists such as John Stuart Mill and John Rawls have agreed with Kant that there is much more to be said about education from a moral point of view if persons are to treat each other with respect, and political education can be reduced to knowing when to trust those who can hold power without abusing it.

Under the influence of Locke and Kant, modern liberal theory has continued to minimize its entanglement with power.[11] This aversion to any direct confrontation with power has led to a revival of interest in the work of Ralph Waldo Emerson. Like Kant, Emerson at times had a strong antipathy for power and an even stronger aversion to entrusting it to ordinary people: "Don't trust children with edged tools. Don't trust man, great God, with more power than he has, until he has learned to use that little better. What a hell should we make of the world, if we could do what we would!"[12] John Stuart Mill, in his criticism of the unequal distribution

9 Jean-Jacques Rousseau, *The Government of Poland*, trans. Willmoore Kendall (Indianapolis: Bobbs-Merrill, 1972), p. 19.

10 Immanuel Kant, "Perpetual Peace," in *On History*, ed. Lewis White Beck (Indianapolis: Bobbs-Merrill, 1963), p. 112.

11 Dunn, " 'Trust' in the Politics of John Locke," p. 34.

12 Ralph Waldo Emerson, journal entry for January 20, 1832, in *Emerson in His Journals*, ed. Joel Porte (Cambridge: Harvard University Press, 1982), p. 81.

of power in the family, revealed a surprisingly similar view. "The love of power and the love of liberty are in eternal antagonism. Where there is least liberty, the passion for power is the most ardent and unscrupulous. The desire of power over others can only cease to be a depraving agency among mankind, when each of them individually is able to do without it." [13] What liberal citizens need, according to Emersonian liberal theory, is a way of seeing the world that is untouched by power. The Emersonian liberal theorist strives for a detachment and self-transparency that renders unspeakable any admission of seducing citizens into using and enjoying power.

Two points should be made about this liberal tradition. First, there is something puzzling about the image of the liberal citizen it projects. Ideal liberal citizens are supposed to know enough about the dangers of pride and envy to keep a watchful eye on each other and the state, and they are supposed to be unbiased toward their fellow citizens as long as those citizens show the same restraint they do in the pursuit of private pleasures. Liberal citizens are supposed to know whom to trust and how far to trust them. But this is surely political knowledge that has to be learned. It is knowledge of what kinds of conflicts and disagreements the political community can withstand, what the state can be trusted to settle impartially, and what kinds of persons are likely to understand and respect these limits. It may be "tacit political knowledge" [14] in the sense that it is not part of any constitution, code, or curriculum. But liberal citizens still will need to know how power affects those who hold it as well as those who do not. They still need an education in power.

Second, pride and envy are no longer obstacles to political trust in the way Hobbes and Locke thought. Political order is no longer threatened by Hobbesian "masterless men" who are too proud to submit to the dominion of others. The state is also no longer so clearly distinct from other structures of power that its officers cannot avoid judging their own cases. In liberal societies the state is part of a maze of competing policymaking arenas. Economic class conflict no longer openly rages in the United States and Great Britain as it did in the mid-nineteenth century, when defenders of the status quo characterized the poor as simply envious. In modern liberal societies like these over the past century, pride has become an interest group slogan and envy has been managed through trickle-down market-

[13] John Stuart Mill, *The Subjection of Women*, in *The Collected Works of John Stuart Mill*, ed. John M. Robson (Toronto: University of Toronto Press, 1963-91), 21:338. (Hereafter cited as *CW*.)

[14] See Sheldon S. Wolin, "Political Theory as a Vocation," in *Machiavelli and the Nature of Political Thought*, ed. Martin Fleisher (New York: Atheneum, 1972), p. 45.

ing techniques that create the illusion of upward mobility.[15] The path to political trust lies elsewhere, and the obstacles are more difficult to decode.

Modern liberal citizens are primarily clients and consumers whose voices are a mixture of deference, interest group protest, appeals to procedural fairness, and requests for personal care. When it is not conducted in the relative intimacy of professional relationships between clients and experts, where tone of voice can make the difference, politics is a spectacle in which Manichean images of enemies, leaders, and social problems compete for market shares and consumer loyalty.[16] For these constituents, government is just part of a fragmented network of policymaking arenas dominated by the domesticated voices of clientism and the bright lights of consumerism. Occasionally events such as the Iran-contra affair bring clients and consumers together; but these moments are ephemeral, surely no improvement from a democratic point of view.

Unlike similar criticisms that have been made by Michel Foucault and Jürgen Habermas, this reading of liberal society emphasizes liberal theory's methods of reasoning, not its regimenting impersonality. It is an interpretation of liberal theory that relies on a Bakhtinian conception of dialogue and the orchestral complexity of the self to explain how the boundaries of politics, the use of power, and most of all the education of citizens have been affected by liberal theory. The voices that liberal theories have recognized and the images they have magnified have been part of a dialogical, but democratically inadequate, construction of expert authority and citizenship.

Can this traditional liberal orientation toward power be made more democratic? Emerson, I argue, had a more complex and potentially more democratic view of power and political education than liberal theory has recognized. In contrast to liberal theory's Emersonian ideal of immaculate perception, there is another Emerson explicitly interested in the dynamics of power and the political education of citizens in a democratic society. For this Emerson, the value of self-reliance is not a plea for individual Millian progress.[17] Democratic self-reliance is the goal of a political education

---

[15] Fred Hirsch, *Social Limits to Growth* (Cambridge: Harvard University Press, 1977), p. 167.

[16] See Michael Rogin, *Ronald Reagan, the Movie and Other Episodes in Political Demonology* (Berkeley and Los Angeles: University of California Press, 1987), and Murray Edelman, *Constructing the Political Spectacle* (Chicago: University of Chicago Press, 1988).

[17] Stanley Cavell emphasizes Emerson's resemblance to Mill in *Conditions Handsome and Unhandsome: The Constitution of Emersonian Perfectionism* (Chicago: University of Chicago Press, 1990). For a reading of Emerson closer to my own, see Christopher Lasch, *The True and Only Heaven: Progress and Its Critics* (New York: W. W. Norton, 1991), pp. 243–77.

in power that emphasizes the importance of poise and sensitivity, not universal mutual respect, where poise is the ability to keep your balance on a crowded, rolling political surface and sensitivity is the ability to hear what you sound like to others when you lose your footing or they lose theirs.

Liberal traditions are not a series of ideals or "switchmen," to use Weber's metaphor, shuttling society along the tracks history has provided.[18] Nor are liberal traditions glacial forces carving their signatures into the social terrain. A liberal tradition is a more fluid set of practices and ways of reasoning that changes course like a river, picks up new material, and deposits the old in a determinate but not entirely predictable way. The banks it simultaneously forms and follows and which can be fortified as well as lowered make up the general political structure of a society.

## The General Structure of Liberal Politics

To understand how the personal voices and spectacular images that modern liberal theory has amplified and magnified have contributed to trust and distrust in expert authority, we have to distinguish three aspects of modern liberal politics: social practices, speech genres, and philosophical methods. Together they form the general structure of modern liberal politics that I will call humanistic corporatism. It is within this structure that liberal theory and political practice are joined through political education.

I explain what lies behind my choice of the term *humanistic corporatism* in the next chapter. At this point I only want to explain what it means for liberal politics to have a general structure and how the tradition of liberal theory as political education has worked within that structure. In doing this, I can show the relation between my own project and other criticisms of liberal theory and liberal politics.

The idea that modern liberal politics has a general structure involves more than what John Rawls calls the "basic structure" of society, that is, its constitutional arrangements and the other "background" institutions, such as a market economy and the family, which shape desires and preferences.[19] The general structure of liberal society is this, but it also refers to the way these "basic" institutions hold together in practice. It is made up of the social practices, self-understandings, and mediating methods of

[18] Max Weber, "The Social Psychology of the World Religions," in *From Max Weber,* ed. Hans H. Gerth and C. Wright Mills (New York: Oxford University Press, 1958), p. 280.

[19] John Rawls, "The Basic Structure as Subject," *American Philosophical Quarterly* 14 (April 1977): 159.

reasoning in modern liberal society, through which political power is created and apportioned. It is within this general structure that the voices of clientism can be heard, the images of consumerism take shape, and political trust in expert authority is constructed.

*Social Practices.* Rawls includes social practices within his definition of the basic structure of society. He defines a practice as "any form of activity specified by a system of rules which defines offices and roles, rights and duties, penalties and defenses, and so on, and which gives the activity its structure."[20] This definition, however, like Rawls's definition of the basic structure, is incomplete. Not only do social practices specify a system of rules that define powers, prerogatives, and membership, they also create a sense of belonging. That is, they define for liberal citizens who they are as a people and who they are not. Social practices are not just patterns of rule-governed behavior. They are self-conscious activities in modern liberal society that define "us" over against "them." We are the people, for example, who work in a certain way; they are not. We treat certain national symbols with respect; they do not. More generally, we can be trusted; they cannot be. Not all social activities are social practices in this sense. What gives social practices their political significance in liberal societies is that they create shared understandings of the nature of collective identity and the legitimate distribution and use of power. In other words, social practices confer political identity.[21]

Clientism and consumerism, as I have said, are the social practices that now dominate liberal politics. The self-descriptions of client and consumer make possible a range of related social practices, including the highly organized and institutionalized forms of action that occur among clients and professionals, the more impersonal consumer demonstrations and demands made against producers and providers of services that may take traditional forms like voting but need not, and the responses of experts in and outside government to these various constituents. As participants in these social practices, clients and consumers share the tacit political knowledge that they need to trust and distrust expert authorities within particular neocorporatist policymaking arenas. This is where most power lies and political membership is determined.

Foucault has suggested one way to identify the close relationship between theory and these modern social practices. His concept of discourse

[20] John Rawls, "Justice as Reciprocity," in *Mill: Utilitarianism,* ed. Samuel Gorovitz (Indianapolis: Bobbs-Merrill, 1971), p. 242 n. 1.

[21] Charles Taylor, "Social Theory as Practice," in his *Philosophy and Human Sciences: Philosophical Papers 2* (Cambridge: Cambridge University Press, 1985), pp. 91-115.

refers to a body of knowledge whose production is organized according to disciplinary principles. Foucauldian discourse analysis emphasizes the way theoretical knowledge constitutes its own subject matter not in an abstract epistemological sense, but by shaping identities and giving determinate content to action as knowledge is deployed. Knowledge is a social process in which the accumulation and circulation of symbols of the self and the other are contested; theories, on this interpretation, are particular knowledge regimes that attempt to influence this process and gain hegemony. According to Gilles Deleuze, with whom Foucault agrees on this point, "from the moment a theory moves into its proper domain, it begins to encounter obstacles, walls, and blockages which require its relay by another type of discourse. . . . Practice is a set of relays from one theoretical point to another, and theory is a relay from one practice to another. No theory can develop without eventually encountering a wall, and practice is necessary for piercing this wall."[22] For Foucault, theory and practice are alternating relays in the dominant modern discourses of sexuality, politics, and truth.

Social practices are discursive in this alternating sense, but this does not tell us how social practices come apart, blend with one another, and are often subverted. Foucault's discursive social practices are too immobile. He tries to inject some life into them with the concept of "knowledge/power," but this remains only a suggestion on which his later work on the creative "care of the self" does not seem to build. Rather than follow Foucault, I prefer to distinguish two levels of theory that have different relations to social practices. I will use the terms *speech genres* and *philosophical methods* to distinguish between two related ways social practices have been theoretically informed and transformed in liberal societies.

*Speech Genres.* Speech genres, Mikhail Bakhtin argues, are "relatively stable types of . . . utterances." These types, whether they are everyday "primary" genres like casual greetings and military orders or more complex "secondary" genres like novels or research monographs, which incorporate primary genres, have three common features. The spoken language or utterances making up a speech genre are bound together by their "thematic content, style, and compositional structure."[23] It is on this basis that we can recognize, sometimes through the slightest hints, the genre in which the language of others is cast and then communicate with them. "If

[22] Gilles Deleuze, "Intellectuals and Power: A Conversation between Michel Foucault and Gilles Deleuze," in Michel Foucault, *Language, Counter-Memory, Practice,* ed. Donald F. Bouchard (Ithaca: Cornell University Press, 1977), p. 206.

[23] M. M. Bakhtin, "The Problem of Speech Genres," in his *Speech Genres and Other Late Essays,* trans. Vern W. McGee, ed. Caryl Emerson and Michael Holquist (Austin: University of Texas Press, 1986), pp. 60-62.

speech genres did not exist and we had not mastered them, if we had to originate them during the speech process and construct each utterance at will for the first time, speech communication would be impossible." For Bakhtin, this kind of command over speech genres is not just a necessity for communicating with others: it is by entering, responding to, and altering the genres we are presented with that we also "reveal our own individuality."[24]

The political trust and distrust peculiar to clientism and consumerism are expressed through the secondary speech genres of policy analysis and professional ethics.[25] These speech genres provide the social practices of clientism and consumerism with the subtleties of voice and gesture they need in order to be flexibly sustained. The limits of client trust and the occasions for consumer demand depend on utterances about the nature of risk, efficiency, autonomy, individuality, fairness, merit, and desert. These are not isolated abstract concepts; they are types of utterances expressed within social practices by the intonations, intimations, and cues that enable clients and consumers to respond in kind. Although clients and consumers are rarely policy analysts or professional ethicists themselves, the dialogues they enter—sometimes with the help of second opinions, lobbyists, and advisers—depend on their acceptance and mastery of these speech genres and their typical utterances.

*Policy analysis* and *professional ethics* are relatively new terms, but the speech genres they name are not. The debates over value neutrality in public administration and the creation of codes of professional responsibility early in this century were concerned with the interplay of these two political speech genres. And though they have begun to mature and take on a more permanent appearance, neither policy analysis nor professional ethics is monolithic. For example, some have argued that policy analysis enables policymakers to avoid the vagaries of democratic politics,[26] while others have argued that policy analysts should respect democratic norms rather than try to make them obsolete[27] and that they should

---

24 Ibid., pp. 79, 80.

25 According to Bakhtin, "We learn to cast our speech in generic forms and, when hearing others' speech, we guess its genre from the very first words; we predict a certain length (that is, the approximate length of the speech whole) and a certain compositional structure; we foresee the end; that is, from the beginning we have a sense of the speech whole, which is only later differentiated during the speech process" (ibid., p. 79).

26 Edith Stokey and Richard Zeckhauser, *A Primer for Policy Analysis* (New York: W. W. Norton, 1978).

27 John S. Dryzek, *Discursive Democracy: Politics, Policy and Science* (Cambridge: Cambridge University Press, 1990).

confront more honestly their own unavoidable value judgments.[28] The debates among professional ethicists are no less heated, though they tend to focus on disagreements over the nature of moral theory rather than over science and value neutrality.[29] There is no single or even dominant theory of policy analysis or professional ethics.[30] To think of policy analysis and professional ethics as speech genres emphasizes how they have provided two interconnected sets of utterances through which client trust is expressed and consumer choices are made within these social practices.[31]

The administration of consumer choices has not replaced clientism, as some have argued.[32] The two reinforce each other, operating as seemingly effective checks on the arrogance of different forms of expertise. Consumerism and the administrative control over professional-client relations have been held in check by resurgent forms of clientism and the demand for personal care and quality, but their ineffectiveness in limiting each other's excesses has made certain philosophical methods of reasoning essential to liberal politics.

*Philosophical Methods.* When social practices grow rigid and the speech genres they depend on become too dissonant, revisions may be necessary and changes may occur. At this point philosophical methods for mediating these disputes may be developed as one possible response. For example, Rawls describes the original position as a "mediating idea" that "enables us to establish greater coherence among all our judgments; and

[28] David Paris and James Reynolds, *The Logic of Policy Inquiry* (New York: Longman, 1983), and Frank Fischer and John Forester, eds., *Confronting Values in Policy Analysis: The Politics of Criteria* (Newberry Park, Calif.: Sage, 1987).

[29] See Arthur L. Caplan, "Ethical Engineers Need Not Apply: The State of Applied Ethics," *Science, Technology, and Human Values* 6 (Fall 1980): 24–32, and Joseph P. DeMarco and Richard M. Fox, *New Directions in Ethics: The Challenge* (New York: Routledge and Kegan Paul, 1986).

[30] For a summary of the evolution of policy analysis, see Peter DeLeon, *Advice and Consent: The Development of the Policy Sciences* (New York: Russell Sage Foundation, 1988). There is no similar study of professional ethics. Joan C. Callahan, *Ethical Issues in Professional Life* (New York: Oxford University Press, 1988), provides an account of the scope of professional ethics. My article "Locating Professional Ethics Politically" and the article by Michael Davis, "The Ethics Boom, What and Why," both in *Centennial Review* 34 (spring 1990), provide brief synopses.

[31] Policy analysis and professional ethics periodically show some signs of coalescing into a single speech genre. See, for example, the essays in James S. Bowman, ed., *Ethical Frontiers in Public Management: Seeking New Strategies for Resolving Ethical Dilemmas* (San Francisco: Jossey-Bass, 1991).

[32] For example, Robert Castel, "From Dangerousness to Risk," in *The Foucault Effect: Studies in Governmentality*, ed. Graham Burchell, Colin Gordon, and Peter Miller (Chicago: University of Chicago Press, 1991), pp. 281–98.

with this deeper self-understanding we can attain wider agreement among one another."[33]

Mediating philosophical methods of reasoning do not directly mediate between clients, consumers, and expert authorities; rather, they mediate disputes among policy analysts, ethicists, and other professional experts who articulate and set the tone of the speech genre in question. Philosophical methods can mediate between these mediators when deep disagreements break out over the core utterances of the speech genre.[34] Deep conflicts within modern social practices, such as those that have erupted over abortion and affirmative action, require this kind of abstract intellectual intervention. Abstractions like the original position, Rawls argues, provide "a way of continuing public discussion when shared understandings of lesser generality have broken down. . . . [T]he deeper the conflict, the higher the level of abstraction to which we must ascend to get a clear and uncluttered view of its roots."[35] Typically the "public discussion" has been continued within the confines of particular policymaking arenas.

The methods that have been especially important in the development of the speech genres and social practices of modern liberal society have been a Millian method of emulation and a Rawlsian method of deliberation. Both John Stuart Mill and Rawls have accepted the need for a politics of expert policymaking. But Mill's contribution to the political education of citizens in this context, I argue, is visual: his method of reasoning, though dialogical in its operation, has gradually and indirectly oriented citizens toward the consumerist imagery of modern politics. In the hands of policy analysts and professional ethicists, Millian practical reason encourages individual citizens to emulate an exemplary political character capable of making hard-and-fast distinctions between production and distribution, self-regarding and other-regarding actions, and expert administration and popular deliberation. By emulating the right kind of character, citizens will be able to see the political world in these dichotomous terms and know when to trust the images of expert policymakers.[36]

In contrast, Rawls's method of deliberation from an "original position" has served to mediate clientistic social practices that represent the objects

[33] John Rawls, *Political Liberalism* (New York: Columbia University Press, 1993), p. 26.

[34] I owe this notion of mediation to Richard T. Peterson. See our article, "The Original Position as Social Practice," *Political Theory* 16 (May 1988): 303–8.

[35] Rawls, *Political Liberalism*, p. 46.

[36] Mill uses the term *emulation* to describe the way in which husbands and wives with good, but different, qualities can benefit from each other's company: "The difference does not produce diversity of interest, but increased identity of it, and makes each still more valuable to the other." John Stuart Mill, *The Subjection of Women*, in *CW* 21:335. My appropriation of this term reflects the importance of the family for Mill's conception of exemplary political character. See chapter 5 below.

of trust in less visual terms. Rawls's method and its less formal contractarian facsimiles let citizens discriminate between the voices of merit, egalitarianism, and fairness. Even though Rawls's liberal theory is replete with visual metaphors such as the veil of ignorance, its practical significance within the speech genres of policy analysis and professional ethics derives from the way it accents professional language and domesticates emotions, not the way it represents trustworthy images and symbols.[37]

This contrast complicates the relation between Mill and Rawls within the liberal tradition. Their methods are different in the sense that for the former visual imagery plays the crucial mediating role whereas for the latter it is the less visible intonations and inflections of voice. Both methods, however, are dialogical in the way they mediate among policy analysts, ethicists, and professional experts within clientism and consumerism. This is what enables them to modify and expand these social practices and their speech genres. These liberal theories have operated like spoken dialogues, blending voices, creating openings for others, and casting suspicious "sideward glances" toward others.[38] Through their methods of philosophical reasoning, Mill and Rawls have instigated what Bakhtin calls internal dialogues that give greater specificity to the generic utterances of autonomy, individuality, merit, fairness, and risk while depreciating other responses to political conflicts. In this way these philosophical methods have served as forms of political education, reshaping clientism and consumerism and the boundaries of trust in expert policymaking. These methods of philosophical reasoning have helped liberal citizens learn which expert policymakers to trust and how far to trust them. Finally, because they share a particular Emersonian ego ideal, neither method has been entirely forthcoming about the way it has oriented citizens toward power, including the educative power of liberal theory.

---

[37] Robert M. Veatch, *A Theory of Medical Ethics* (New York: Basic Books, 1981), pp. 119–21, and idem, *The Patient-Physician Relationship* (Bloomington: Indiana University Press, 1991), pp. 28–32.

[38] Mikhail Bakhtin, *Problems of Dostoevsky's Poetics*, trans. Caryl Emerson (Minneapolis: University of Minnesota Press, 1984), p. 201.

# CHAPTER TWO

# Liberal Theories
# and Their Problems

"However monological the utterance may be, for example, a scientific or philosophical treatise," Mikhail Bakhtin has argued,

> however much it may concentrate on its own object, it cannot but be, in some measure, a response to what has already been said about the given topic, on the given issue, even though this responsiveness may not have assumed a clear-cut external expression. It will be manifested in the overtones of the style, in the finest nuances of the composition. The utterance is filled with *dialogic overtones.* . . . After all, our thought itself—philosophical, scientific, and artistic—is born and shaped in the process of interaction and struggle with others' thought, and this cannot but be reflected in the forms that verbally express our thought as well.[1]

The dialogic overtones of liberal theory have enabled it to be at times a catalyst, at other times an analgesic and a lubricant, for the two speech genres of policymaking and professional ethics. Liberal theory's inspiring portraits, domesticated voices, and suspicious "sideward glances"[2] — more than its regulative principles—have kept the politics of policymaking moving through hard times.

The argument I outlined for this thesis presupposes the truth of a mixed corporatist and pluralist description of modern liberal political economy, and it also depends on two related distinctions. One distinction is be-

[1] M. M. Bakhtin, "The Problem of Speech Genres," in his *Speech Genres and Other Late Essays*, trans. Vern W. McGee, ed. Caryl Emerson and Michael Holquist (Austin: University of Texas Press, 1986), p. 92.

[2] Mikhail Bakhtin, *Problems of Dostoevsky's Poetics*, trans. Caryl Emerson (Minneapolis: University of Minnesota Press, 1984), p. 201.

tween a theory *of* political education and theory *as* political education; the other is between the *traditional* problem of liberal political education and the *modern* problem of liberal political education. The truth of the mixed corporatist and pluralist description of modern liberal society and the clarity of these two distinctions by themselves are not enough to sustain my thesis. They are, however, necessary if the criticism of liberal theory as a political education for humanistic corporatism is to make sense.

In the final section of this chapter I discuss the importance of metaphor for my reconstruction of liberal theory as political education. Political theories depend on metaphors to generate and support their practical implications. This function includes explicit metaphors in the text, but also metaphors of theorizing itself that orient readers toward power and citizenship in certain ways. Different liberal metaphors of theorizing highlight different "dialogic overtones" in the text, some more revealing than others of liberal theory as political education.

## Theory *of* and Theory *as*

The goal of liberal theories *of* political education has been to identify who should have the power to educate citizens and what the limits on that power should be, given the deep disagreements within liberal societies and their commitment to individual liberty.

To reach this goal, liberal theorists of political education have divided their project into three parts. First, a liberal theory of political education specifies what it means to be a citizen in liberal society—that is, the difference between citizenship and other forms of individual and group identity. Second, it specifies what knowledge, skills, habits, and dispositions citizens must have if liberal society is to be stable. This may involve knowledge of power, in some form, as it did for Hobbes and Locke, or the emphasis may be on other deliberative skills and dispositions, as in Rousseau and Kant. Third, generally speaking a liberal theory of political education tells us something about how citizens can acquire the attributes politics requires of them and tells who is eligible for this education and capable of benefiting from it.

Liberal theories of political education are not simple deductions from an ideal of citizenship, but the ideal of citizenship that a theory of political education favors will have a strong influence on what citizens are supposed to know and be like, and on how they can learn to be good citizens. In the case of liberal theories, old and new, the stated ideal of citizenship has been fairly constant.

According to liberal theories of political education, citizens are property owners, workers, friends, relatives, and neighbors first, intermittent voters and episodic participants in political life second. Citizens vote and participate in order to protect their families, friends, jobs, and possessions. They are primarily private citizens and members of organized interest groups.

Some liberal theories of political education accept this hierarchy on metaphysical grounds: first things should come first. Michael Walzer argues that the liberal ideal of citizenship is a product of the structure of modern societies themselves. "Citizenship is unlikely to be the primary identity or the consuming passion of men and women living in complex and highly differentiated societies, where politics competes for time and attention with class, ethnicity, religion, and family, and where these latter four do not draw people together but rather separate and divide them. Separation and division make for the primacy of the private realm."[3] This view of liberal citizenship, which professes to be based on the complexity of pluralist society, is opposed to other models of citizenship that stray too far from the fact of separation and division, especially participatory theories that assume politics is the highest form of human activity. According to Walzer, the desire to reverse the primacy of "man" over "citizen" and recapture the intimacy of classical Greek and Roman politics is not just archaic but leads to a Jacobinism that "enacts an inauthentic autonomy, and fails because it cannot sustain the enactment without continuous violence."[4]

What are the skills, knowledge, habits, and dispositions that citizens in such a pluralist society must know and have? Here we begin to see some variety. Three general liberal positions can be distinguished. All emphasize informed toleration; beyond that, however, there are important differences in how they construe political participation. Hobbesian theorists emphasize instrumental knowledge and skills of rational choice.[5] Others, sympathetic to but not uncritical of Rousseau, stress mutual respect and the skills of collective deliberation and compromise.[6] Still others hold to a Lockean notion of individual rational deliberation and the ability to take

[3] Michael Walzer, "Citizenship," in *Political Innovation and Conceptual Change*, ed. Terence Ball, James Farr, and Russell L. Hanson (Cambridge: Cambridge University Press, 1989), p. 218.

[4] Ibid., p. 213. Also Michael Walzer, "What Does It Mean to Be an 'American'?" *Social Research* 57 (fall 1990): 591–614, and John Rawls, "The Idea of an Overlapping Consensus," *Oxford Journal of Legal Studies* 7, no. 1 (1987): 4.

[5] David Gauthier, *Morals by Agreement* (Oxford: Oxford University Press, 1986).

[6] For example, Benjamin Barber, *Strong Democracy: Participatory Politics for a New Age* (Berkeley and Los Angeles: University of California Press, 1984).

responsibility for oneself, avoiding both what they consider unrealistic rationalism and an equally dangerous faith in participatory democracy.[7]

Beyond these skills and habits of toleration and participation, liberal citizens also ideally possess certain dispositions. They have an affection for their country but one that is moderate and secular, not zealous. They will do their share of public service, but locally and only from time to time. They will look down on vigilante justice and feel a duty to obey the law. These dispositions—what Michael Walzer calls "loyalty, service, and civility"—will vary from one liberal society to another in their intensity.[8] But they seem no less essential to the liberal ideal of citizenship than the more familiar values of tolerance and participation.

How are liberal citizens going to acquire this knowledge and learn these skills, habits, and dispositions? Obviously, with so much to be learned, liberal political education has to proceed on several fronts. One is what contemporary liberal theorists call political socialization. If citizens are socialized in the normal way in a pluralist society, they will be able to compete and cooperate with one another as members of private interest groups, respect each other's individual rights and duties, and keep the power of the state in check. Socialization should be enough to meet their needs in most cases, and so liberal citizens will not be too much inclined to participate in politics. When they have to do so they can, but they will be wary of those who always seem ready to step into the public arena or resort to political remedies.[9]

But liberal theorists have recognized that socialization, even in a pluralist society, is imperfect, and so formal schooling also has a place in their ideas on political education. For example, Amy Gutmann has argued that schools should teach students the deliberative skills and moral sentiments that liberal democracy depends on, especially toleration, mutual respect, and compromise. To do this, adult citizens and gradually students

[7] William A. Galston, *Liberal Purposes: Goods, Virtues, and Diversity in the Liberal State* (New York: Cambridge University Press, 1991).

[8] Michael Walzer, *What It Means to Be an American: Essays on the American Experience* (New York: Marsilio Publishers Corporation, 1992), pp. 81–101.

[9] The classic texts on political socialization are Charles E. Merriam, *The Making of Citizens: A Comparative Study of Methods of Civic Training* (Chicago: University of Chicago Press, 1931); Gabriel A. Almond and Sidney Verba, *The Civic Culture: Political Attitudes and Democracy in Five Nations* (Boston: Little, Brown, 1973); and Jack Dennis, ed., *Socialization to Politics: A Reader* (New York: John Wiley, 1973). More recent work includes Robert Brownhill and Patricia Smart, *Political Education* (London: Routledge, 1989); Richard Pratte, *The Civic Imperative: Examining the Need for Civic Education* (New York: Teachers College Press, 1988); David C. Bricker, *Classroom Life as Civic Education* (New York: Teachers College Press, 1989); Orit Ichilov, ed., *Political Socialization, Citizenship Education, and Democracy* (New York: Teachers College Press, 1990); and Roberta S. Sigel, ed., *Political Learning in Adulthood: A Sourcebook of Theory and Research* (Chicago: University of Chicago Press, 1989).

must have the opportunity to participate in education policymaking, and professionals must oversee schooling to ensure that moral principles of "nondiscrimination" and "nonrepression" are not violated. The authority for liberal democratic education should rest in part with private citizens capable of democratic deliberation, but their views must be moderated by professional interpretations of these two moral principles.[10]

Gutmann's theory of political education combines a concern for citizens as members of families, private associations, and interest groups as well as individual moral persons with a concern for them as clients of professionals and consumers of educational policies. In the former sense citizens are active political participants. In the latter sense they accept, reject, and sometimes trust in and advance the judgments of professionals to help them locate the line dividing their private lives from their place within the public realm. In their private lives citizens have more autonomy and control over the education of their children; in the public realm professionals can exercise greater authority and discretion over what citizens need to become free and equal participants in political life. The role of the liberal theorist of political education, Gutmann argues, is to advise professional policymakers, from classroom teachers to local administrators to national officials, on questions of political morality so that the separation between public power and private life is not obscured by the arrogant abuse of professional authority or the recalcitrance of private interest groups.

Unfortunately, this effort to sustain the public/private distinction in liberal society, in one form or another, is becoming increasingly Quixotic. This development is especially true for liberal theories of political education, which struggle to teach professional policymakers what Walzer calls the "art of separation." He admits that experts, not citizens, draw the line between public and private, and they usually do it in self-serving ways.[11] The reason for this change is not simply the absence of compelling theoretical arguments. The distinction, in its various forms, has become anachronistic. We cannot yet do without the terms *public* and *private*, but, because they no longer describe the boundaries of legitimate political power and membership, we are gradually sloughing them off in favor of such terms as *industrial* and *family policy*. Consider the following description, in which these terms are put in quotation marks to point up their inadequacy.

Not only have "private" producers been regulated more heavily and integrated more thoroughly into the policymaking process, but "private" life generally has been organized according to "publicly" authorized professional standards and administrative guidelines. And as the large interest

[10] Amy Gutmann, *Democratic Education* (Princeton: Princeton University Press, 1987).

[11] Michael Walzer, "Liberalism and the Art of Separation," *Political Theory* 12 (August 1984): 328.

groups that dominate "private" life have gained "public" status through state subsidies, tax exemptions, legally enforceable rules regarding membership, and privileged positions within the policymaking process,[12] the traditional liberal "public sphere"[13] has been transformed. According to Habermas, this older "public sphere" made up of representative government and the press, where private interest groups could voice their differences and private citizens could critically debate the scope and purposes of state power in their own lives, has been overshadowed by new social arrangements and policymaking arenas. Now legitimate political power, in the form of both professional and government experts, and organized interest groups with an official status occupy a social space that is insulated from critical debate. State power does not take its direction from the bargains worked out between private interests. Policies are the products of expert initiative and various forms of organized consumer and clientele acquiescence and resistance within a more fragmented and less accessible social domain. Terence Ball has described this transformation in terms of an "epistemocratic ideal" of political power "in which politicians are replaced by planners and citizens by clients. It is an ideal," he continues, "to which political reality in some respects increasingly corresponds."[14]

Liberal societies have tipped: liberal citizens in the twentieth century are primarily political clients, consumers, and policymakers entangled in an unstable nexus of trust and expert authority. They are divided and separated, but not by Tocquevillean private associations and affiliations. They are skeptical of politics and politicians, but they do not measure their distance from them simply in terms of individual political and civil rights that protect them from state power. For clients of professionals, consumers of public policies, and policymakers in nominally public and private organizations, the lines that divide and separate liberal citizens are drawn along the dimensions of trust and expertise, not private rights and state powers.

Trust in expert authority—sometimes grudging and skeptical, sometimes rash, and sometimes calculated—is what liberal theory *as* political education has taught citizens to extend and to withhold. This is not to say that liberal theorists have not continued to champion individual rights or

[12] See Claus Offe, "The Attribution of Public Status to Interest Groups," in *Disorganized Capitalism: Contemporary Transformations of Work and Politics*, ed. John Keane (Cambridge: MIT Press, 1985), pp. 236–42.

[13] Jürgen Habermas, "The Public Sphere," *New German Critique*, no. 3 (fall 1974): 54.

[14] Terence Ball, "Authority and Conceptual Change," in *Authority Revisited: NOMOS XXIX*, ed. J. Roland Pennock and John W. Chapman (New York: New York University Press, 1987), p. 50. See also *Habermas and the Public Sphere*, ed. Craig Calhoun (Cambridge: MIT Press, 1993).

that the ideal of citizens bearing protective individual rights is not invoked by professional associations, multiclient lobbyists, and large corporations to justify their aggressive behavior in the policymaking process. The advocacy of political and civil rights, especially freedom of religion and the extension of the franchise, by theorists such as Locke, Kant, and Mill was instrumental in redefining the boundaries of the political domain and the terms of cooperation within it in the eighteenth and nineteenth centuries. The rights of citizens in those days were the main counterweights to state powers, and on occasion they still play an important role.[15]

Since the New Deal and the growth of administrative law, however, these values have radically underdetermined political membership and social cooperation in these societies. Landmark judicial decisions and legislative acts set only vague boundaries for the articulation and resolution of political conflicts. Increasingly, the rules and regulations of policymakers, especially at subnational levels, initially determine what these vague pronouncements mean, and the responses to these policies by clients, consumers, and other professionals give them their final content. The language of rights, like the public/private distinction, is still with us, but actual political practice depends more on the constitution of trust in expert authority and the images of political spectacles than on the protection of rights for those who can afford it. In Anthony Giddens's words, "The nature of modern institutions is deeply bound up with the mechanisms of trust in abstract systems, especially in expert systems."[16]

Andrew Shonfield, one of the first to carefully examine this profound shift, summarized the situation this way.

> This corporatism is not the authoritarian system of management familiar from the experience of fascism. It is, by contrast, *a systematic dialogue between interest groups both private and public;* at its best, it succeeds in putting order and a priority ranking based on recognized standards of social justice into the expression of divergent voices which characterizes the pluralist democracies. This form of government is usually benign—though not, unfortunately, invariably so. Its effectiveness and its acceptability both depend on the adaptation of existing institutions, adjustments which are political as well as economic. Behind these adaptations is the ultimate aim of moderating and mediating conflicts between the needs, aspirations and claims of the various competing interest groups. [Emphasis added][17]

15 See T. H. Marshall, "Citizenship and Social Class," in *Class, Citizenship, and Social Development: Essays by T. H. Marshall* (Garden City, N.Y.: Doubleday, 1965), pp. 71–134.

16 Anthony Giddens, *The Consequences of Modernity* (Stanford: Stanford University Press, 1990), p. 83.

17 Andrew Shonfield, *In Defence of the Mixed Economy*, ed. Zuzanna Shonfield (Oxford: Oxford University Press, 1984), p. 127.

It is in this mixed pluralist and corporatist context that Shonfield and others have described that trust in expert authority among clients, consumers, and policymakers has been sustained, in part, by liberal theories as political education. No priority ranking based on recognized standards of justice has been found to harmonize the needs, aspirations, and claims of the various competing interest groups in modern liberal societies. Trust between these groups and government officials cannot be legislated according to recognized standards. But many, though certainly not all, have been mediated through a variety of structured dialogues, social contracts, and designed conversations for which liberal theory has set the tone. Liberal theorists have not produced universally accepted standards of social justice, but the "overtones" of their methods of practical reason have made the mediating dialogue Shonfield valued more possible. Whether this form of mediation has been as "benign" as he says is another matter. My view is that Shonfield and others understate the price we have paid for mixed corporatist and pluralist stability while either overstating the obstacles to alternative forms of democratic citizenship or too quickly equating them with Jacobinism.

If this account of the shift in citizenship from pluralist competition based on individual rights to client and consumer trust in expert authority is true, does it mean that liberal theory, which has been preoccupied with recommending rights-based regulative principles to policymakers, has had little to do with the making of political clients and consumers? On the contrary. But to understand the role modern liberal theory has played in the making of clients, consumers, and expert authorities, we have to distinguish between what liberal theorists say in their theories *of* political education and what their "dialogical" methods of reasoning have meant in practice *as* political education.

## The Traditional Problem

The traditional problem of liberal political education is organized around the question, How can individuals be taught to meet their impersonal political obligations when (1) they view these obligations as a burden and a threat to the personal moral relationships they prize and within which they believe they are truly free, and (2) they think sometimes they can justifiably avoid these impersonal political obligations with impunity?

John Locke, a firm believer in the need for religious training and a strict diet, recognized the need for this kind of traditional political education. He believed that a constitutional government could be organized well enough to preserve the sphere of private morality and that most citizens would recognize that it was in their interest and consistent with their religious beliefs to support such a constitutional government, but this was not enough. The Lockean task of political education was one of instilling, especially in the peerage, a civil commitment to life, liberty, and property so that leaders could meet their political obligations and sit impartially in judgment on others.[18]

Locke took a dim view of extending love and friendship to political life in order to curb the tendency to shirk one's political duties. In his rejoinder to Richard Hooker, who thought he must find some way of deducing an "obligation to mutual love" from mankind's natural equality, Locke made it clear that this search was more than unnecessary—it was a serious error. Gentlemen could be educated for liberty without diluting their private moral sentiments by extending them to strangers in the form of "mutual love." What they needed was the ability to recognize and defend the value of liberty for its own sake and for the preservation of life and property. It is an essential part of a gentlemanly education, but it is not all of moral character, which includes other virtues like liberality, humanity, industry, and thrift.[19] Once a gentlemanly sense of justice has been taught, these Lockean leaders can be counted on "to preserve the rest of mankind" without putting their own moral character at risk.[20]

Many historians of the American founding have argued that this Lockean understanding of the relation between politics and moral virtue lies behind Madison's famous aphorism on angelic politics.[21] It is better to depend on the ordinary desires and religious beliefs of individuals and groups, limited by "republican government" and led by gentleman capable of rational deliberation, than to risk both the political corruption of personal morality and the disruption of political order through widespread moralizing on public issues. Where does this leave political education? It is primarily a matter of Stoic training for a male elite. Gentlemen must learn to separate their moral sentiments from the narrower political sense

[18] See Rogers M. Smith, *Liberalism and American Constitutional Law* (Cambridge: Harvard University Press, 1985).

[19] John Locke, "Some Thoughts concerning Reading and Study for a Gentleman," in *The Educational Writings of John Locke*, ed. James L. Axthell (Cambridge: Cambridge University Press, 1968).

[20] John Locke, *Two Treatises of Government*, ed. Peter Laslett (New York: New American Library, 1965), II, secs. 5–6, pp. 310–11.

[21] Alexander Hamilton, James Madison, and John Jay, *The Federalist Papers* (New York: New American Library, 1961), no. 51, p. 322. See Lorraine Smith Pangle and Thomas L. Pangle, *The Learning of Liberty: The Educational Ideas of the American Founders* (Lawrence: University of Kansas Press, 1993).

of justice they may need to identify impartially the content of impersonal public duties and to judge how well they are being fulfilled. If they do not, both politics and morality will suffer.

Rousseau offered a very different response to the original problem. Natural self-love (*amour propre*) must be transformed into public devotion through a long process of tutoring and participation in public rituals, spectacles, and customs. Only then will each citizen "vie with his fellows to win the palm of public esteem."[22] Yet Rousseau's own solution also tended to be elitist. It turns on the virtuousity and selflessness of a "lawgiver" who is above the law rather than at the center of it. In Rousseau's words, "He who would try his hand at founding a nation must learn to dominate men's opinions, and through them to govern their passions."[23] This ultimate Rousseauian device for teaching citizens to vie for public esteem rests on a misguided Jansenist faith that such a lawgiver will descend, establish a new political order, and then quietly depart leaving citizens to govern themselves.

The French Revolution and the Napoleonic wars had a profound effect on liberalism, including its view of the traditional problem of political education. The solution to the traditional problem, argued Alexis de Tocqueville, will have to be more moderate than Rousseau's but more broadly based than Locke's.

According to Tocqueville, the solution to the traditional problem, if it is to be found at all, exists in the interstices of social life, not in the skills of rational deliberation, the balancing effects of constitutional arrangements, or the glorious deeds of founding fathers. If individuals have the freedom to address their immediate social and religious concerns, argued Tocqueville, this latitude may eventually "induce a greater number of citizens to value the affections of their kindred and neighbors . . . and force them to help one another"[24] so that a modest form of civic virtue, "self-interest properly understood," may gradually emerge.[25] Only then, Tocqueville averred, can the destabilizing passions for democratic equality be contained.

Members of Tocquevillean voluntary associations in liberal societies sometimes have quietly devoted part of their lives to the less fortunate

---

[22] Nannerl O. Keohane, *Philosophy and the State in France: The Renaissance to the Enlightenment* (Princeton: Princeton University Press, 1980), p. 441.

[23] Jean-Jacques Rousseau, *The Government of Poland*, trans. Willmoore Kendall (Indianapolis: Bobbs-Merrill, 1972), p. 18.

[24] Alexis de Tocqueville, *Democracy in America*, trans. George Lawrence, ed. J. P. Mayer (Garden City, N.Y.: Anchor Books, 1969), p. 511.

[25] Ibid., p. 526.

members of society. The cumulative effect of these voluntary associations may be to strengthen the bonds of community as the individuals who work within these social and religious associations take an interest in the interests of others and finally in the activities they share with others and see those activities as constitutive of a common good. Robert Bellah and his associates have contrasted these engaged "independent citizens" with more familiar, self-seeking liberal citizens, and Bellah urges us to keep these civic conversations going so that our understanding of and commitment to the common good will grow.[26] The only way to renew cooperative social and religious "habits of the heart," according to Bellah, is "by the reciprocal action of men one upon another."[27]

On this Tocquevillean view, then, the task of liberal political education is the gradual development of republican virtues. Without them, personal morality will always outweigh public duties. In fact, this view has received a great deal of attention from historians, political theorists, and legal scholars of late, and some have argued that even stronger communitarian sentiments than Tocqueville thought he detected have periodically existed within liberal societies. But it is easy to forget the original elitism in the theory of civic republicanism and how this has manifested itself in the twentieth century. Many modern civic associations have been designed with very little interest in the inchoate republican virtues of "the masses" or "the crowd." In the United States in the first half of the twentieth century, clubs for the elderly, co-opting foremen's clubs, and even the YMCA were consciously designed to arrange and contain mass political passions, not to nurture civic virtue. The purpose of these associations was "social engineering," and there was very little interest in the political education of the members.[28] Not only was the original doctrine of civic republicanism exclusionary, but its contemporary supporters have underestimated the manipulative way many such voluntary associations have operated within mixed corporatist and pluralist political economies.

In response to criticism of this sort, the Bellah team has taken a second look at the institutional context within which they have called for public conversation, and they have found it wanting. Their sequel, *The Good Society*, corrects the romantic impression created by *Habits of the Heart*. They underscore the need for democratizing the workplace and restruc-

---

[26] Robert N. Bellah, Richard Madsen, William M. Sullivan, Ann Swidler, and Steven M. Tipton, *Habits of the Heart: Individualism and Commitment in American Life* (Berkeley and Los Angeles: University of California Press, 1985).

[27] Tocqueville, *Democracy in America*, p. 515.

[28] See William Graebner, *The Engineering of Consent: Democracy and Authority in Twentieth-Century America* (Madison: University of Wisconsin Press, 1987).

turing the administrative state if civic virtue is to take hold and amount to much.[29] They recognize that the civic conversations they call for will have to be among people who will continue to disagree sharply.[30] Trust, they argue, is the essential glue of democratic society; and we should become "ambassadors of trust in a fearful world."[31] But the problem of political trust among citizens of the same political society is not one ambassadors can solve.

## The Modern Problem

Like the traditional problem of liberal political education, the modern problem deals with membership and social cooperation. But as I have said, the terms of membership and the boundaries between members and non-members since the latter half of the nineteenth century have changed dramatically in liberal societies. Other shifting boundaries between political clients, consumers, and experts have made the public/private distinction much less salient in practice.

As countries have been partitioned and then have struggled for and against reunification, as religious and ethnic minorities have sought political asylum and a homeland, and as the globalization of economic production has perforated national boundaries, who deserves to be a member is no longer a matter of the claims of necessity voiced by outsiders against insiders' counterclaims of national identity. This is not just a problem for developing countries or unstable nondemocratic regimes, although it is certainly true for them. In the United States and Great Britain it is also not clear who is an outsider and who is an insider, because it is not clear where the line dividing outside from inside is. Economically and socially, these countries are no longer self-sufficient nation-states. Economic interdependence and patterns of immigration have made their national boundaries a maze of exceptions and shifting eligibility requirements rather than a continous line.

Similarly, the equally important internal boundaries or district lines within liberal societies are in disarray. The proliferation of administrative agencies and the districts and jurisdictions they oversee has made existing legislative boundaries almost invisible. Most citizens are ignorant of their legislative districts' boundaries and their local elected representatives' identities but well aware of the administrative agencies, from the

[29] Robert N. Bellah, Richard Madsen, William M. Sullivan, Ann Swidler, and Steven M. Tipton, *The Good Society* (New York: Alfred A. Knopf, 1991), p. 81.

[30] Ibid., p. 293.

[31] Ibid., pp. 285–86.

drain commission and the quasi-public utilities to the school district, with which they must negotiate for changes or improvements in public services. With each new administrative agency, a new set of "members" is created, and the terms of membership in this chaotic world must be based on negotiated trust relations, not on fixed principles of national or ethnic identity or necessity.[32] Within the politics of policymaking, de facto political membership is at the mercy of the stress that social and economic problems place on administrative systems designed to manage interest groups and also the client and consumer counterdemands this system elicits.

Given the complexity of membership and social cooperation, the modern problem of liberal political education goes beyond the traditional problem of teaching private citizens to respect the rights of others and do their duty; it has been one of creating an appropriate system of trust and expert authority. For politics as policymaking to work, citizens must learn to trust in expert authority as both clients and consumers. They must learn to trust authorities who are responsible for the interpretation and satisfaction of needs, and they also must learn to trust themselves as sovereign consumers of expert services and information. This system of skeptical trust in expert authority cannot be engineered any more than it can be spontaneously generated through voluntary associations.

To the extent that classical liberal theorists were interested in the dynamics of political trust, they reduced it to a rigid deference to patriarchal authority, sometimes with divine trappings. This was especially true of Locke. Kant was different, and his political theory represents a transition to the modern problem of political education. Kant sensed that the skills needed in the modern world would have to be acquired through discursive trust building. He implored men (only) to think for themselves, but he realized that the kind of thinking these new "independent" liberal citizens would be called on to do would require new forms of trust in their own faculties as well as the expert faculties of a more modern university.

Max Weber was the first to flesh out this Kantian vision of society by identifying the central place of expert authority. Weber argued that the dominant form of authority in modern liberal societies has become the authority of those who have organized the production of scientific and technical knowledge and have retained exclusive jurisdiction over its interpretation and deployment. One of the keys to this enterprise has been the development of specialized languages and methods—principles, laws, and rules. These abstractions have become the coin of the realm. This is why Weber called modern expert authority "rational-legal" authority. Accord-

---

[32] See Michael Walzer, *Spheres of Justice: A Defense of Pluralism and Equality* (New York: Basic Books, 1983), chap. 2.

ing to Weber, it is through compliance with the judgements of experts, rationally articulated in formal terms, that the modern secular values of security, procedural fairness, and wealth have been better realized. The Kantian republic requires Weberian organization.

In a world organized according to principles, laws, and rules that promise these modern values, it is primarily expert interpretations that have defined the boundaries of human needs, and it is the authority of expert pronouncements that has been decisive in mediating conflicts over the satisfaction of these needs. What, for example, is the status of the need for workers' compensation insurance, a minimum wage, or child care? Do they constitute a legal right, a means-tested entitlement, a market commodity, or a mother's duty? The principles, rules, and laws that provide the answer and function as methods for mediating between competing views themselves have to be interpreted and applied by expert authorities ranging from private legal counsels and academic researchers to administrative law judges and budget officers. The same is true for scientific research in biotechnology or nuclear energy. The ostensible need for advanced work in these areas is a matter of interpretation and mediation by a wide range of expert authorities. It has been the expert interpretation of needs, couched in the "rational-legal" language of principles, rules, and laws, that has given the secular values of security, procedural fairness, and wealth their determinate content.

In Weber's Germany these expert interpretations and pronouncements were made primarily by a large class of "government officials."

> Of course the official, even the specialized official, is a very old constituent of the most various societies. But no country and age has ever experienced, in the same sense as the modern Occident, the absolute and complete dependence of its whole existence, of the political, technical, and economic conditions of its life, on a specially trained organization of officials. The most important functions of the everyday life of society have come to be in the hands of technically, commercially, and above all legally trained government officials.[33]

Historically, in the United States and Great Britain expert authorities have not held official government positions to the same extent as they did in Germany in the late nineteenth and early twentieth centuries, but they have often performed the same function as gatekeepers, interpreters, and de facto mediators. Authorities such as professors, physicians, and lawyers, even if they are privately employed or self-employed, have functioned like

---

[33] Max Weber, *The Protestant Ethic and the Spirit of Capitalism*, trans. Talcott Parsons (New York: Charles Scribner's Sons, 1958), p. 16.

"government officials." Because access to expertise has become essential for full membership in modern liberal society, it could even be said that private professionals function as de facto government officials.

Political clientism and consumerism are now the dominant conceptions of citizenship in an age of expert authority.[34] Clientism and consumerism define the de facto boundaries of membership in the political community and the political roles that citizens occupy within it. Those without the public status, opportunities, resources, and abilities to participate as clients, consumers, or policymakers may formally still be voting members and possess other individual rights, but in fact they will be politically marginal. Their voices will not be audible to expert authorities, and they will not be heard within the policymaking process. Neither their expertise nor their trust will be sought by other citizens. Conversely, some powerful clients, consumers, and policymakers in liberal societies may lack de jure citizenship but still be de facto citizens. They may, for example, influence industrial policy because of their control over investments in land and capital even though they are legally citizens of a foreign country.

As political clients, liberal citizens look to professionals, public planners, and a wide variety of other policymakers all the way down to the "street level"[35] for advice, assistance, and expert services. Citizens rely on them to provide the specialized services they cannot provide for themselves and to simplify complex decisions on issues ranging from access to medical services to nuclear deterrence. In return, political clients tolerate, within limits, the oligopolistic power of professionals and other expert authorities. They look to the system of planners, social workers, health care workers, teachers, and other professionals that dominate the politics of policymaking to interpret and meet many of their needs and respond to their interests. They want to trust in these expert authorities. Under some conditions they will speak out, however, sometimes in very organized ways, if they think their interests are being ignored and their own careers are in jeopardy. As they become political consumers, they reserve the right to make some final choices themselves. They lobby government bureaucrats, pressure private firms, and hire expert witnesses in order to influence public policy on issues like abortion, school prayer, and environmental pollution.

The line dividing clientism from consumerism is not just another version of the public/private distinction, nor is it fixed. Even technically complex issues like nuclear deterrence and access to medical care can become subjects for intense consumer debate. Conversely, experts can exercise

[34] Daniel Bell, *The Coming of Post-Industrial Society* (New York: Basic Books, 1973).
[35] Michael Lipsky, *Street-Level Bureaucracy: The Dilemmas of the Individual in Public Services* (New York: Russell Sage Foundation, 1980).

considerable influence over the formulation and implementation of policies even where there are many relatively informed and concerned consumers. Modern liberal citizens have an ambivalent attitude toward the relative merits of the competitive and oligopolistic markets in which expert authority is traded and public policies are made. As clients, they want experts to make and carry out the right policies. As consumers, they are much less trusting. Depending on their level of solidarity, the opportunities for organized collective action afforded by the political system, and the level of organized resistance from producers and professionals, clientism and consumerism will vary considerably.[36]

## Humanistic Corporatism

I will call the nexus of trust and expertise that defines the modern problem of political education, that political clients and consumers operate within, and that liberal theory as political education has worked to perfect, *humanistic corporatism*. It is the general structure of politics as policymaking that liberal theorists have accepted and have taught clients, consumers, and policymakers how to come to terms with since the Great Depression of the 1930s. There are intimations of it in the latter half of the nineteenth century, and it finally has reached maturity in the last two decades of the twentieth century in the United States and Great Britain.

Corporatism refers to the organization of elites within government bureaucracies, labor and consumer groups, and private owners and managers who preside over the formulation and implementation of public policy, relatively free from the constitutional checks and restraints that exist within electoral and legislative arenas in advanced capitalist societies. This kind of corporatism (sometimes called neocorporatism or societal corporatism), as distinguished from authoritarian state corporatism, describes those political processes in advanced capitalist societies that cannot be characterized in simple pluralist or elitist terms. At the same time, according to Philippe Schmitter, corporatism should not be described as "the result of the wilful calculation of some autonomous state actor or the hegemonic project of some progressive class fraction." Corporatist arrangements in almost all cases, Schmitter continues,

> have been the largely unintended outcome of a series of disparate interest conflicts and policy crises in which none of the class or state actors involved

[36] Alan Cawson, "Is There a Corporatist Theory of the State?" in *Democracy and the Capitalist State*, ed. Graeme Duncan (Cambridge: Cambridge University Press, 1989), pp. 233–52.

was capable of imposing its preferred solution upon the others. Typically, they began as second-best compromises which no one really wanted or defended openly: hence their general invisibility, their uneven distribution and their precarious legitimacy. State actors would usually have preferred authoritative regulation; business representatives an allocation through market forces; and labour leaders a redistribution of wealth and/or a redefinition of property rights. Neo-corporatism satisfies none of these projects, but incorporates elements of all of them. It is, therefore, both conservative in that it reflects existing property and power relations, and potentially transformative in that it subjects them to explicit and repeated negotiation. Class compromise is thereby moved from the plane of individualistic adaptation and parliamentary manoeuvre to that of inter-organizational bargaining and contract formation.[37]

Schmitter and other corporatist theorists have been justly criticized for the looseness of formulations like these.[38] More certainly needs to be done to clarify the relation between organized interests and the state under neo-corporatism, and more careful distinctions need to be drawn between and within neocorporatist societies, even if we think of corporatism, following Offe, as just one "axis of development" within liberal societies.[39]

In return for their place as functional representatives in the policymaking process, the leaders of corporatist groups have ensured the acquiescence of their "constituents." [40] For the representatives of organized labor, this is sometimes a matter of co-opting or dividing workers. At other times, when the problems are not matters of economic conflict or labor-management disagreements, organized interest groups must develop new institutions that will mediate social conflicts through administrative and professional speech genres. Experts (from doctors and lawyers to city

[37] Philippe C. Schmitter, "Neo-corporatism and the State," in *The Political Economy of Corporatism*, ed. Wyn Grant (London: Macmillan, 1985), p. 37.

[38] See Peter J. Williamson, *Varieties of Corporatism: A Conceptual Discussion* (Cambridge: Cambridge University Press, 1985), and idem, *Corporatism in Perspective* (London: Sage, 1989).

[39] Claus Offe, *Disorganized Capitalism*, ed. John Keane (Cambridge: MIT Press, 1985), p. 236. Recently, Jeffrey J. Anderson, *The Territorial Imperative: Pluralism, Corporatism, and Economic Crisis* (Cambridge: Cambridge University Press, 1992).

[40] Philippe Schmitter defines corporatism "as a system of interest representation in which the constituent units are organized into a limited number of singular, compulsory, non-competitive, hierarchically ordered and functionally differentiated categories, recognized or licensed (if not created) by the state and granted a deliberate representational monopoly within their respective categories in exchange for observing certain controls on their selection of leaders and articulation of demands and supports." See his "Still the Century of Corporatism," in *Trends toward Corporatist Intermediation*, ed. Philippe Schmitter and Gerhard Lehmbruch (Beverly Hills, Calif.: Sage, 1979), p. 13.

planners and social workers) have played a distinctive role in this kind of mediated corporatist politics in the United States and Great Britain, where the political culture has been less hospitable to centralized national planning. It is within this subnational "meso-corporatism"[41] that experts, especially policy analysts and professional ethicists, are playing new mediating roles and political clients and consumers are most active.

Note how pervasive and heavily mediated these partnerships have become at the state and local levels. Universities and "private" research institutes, often with government support, provide help to industry through applied forms of research. Subsidies to retrain older workers and prepare new workers for an entrepreneurial environment have been hailed as necessary measures within these new partnerships as well. Risk or venture capital has been made available to private firms through government programs, sometimes using public employee pension funds. And in some cases, supportive social services that couple income assistance with job training and child care have been developed.[42] These are only the most common forms mesocorporatism has taken in the late 1970s and 1980s, and in carrying out these public policies experts have played key roles. Whether they have specialized in new forms of revenue raising for the state, new ways to enhance the entrepreneurial climate and open up markets, or new forms of counseling, government experts and other professionals have tried to work cooperatively with one another and, in some cases, with representatives of labor, neighborhood groups, and client groups concerned about the pattern and social impact of these new partnerships. The crucial characteristic of all these partnerships, and many similar measures, is that policies are formulated and implemented largely outside the electoral political arena. Periodically they may be subject to referenda or trigger recall elections, but the normal process is one of expert study, commission recommendation, collaboration between government and nongovernment producers, consultation with marketing and advertising firms, and the implementation of related services to deal with the flak and cleanup. This is the major axis of mesocorporatism.

I already have stated that I do not believe corporatism is a complete description of the political economies of the United States and Great Britain in this modern period. Pluralist bargaining and competition remain important in some sectors. But the term corporatism does capture the direction important features of these political economies are moving, and

[41] This is Alan Cawson's term in *Corporatism and Political Theory* (Oxford: Basil Blackwell, 1986).

[42] David Osborne, *Laboratories of Democracy* (Boston: Harvard Business School Press, 1988), and R. Scott Fosler, ed., *The New Economic Role of American States* (New York: Oxford University Press, 1988).

this point is what even the most complicated pluralist theories miss: specifically, the reduction of the traditional public sphere, a new official status for some organized interests, and the creation of new political clients and consumers. Corporatism, again in Offe's words, "is a concept that does not describe a situation, but rather an 'axis' of development."[43] The more organized interest groups depend on official recognition, the more citizens think of themselves as clients and consumers and behave accordingly, and the more political debate and discussion are conducted within the restricted boundaries of administrative rules and professional norms, the more corporatist a society is. That some forms of pluralist bargaining persist and that some revised pluralist theories can incorporate these dramatic changes at a very high level of abstraction does not negate the significance of this development.

*Humanistic* corporatism combines policy planning and implementation outside traditional legislative channels by state officials, corporate and labor leaders, and professional elites with a belief that these methods can and should be guided by nondiscriminatory forms of moral and political reasoning. At a minimum, humanistic corporatism is free of the discrimination that denies full political standing to those confined to the household and similar forms of work.[44] Beyond that, it strives to change the way those who implement as well as formulate public policies in and outside government think through the moral and political problems of clients and consumers. It strives to change the way those who make public policies and those dependent on these authorities think about their needs, their political identities, and the sense in which they can trust each other and themselves.

To clarify this deeper meaning, it is helpful to recall earlier forms of humanism. First, humanistic corporatism draws on a post-Reformation secular approach to moral and political reasoning that is doubtful of the possibilities of dialogue when religious beliefs are accepted as the grounds for moral and political arguments. For humanists, religious disagreements have proved too volatile and religious majorities too intolerant to include in policymaking.[45] For some liberal theorists this is not just a matter of historical record; they argue that religious beliefs themselves are more categorical and unsubstantiated than other moral and political beliefs and therefore cannot and should not count as claims to legitimate political power in a mixed corporatist and pluralist political society.[46] Humanistic

---

[43] Offe, "*Disorganized Capitalism*," p. 236.

[44] Susan Moller Okin, "Humanistic Liberalism," in *Liberalism and the Moral Life*, ed. Nancy L. Rosenblum (Cambridge: Harvard University Press, 1991), pp. 39-53.

[45] Rawls, "Idea of an Overlapping Consensus," pp. 11-12.

[46] Thomas Nagel, "Moral Conflict and Political Legitimacy," *Philosophy and Public Affairs*

corporatism attempts to cordon off religious beliefs so that policymaking can proceed civilly.

Second, humanistic corporatism is humanistic in an elitist Ciceronian sense. Clients and consumers should serve as the judges of policymaking, and they should judge according to independent, cultivated tastes and standards of excellence. Hannah Arendt has been one of the most eloquent defenders of this Ciceronian humanism, which she believed was the best—perhaps the only—way to contain the rule of professional and bureaucratic experts.

> What Cicero in fact says is that for the true humanist neither the verities of the scientist nor the truth of the philosopher nor the beauty of the artist can be absolutes; the humanist, because he is not a specialist, exerts a faculty of judgment and taste which is beyond the coercion which each specialty imposes upon us.... As humanists, we can rise above these conflicts between the statesman and the artist as we can rise in freedom above the specialities which we all must learn and pursue. We can rise above specialization and philistinism of all sorts to the extent that we learn how to exercise our taste freely.[47]

Arendt's formulation is archaic, but the sentiment behind it is still popular. Liberal education understood as the education appropriate to a leisured, cultivated class is the modern form in which this sense of humanism has been expressed in our century. The liberally educated humanist must be able to understand expert jargons and judge them according to common human values in the way a knowledgeable spectator judges the performance of a virtuoso.[48]

Finally, and most important, the discourse of humanistic corporatism is humanistic in a Socratic sense. It demands that moral and political inquiry be a common enterprise based on egalitarian mutual respect. It underscores the importance of accounting for the familiar and the particular and not being lulled by generalizations. It recognizes that experts must be able to maieutically bring out the immanent knowledge that ordinary citizens have so they can formulate complex issues in their own words, and it also recognizes that this may have to be done ironically in order to win the trust of ordinary citizens. Unlike secular and Ciceronian humanism, which emphasize the like-mindedness of those engaged in argument

---

16 (1987): 215–40. But see his *Equality and Partiality* (New York: Oxford University Press, 1991), chap. 14, for a change of mind.

[47] Hannah Arendt, "The Crisis in Culture: Its Social and Its Political Significance," in her *Between Past and Future* (New York: Viking Press, 1968), p. 225.

[48] See Robert Paul Wolff, "What Good Is a Liberal Education?" *Salmagundi*, no. 84 (fall 1989): 109–25.

and judging, Socratic humanism is above all committed to dialogue and conversation across the lines that separate consumers and clients from policymaking professionals and government officials. Although humanistic corporatism is secular and at times elitist in a Ciceronian sense, it is primarily Socratic. It breeds a modest trust in oneself and a guarded skepticism toward others. There is, the Socratic humanist might say, probably more going on, inside and outside, than we can see.[49]

The ground for the acceptance of humanistic corporatism was first tilled by Tocqueville's contemporary John Stuart Mill, who accepted Tocqueville's approach to political education but not his belief in the need to revive republican civic virtue. Tocqueville's detailed account of the problem of political education was too backward-looking for Mill. Tocqueville had sought ways of inculcating republican civic virtue as a surrogate for aristocratic virtue. Mill accepted and improved on Tocqueville's view of how political education operates within the general structure of a society, but Mill's orientation toward that structure was forward-looking and at times prescient, not reactionary. In other words, like Tocqueville, Mill believed that the education of good citizens should aim at the knowledge, habits, and skills that can be taught within the existing general structure of society. But—and this is where Mill is most prescient—that basic structure was becoming a contradictory mix of steering institutions and resistance to them, and its indigenous skills and habits were becoming a combination of trust in authority and skepticism toward custom and majority opinions.

To sharpen this contrast, consider Tocqueville's account of jury duty. He argued that jurors in civil cases can learn to feel responsible for their own actions, learn that all citizens are equally liable under the law, and learn a form of social responsibility that helps to "combat that individual selfishness which is like rust in society." But the "greatest advantage" of this "magisterial office" is that it instills "the habits of the judicial mind into every citizen, and just those habits are the very best way of preparing people to be free." By coming into contact with the "best-educated and most enlightened members of the upper classes," ordinary citizens who are

---

[49] Arendt argues that Socrates correctly rejected the Platonic method of visualizing the beautiful and the good. Omniscient experts may be able to see "the truth in solitude and remoteness," but this is dangerous when the object in question is the good of the political community. Then violence will masquerade as authority. See Hannah Arendt, "What Is Authority?" in her *Between Past and Future*, pp. 115–16. Arendt's criticism of Plato and defense of Socrates is not a position that liberal theory has accepted, since, as I will argue, the Socratic ideal in liberal theory is overtly visual. For a reading of Socrates similar to Arendt's see Sheldon S. Wolin, "On the Theory and Practice of Power," in *After Foucault: Humanistic Knowledge, Postmodern Challenges*, ed. Jonathan Arac (New Brunswick, N.J.: Rutgers University Press, 1988), p. 192.

too easily moved by a passion for equality learn to understand the rights that protect their freedom. The most powerful influence on the jurors in this regard is the judge, who "appears as a disinterested arbitrator between the litigants' passions." By virtue of the judge's ability to sort through the opposing arguments and complexities of the law, he "has almost unlimited influence" over the jurors. He is the aristocratic counterweight that a liberal society needs, and his courtroom is "the most effective means of popular education at society's disposal."[50] According to Tocqueville, citizens' weak commitment to political freedom can be partially corrected through jury duty, and it is the "first duty" of statesmen in a liberal society to "educate democracy" by establishing such institutions in addition to vicarious participatory practices like the political debates staged in the mainstream press.[51]

Mill agreed with Tocqueville that social conformity could lead to political complacency and eventually to some sort of despotism. The best way to fight this off, Mill argued, is to protect the diversity of social and economic associations on which liberty and a healthy skepticism toward the wisdom of majority rule depend, but also to put experts in positions of political and economic authority. "The interests dependent on the acts done by a public department, the consequences liable to follow from any particular mode of conducting it, require for weighing and estimating them a kind of knowledge, and of specially exercised judgment, almost as rarely found in those not bred to it as the capacity to reform the law in those who have not professionally studied it."[52] The public education that local institutions, even jury duty, provided was no longer enough. The diversity of social and economic associations should be a mix of centralized and professionalized institutions on one side and local associations and cooperative experiments on the other. In addition, Mill joined Tocqueville's emphasis on the influence of associative activity and organizational structure on political character with an appreciation of the self-reflective complexity of the process of political education. Mill believed that social and economic conflicts could be resolved only when individual forms of mutual recognition and self-recognition were put in order. There was a need for an egalitarian understanding of the family, a mixture of planning, cooperation, and competition in the marketplace, and a variety of cosmopolitan and local expert points of view within politics. Political education must address how citizens think through particular conflicts within local,

[50] Tocqueville, *Democracy in America*, pp. 274–75.

[51] Ibid., p. 12.

[52] John Stuart Mill, *Considerations on Representative Government*, in *The Collected Works of John Stuart Mill*, ed. John M. Robson, vol. XIX (Toronto: University of Toronto Press, 1963-91), 19:425-26. (Hereafter cited as *CW.*)

cooperative, but also centralized institutions and practices, how they interpret the indeterminate principles and rules of these institutions and practices, and how carefully they reexamine their own evolving identities within the process of experimentation and reform. Only against the backdrop of these mixed basic social and economic institutions, as they are interpreted by individual citizens wrestling with their own changing identities, can constitutional arrangements resolve class conflicts and moderate public opinion. The demands on citizens had become much greater— it was not just a matter of balancing private freedom with periodic public service—and so their political education would have to become more complex if they were to meet these demands.

Mill's counterpart in the twentieth century is John Rawls. Though he is less engaged in politics than Mill was and vaguely sympathetic to the concerns of civic republicanism,[53] Rawls's orientation toward the demands of citizenship is still much more like Mill's than Tocqueville's. Following Mill, Rawls considers the individual freedoms of association and expression the most distinctive and valuable characteristic of post-Reformation liberal societies.[54] But though he believes that pluralism within reasonable limits is a prerequisite for stable democracy, Rawls does not seem committed to the more controversial claim about pluralism that mainstream political scientists have made for the past twenty-five years. Correctly, he does not assume that government decisions in liberal societies are usually made in response to shifting majority coalitions among diverse interest groups and that this process moderates the exercise of political power while it satisfies most people's expressed preferences. His account of how the state should be organized to "mediate society's deepest conflicts"[55] is driven by the functional needs of the political economy as well as by the ideals of political liberty and equal opportunity.[56]

Also, Rawls's account of mediation within a mixed corporatist political economy, like Mill's theory of representative government, is psychologically complex. The mediation he favors combines participation within this mixed corporatist structure with the cultivation of a humanistic method of practical reasoning for expert public officials, professionals, and their

[53] Rawls distinguishes between classical republicanism, which he argues is a political doctrine concerned to cultivate political virtues and informed participation as a means to other ends, consistent with justice as fairness, and civic humanism, which is a comprehensive moral doctrine that identifies political activity with "the good," and which he rejects. See John Rawls, "The Priority of Right and Ideas of the Good," *Philosophy and Public Affairs* 17 (fall 1988): 272–73.

[54] Rawls, "Idea of an Overlapping Consensus," p. 4.

[55] Ibid., p. 24.

[56] John Rawls, *A Theory of Justice* (Cambridge: Harvard University Press, 1971), pp. 224–26.

clients and customers. We can have, he claims, a "reasonable faith" that "free public reason" and "deliberative rationality" in "the original position" will teach policymakers, professionals, and other mediators how to trust one another.[57]

To say that Mill was able to speak to political economists, poets, politicians, and philosophers understates the important educative role his theory played at a time when political economy was the established framework within which economic class conflict was being interpreted and contained. Mill was not simply a polymath who enjoyed Bentham as well as poetry. He sought a method of reasoning that could mend the political economy by bridging the gap between competing speech genres from utilitarianism to romanticism. Similarly, Rawls's ability to be taken seriously by economists, lawyers, physicians, social psychologists, political scientists, and philosophers is not simply testimony to the breadth of his learning. Many of these professionals have listened to him, even when they have rejected his conclusions, because of the rigidified conflicts they are embroiled in: practical adaptations of his methods of practical reasoning, like normative policy analysis and professional ethics, give them a purchase on these conflicts. The current rise of normative policy analysis and professional ethics testifies to the willingness of established experts and government officials to look to liberal theory and its offspring for this kind of second-order theoretical mediation. In the words of Robert Reich, an enthusiastic and prolific advocate for more theoretically informed mediation, "The responsibility of government leaders is not only to make and implement decisions responsive to public wants. A greater challenge is to engage the public in an ongoing dialogue over what problems should be addressed, what is at stake in such decisions, and how to strengthen the public's capacities to deal with similar problems in the future."[58]

Joshua Cohen and Joel Rogers have argued that a neocorporatist society can be democratic if the groups and associations that participate in the policymaking process and the process itself meet certain democratic standards. Their argument for "associative democracy" is a self-conscious attempt to spell out some of the institutional reforms that are possible in a neocorporatist society consistent with general Rawlsian principles of justice. Rawls may not say more than a few words about the functional branches of government (and nothing on functional representation), but Cohen and Rogers correctly infer that his model of a well-ordered society is much closer to neocorporatism than to the anachronistic theories of neoliberal constitutionalists and egalitarian pluralists. The mix of a terri-

---

[57] Rawls, "Idea of an Overlapping Consensus," pp. 20–21.
[58] Robert B. Reich, ed., *The Power of Public Ideas* (Cambridge: Ballinger, 1988), p. 6.

torially based system of representation and a more democratic system of functionally represented quasi-public associations, they argue, "is not an ideal that lies beyond the reach of human beings as they are, and institutions as they can be."[59]

What makes democratic institutional reform possible within neocorporatism, Cohen and Rogers argue, is a guiding public policy that can improve the democratic quality of associations. Government leaders, as Reich says, will have to use policy tools such as taxes, subsidies, and legal sanctions to cajole and constrain associations so that a more democratic process of interest intermediation, assisted by normative policy analysts and professional ethicists, can develop.

Nevertheless, Rawls has insisted that his own work is not "mere politics" and that it "takes the longest view."[60] He has been concerned that he not misunderstood when he says that his theory is "political not metaphysical." A political theory, he argues, is one that does not presuppose a comprehensive moral theory but rather recognizes "the fact of pluralism" and depends on the "fact of reasonable pluralism." He maintains that his theory is not political in the sense that it simply sums up the views of liberal citizens or otherwise enables citizens to come to some overlapping consensus about justice, whatever that may turn out to be. It is political, he argues, in the sense that it tries to work out a normative ideal of social cooperation for free and equal citizens who may well differ about religion, metaphysics, and morality within certain reasonable limits.[61]

Recently, however, Rawls has taken his account of the political nature of his theory one step further. He seems to recognize, albeit hesitantly, that political theory in general can have an "orientation" and even a "reconciliation" effect on its readers.[62] It should orient them toward their political society as a whole from the perspective of citizens, and in some cases it should even calm them down enough so they can see why their political institutions and practices have had to develop the way they have. Reconciliation is not a matter of political passivity but rather entails being "real-

[59] Joshua Cohen and Joel Rogers, "Secondary Associations and Democratic Governance," *Politics and Society* 20 (December 1992): 447.

[60] Rawls, "Idea of an Overlapping Consensus," p. 24.

[61] John Rawls, "The Domain of the Political and Overlapping Consensus," *New York University Law Review* 64 (May 1989): 233–54.

[62] I say hesitantly because the concepts of "orientation" and "reconciliation" found in the manuscript "Justice as Fairness: A Briefer Restatement" (Harvard University, 1989) appear to have been minimized in the work's final published form, *Political Liberalism* (New York: Columbia University Press, 1993). See, for example, *Political Liberalism*, p. 157, and *Theory of Justice*, pp. 221, 512; see also Michael O. Hardimon, "The Project of Reconciliation: Hegel's Social Philosophy," *Philosophy and Public Affairs* 21 (spring 1992): 165–95.

istically utopian." [63] In the same vein, he has argued that his own theory has a kind of educational force. To the extent that a political society conforms to "justice as fairness," its basic structure "should encourage the cooperative virtues of political life: the virtues of reasonableness and a sense of fairness, of a spirit of compromise and a readiness to meet others half way, and the like." [64] This is "the educational role of a public political conception" of justice. [65]

To what extent, if any, do more abstract methods of liberal reasoning have a comparable educational impact? Gutmann explicitly avoids Rawls's method of reasoning from the "original position" in formulating and applying her own regulative moral principles for educational policymaking. [66] Only if we can identify the "dialogic overtones" in these methods as factors within the general structure of liberal politics will they prove to have a role in liberal political education. To read liberal theory as political education within humanistic corporatism rather than thinking of it as a reservoir of principles to be applied to humanistic corporatism, we have to step back from the traditional problem of political education and the particular policy issues that dominate the modern problem. We have to ask what metaphors, with what "overtones," guide our encounter with liberal theory.

## Metaphors of Theory

In politics metaphors bear considerable weight. The organization of power and the education of citizens depend on the implications and limitations of political metaphors like the body politic, the ship of state, and more recently, the policymaking process. How citizens learn to distinguish themselves from others and organize the power they share among themselves depends on metaphors like these that build bridges between private and public life. The body politic has its natural boundaries, life cycles, and preconditions, the ship of state its division of labor and destination, and the policymaking process its own borrowed manufacturing ideals of coordination and integration. Quite a bit rides on which political metaphors a society accepts.

---

[63] Rawls, "Justice as Fairness: A Briefer Restatement," pp. 2–3.

[64] Ibid., p. 83. The parallel passages in *Political Liberalism* are pp. 122, 139, and 194.

[65] Rawls, "Justice as Fairness: A Briefer Restatement," p. 90. See *Political Liberalism*, p. 71. Rawls alludes to this in passing in *Theory of Justice*, p. 133, when he says that a "general awareness" of the "universal acceptance" of principles of justice "should have desirable effects and support the stability of future cooperation."

[66] Gutmann, *Democratic Education*, p. 17.

Within liberal theory, metaphors influence the terms of political membership and the boundaries of the political domain on three levels. The first is the level of ordinary language.[67] Metaphors like John Locke's reference to freedom as the best "fence" against insecurity[68] expand the meaning of political concepts by joining them with ideas and images we do not ordinarily associate with politics. His description of majority rule as a natural gravitational force has the same effect: "It is necessary that the Body should move that way whither the greater force carries it, which is the consent of the majority."[69] Whether this is a matter of supplementing literal meaning with figurative meaning or whether it is more accurately described as using literal meaning for a metaphorical purpose is a matter of some disagreement that we will not have to resolve here.[70] Liberal theory, like all other political theory, depends on the metaphors of its day to make its arguments compelling.

Metaphors are also important because they have the generative power to create larger frameworks of meaning.[71] This is how the metaphor of the watch operates in Thomas Hobbes's author's introduction to *Leviathan*. It suggests the kinds of reforms possible if the delicate balance in Leviathan state is to be maintained. Unlike a body politic, Leviathan state can be repaired by removing and replacing its broken parts. The whole does not have the same integrity as an organic body or the same resistance to foreign objects. In contrast to both of these generative metaphors, Locke asserts that in a "Political Society . . . the Community comes to be Umpire, by settled standing Rules, indifferent, and the same to all Parties."[72] Politics is a matter not of mechanical balance but of competitive striving, and the watchmaker is replaced by an impartial judge who can interpret and enforce the rules.

The dominant generative liberal metaphor today is the policymaking process, which legitimates expert authority, defers to professional judgments, couches political problems in terms of the imperfections of administrative rules and noncompliance with them, and defines possible remedies in terms of plebiscitary mandates and a smoothly functioning bureaucracy. This is the integrated process within which policies are made.

[67] George Lakoff and Mark Johnson, *Metaphors We Live By* (Chicago: University of Chicago Press, 1980).

[68] Locke, *Two Treatises of Government*, vol. 2, sec. 17, p. 320.

[69] Ibid., vol. 2, sec. 96, p. 375.

[70] See the range of opinions in Sheldon Sacks, *On Metaphor* (Chicago: University of Chicago Press, 1979).

[71] Donald A. Schön, "Generative Metaphor: A Perspective on Problem-Setting in Social Policy," in *Metaphor and Thought*, ed. Andrew Ortony (New York: Cambridge University Press, 1979).

[72] Locke, *Two Treatises of Government*, vol. 2, sec. 87, p. 367.

In addition to this generative liberal metaphor, however, liberal theorists have introduced other generative metaphors that humanize the policy-making process. John Stuart Mill's metaphor of a marketplace of ideas and John Rawls's simile of justice as fairness, which likens politics to a fair game, operate on this level.

Finally, the term *orienting metaphor* describes the metaphors that political theories have relied on to orient their readers toward competing generative metaphors. This aspect of metaphor in liberal theory is commonly overlooked, and it is at the heart of my interpretation of liberal theory *as* political education.

The orienting metaphor of analysis emphasizes the binding power of logical consistency. It represents politics in terms of the motivational principles that generate action and the regulative principles that constrain it. In this kind of political world, citizenship is a matter of maintaining equilibrium while making one's way through a field of opposing forces. The power of liberal theory, read this way, is the power a tightly argued theory has to map out the political domain for individuals and inform them of the individual and collective resources at their disposal. It tells them about the future and the relative strengths of internal and external forces. The rest is up to them. "Reading is analyzing" implies "seeing" opposing forces and one's place as a citizen within them.

Analytic reading, as John Stuart Mill suspected when he characterized the methods of Macaulay, Bentham, and his father, is sometimes like a chemical process capable of distilling the political world into its constituent parts and then combining them according to their proper valences. At other times it is more deductive.[73] When read through the eyes of a chemist, the text operates like a centrifuge that drives related arguments together and unrelated ones apart; the reader then uses counterexamples to further separate the arguments that have been precipitated out until the logical structure of the theory is apparent. Alternatively, when done by a geometer like Hobbes, perhaps even more than by James Mill and Bentham, analysis is less experimental. Hobbes invites the reader to think about politics and morality with the help of a "resolutive-compositive" method.[74] On this reading, *Leviathan* begins in introspection as we look into ourselves to resolve Leviathan state into its constituent parts. This is followed by a series of dilemmas and deductions that provide regulative principles to guide its reassembly.

Architectural metaphors represent political life and the power of political theory very differently as fortifications that protect a besieged moral

[73] John Stuart Mill, *A System of Logic, Ratiocinative and Deductive* in *CW*, 8:879-94.

[74] Hobbes, *Leviathan*, in *The English Works of Thomas Hobbes*, ed. Sir William Molesworth, 11 vols. (London: J. Bohn, 1839-45), 3:x-xi.

self. This way of reading political theory, "reading is rebuilding," encourages the reader to look for and repair the foundations of liberal society. Typically these foundations are made out of materials like "human nature," which are thought to have a durability we can intuit. They are our most reliable building blocks if we want to secure ourselves against hunger and war.

Kant's practical philosophy invites this kind of reading, but so do the seemingly very different *Federalist Papers*. Both envision political life as a process of building institutions that will stabilize political power, and both envision two classes of citizens: the majority of citizens will pursue their own private interests, while a virtuous few will oversee the well-balanced institutions that keep the peace. The power of these theories is their ability to build an architectural model of the kingdoms or realms within which political institutions and practice can then rest. In Kant, this architectonic vision sweeps across a field in which practical reason is contained in property relations and then extended to republican government.[75] In the case of Madison and Hamilton, the image is more Newtonian: the satisfaction of human desires depends on seeing to it that public and private spheres remain in their proper orbits.

In Kant's case political institutions are built on moral ground, but actual moral life is possible only when private and public life can be organized so as to make acting for the sake of the moral law more rather than less likely. Active political life is only one choice among many for Kantian individuals, and to make this choice moral education, not political education, is needed. For the Federalists, the ground is a very different vision of human nature, but it serves the same foundational purpose, and political education is again depreciated. Instead of supplanting political education with moral education, this time experience in an "expanded *commercial* republic" is the best preparation for life in a society organized around property and privacy and under rules of representation and interest group bargaining. In Richard Krouse's words, for Madison "participation in the life of the political community and the cultivation of public spirit through political education" have been abandoned.[76]

Archaeological excavation points us in the direction of a natural history, which will give us a greater understanding of our roots. It is backward-looking instead of forward- or upward-looking, but it is still visual. Read

[75] For a subtle interpretation of the relation between architectural metaphor and foundationalism, see Onora O'Neill, "Vindicating Reason," in *The Cambridge Companion to Kant*, ed. Paul Guyer (New York: Cambridge University Press, 1992), p. 291.

[76] Richard W. Krouse, "'Classical' Images of Democracy in America," in *Democratic Theory and Practice*, ed. Graeme Duncan (Cambridge: Cambridge University Press, 1983), pp. 66–67.

through this third visual metaphor, political life has a potential organic unity. Citizenship is not something to be chosen but rather something citizens inherit and then grow into. Liberal theory is part of this collective inheritance, and it is not possible to separate its arguments or foundations from its past use. The arguments and foundations are historical artifacts whose meanings depend on the questions that gave birth to them and that sustain them over time. Through insight into the buried past, citizens can ideally transcend the limits of individualism and rationalism that the metaphors of analysis and reconstruction impose on their political self-understanding.

Hegel was probably the most enthusiastic archaeologist of classical liberal theory, and Nietzsche its greatest archaeological critic. In our time, historians like Pocock and Skinner have sympathetically adopted the metaphor "reading is excavating," albeit much more cautiously than Hegel, while Gadamer and Foucault have been the most important contributors to the Nietzschean revival in political theory. In every case, however, an allegedly metamorphosizing recovery of the history of liberal theory has been sought to take the place of a programmatic conception of political education.

All three of these sight-based orienting metaphors pit liberal theory against a hostile environment that we must initially withdraw from before we can see it clearly. All three undervalue liberal theory's power as a form of political education. When we analyze, rebuild, or excavate liberal theory, it has the power to resist, fortify, or retrieve, but not the power to respond to or inquire of citizens or teach them to discuss and revise the terms of political membership and social cooperation.

Orienting and generative metaphors have very different structures in political theory. Unlike generative metaphors, which strive for unity and coherence, orienting metaphors synesthetically rely on each other. Generative political metaphors designed to connect personal feelings and other private experiences directly with the organization of power and the education of citizens strive for hegemony. They give political theory its commanding tone. Orienting metaphors translate the experiences of one sense into that of another in order to be more persuasive.

Certainly good political theory, like all good writing, tries to block its metaphors. The prejudice against mixed metaphors, however, whatever its merits as a matter of literary style and logic, is misleading in politics, where mixed orienting metaphors of sight, sound, and to a slightly lesser extent touch are necessary for political theory *as* political education.

To illustrate the complex blending of orienting metaphors in liberal theory and their relation to the politics of policymaking, it is helpful to look just outside the borders of liberal theory and then gradually move back inside. The first two examples deal with the recognition of citizens and the effects of power, but they are not theoretical in the sense of favoring any particular generative metaphor. They illustrate the complex interplay of metaphors of sight and sound in politics that orienting metaphors of liberal theory incorporate and subtly exploit.

Janie Crawford, the heroine of Zora Neale Hurston's 1937 novel *Their Eyes Were Watching God*, experiences the effects of power up close. As the wife of Mayor Joe Starks, Janie finds herself increasingly shut off from neighbors and friends in the poor black southern town of Eatonville. She shares in her husband's power, but it is not a power she either enjoys or can control. "There was something about Joe Starks that cowed the town. It was not because of physical fear. He was no fist fighter. His bulk was not even imposing as men go. Neither was it because he was more literate than the rest. Something else made men give way before him. He had a bow-down command in his face, and every step he took made the thing more tangible." [77] Steadily Joe Starks silences Janie. ("It must have been the way Joe Starks spoke out without giving her a chance to say anything one way or another that took the bloom off of things" [p. 70]. But, Hurston tells us, it is not just the bow-down command in his face. As one of Joe Starks's acquaintances remarks, "You kin feel a switch in his hand when he's talkin' to yuh" (p. 78). There is a feel that power has when it is intimated in voice. And as Janie's love for Starks declines, she reflects "back and forth about what had happened in the making of a voice out of man" (p. 134). Though her eyes may be watching God, Janie Crawford also learns to listen to the commanding voice of political power as it oversteps the bounds of decency and mutual respect. Once she can hear the switch in his hand, that is all he is to her.

The voices and faces of power take on even greater complexity in the question raised in 1947 by Ralph Ellison's narrator in *Invisible Man*. "And so I play the invisible music of my isolation . . . you hear this music simply because music is heard and seldom seen, except by musicians. Could this compulsion to put invisibility down in black and white be an urge to make music of invisibility?" [78] The invisibility of his blackness, which first drives Ellison's narrator to strike out in violent anger at those who look right through him, later drives him underground to a basement apartment— well lit and off the meter. There, in his cave of solitary reflection, he is able to sing out about what has made him "so Black and blue." [79] *Invisible Man*

[77] Zora Neale Hurston, *Their Eyes Were Watching God* (Urbana: University of Illinois Press, 1979), p. 75.

[78] Ralph Ellison, *Invisible Man* (New York: Vintage, 1989), p. 13.

[79] See Barry Singer, *Black and Blue: The Life and Lyrics of Andy Razaf* (New York: Schirmer Books, 1993).

makes blackness, the color of the other, visible on the page by playing the invisible music of isolation.

Is music ever visible? Can color carry a melody? Are these mixed metaphors more confusing than enlightening? Psychologists have tried to map this phenomenon of synesthesia, especially in early childhood before the prohibition against mixing metaphors has taken hold.[80] Artists have tried to exploit it. In Rimsky-Korsakov's musical lexicon, C major was white; to Scriabin it was red. Nabokov believed the English long *a* has the tint of "weathered wood, but a French *a* evokes polished ebony."[81] For Ellison the interplay of sight and sound serves a political purpose. Where blackness cannot be seen, perhaps it can be heard. By finding his own voice in black and white, the invisible man hopes to redirect his anger, take responsibility for himself, and teach us something about what it is like to struggle against racism.

Now, if we take a step closer to political theory, we can see how Hurston's and Ellison's metaphors can help us think more critically about the presuppositions of the generative metaphor of policymaking.

By 1962 when Michael Harrington wrote *The Other America*, invisibility had spread. Ellison's song had fallen on deaf ears. "The other America, the America of poverty, is hidden today in a way that it never was before. Its millions are socially invisible to the rest of us."[82] Fifty million Americans, Harrington estimated, had become invisible. Racial minorities were joined by the elderly and rural poor whose poverty was made invisible by geographical segregation and a consumer market flooded with cheap imitations. Despite the eloquence of poets and writers like Ellison, the voices of the invisible poor, Harrington argued, were not being heard. "And finally, the poor are politically invisible. It is one of the cruelest ironies of social life in advanced countries that the dispossessed at the bottom of society are unable to speak for themselves. The people of the other America do not, by far and large, belong to unions, to fraternal organizations, or to political parties. They are without lobbies of their own; they put forward no legislative program. As a group, they are atomized. They have no face; they have no voice" (p. 13). Certainly there have been exceptions. Welfare mothers, the unemployed, and even undocumented foreign workers at times have managed to ignore the stigmas attached to their status in society and accept the costs of coming forward on their own behalf. In general, however, Harrington is still right. Political invisibility

[80] Lawrence E. Marks et al., "Perceiving Similarity and Comprehending Metaphor," *Monographs of the Society for Research in Child Development* 52 (1987), 1, Serial No. 215.

[81] Diane Ackerman, *A Natural History of the Senses* (New York: Vintage, 1991), pp. 290–91.

[82] Michael Harrington, *The Other America: Poverty in the United States* (Baltimore: Penguin, 1963), p. 10.

has meant that the poor have had to depend on the voices of others to be heard within the politics of policymaking. Professional advocates, friends, and family have had to remind the rest of us (and as a university teacher I include myself in this majority) that the "other America" deserves our help. As middle-class consumer movements have become more vocal and clients and professionals more organized,[83] the other America has found it increasingly difficult to speak for itself.

In short, as policymaking has become more streamlined, the ranks of the other America have continued to swell. Race is still a cruel dividing line,[84] but it is not the only one. In 1992 the working poor made up nearly 40 percent of the workforce, and they earned "wages so low that the average hourly pay lifts a family of four barely to the margins of poverty even if the worker is employed full-time the whole year."[85] At roughly 1½ times the poverty level, the "economy budget" of these families usually includes no health insurance, no savings, and little money for new clothes and school supplies. For the "forgotten Americans" who work hard just to get by, the level of despair and powerlessness is painfully high.

For example, Paul is a middle-aged high-school graduate, working two part-time jobs. He and his wife, a full-time secretary, make just enough to pay the rent on their mobile home and keep their two children in school clothes. His interviewer recorded the following conversation.

> Paul looked straight at me: "You know," he said, "I was talking to a friend of mine the other day. We want to make a decent living. We've been eating it. For a long time—for many years—we've been on the other end of the stick. We've been beat into a corner. How do you get to where we can do what we need to do to survive? I've got other friends like this. They're crazed because they can't make it. I don't care if I leave." Stunned at the sudden turn of the conversation, I said, "You mean 'die'?" He reflected a moment, his eyes looking toward the floor. "Yes," he said.[86]

Although Medicare and other social assistance programs have periodically reduced some of the invisibility Ellison and Harrington described,[87]

[83] Mark E. Kann, *Middle Class Radicalism in Santa Monica* (Philadelphia: Temple University Press, 1986).

[84] William W. Goldsmith and Edward J. Blakely, *Separate Societies: Poverty and Inequality in U.S. Cities* (Philadelphia: Temple University Press, 1992), and Andrew Hacker, *Two Nations: Black and White, Separate, Hostile, Unequal* (New York: Macmillan, 1992).

[85] John E. Schwarz and Thomas J. Volgy, *The Forgotten Americans* (New York: W. W. Norton, 1992), p. 14.

[86] Schwarz and Volgy, *Forgotten Americans*, pp. 23–24.

[87] Michael Walzer, "Politics in the Welfare State," in *Beyond the Welfare State*, ed. Irving Howe (New York: Schocken Books, 1982).

the political changes they wanted have not occurred. The voices of the invisible are still rarely heard, and are easily forgotten.

This suggests that metaphors of sight and sound not only are inextricably connected but may also be in conflict. For Harrington, the invisible were voiceless. Now, visibility within the policymaking process may deny one a voice. The painful limits of metaphors of visual equality are recorded in Patricia J. Williams's *The Alchemy of Race and Rights:*

> My parents were always telling me to look up at the world; to look straight at people, particularly white people; not to let them stare me down; to hold my ground; to insist on the right to my presence no matter what. They told me that in this culture you have to look people in the eye because that's how you tell them you're their equal. . . . What was hardest was not just that white people saw me, . . . but that they looked through me, as if I were transparent.
>
> By itself, seeing into me would be to see my substance, my anger, my vulnerability and my raging despair—and that alone is hard enough to show. But to uncover it and have it devalued by ignore-ance, to hold it up bravely in the organ of my eyes and to have it greeted by an impasssive stare that passes right through all that which is me, an impassive stare that moves on and attaches itself to my left earlobe or to the dust caught in the rusty vertical geysers of my wiry hair or to the breadth of my freckled brown nose— this is deeply humiliating. It rewounds, relives the early childhood anguish of uncensored seeing, the fullness of vision that is the permanent turning-away point for most blacks.
>
> The cold game of equality staring makes me feel like a thin sheet of glass: white people see all the worlds beyond me but not me. They come trotting at me with force and speed; they do not see me. I could force my presence, the real me contained in those eyes, upon them, but I would be smashed in the process. If I deflect, if I move out of the way, they will never know I existed.[88]

For Williams, a lawyer and teacher writing in the Reagan years, partial legal equality, beginning with the *Brown* decision and the civil rights legislation of the 1960s, had made the surfaces of her body visible while transforming the substance within it (her anger, vulnerability, and raging despair) into an unoffending, transparent gel. The struggle to overcome invisibility revealed to her the limits as well as the power of this political metaphor.

Why do we so rarely hear the voices of these invisible men and women? Why do we forget what they sound like even when they do not drop out of sight? At some level we know they are there, yet the language we use to

[88] Patricia J. Williams, *The Alchemy of Race and Rights* (Cambridge: Harvard University Press, 1991), p. 222.

speak about them and with them remains foreign and often threatening to them. We are tone deaf to what Ellison called the "music of invisibility." This is not always a product of ill will; it is often more like what Harrington called "well-meaning ignorance." But it is a costly ignorance: the suspicion in our own voices weakens their political agency. As the political alienation of these others has increased, we have acquired a full register of liberal voices—not just tolerance but the arrogance of expertise, the deference of clients, and the persistence of consumers—that sets the boundaries of authority and the terms of citizenship beyond their grasp; like Williams, they feel like see-through citizens who are visible only in their contours and outlines—and are not to be trusted. Trusting and trustworthy modern liberal voices are at once humanistic and deaf to the music of invisibility. Until we can hear our own all too familiar liberal voices more clearly— until we listen to them on the page in "black and white"—we are not going to know how to adjust them to a more democratic politics.

This will take something more than self-critical reflection. If we who have a voice in liberal society are to listen to the invisible, the forgotten, and the transparent, we must first learn to listen to how our own voices overshadow and discourage the voices of others. This requires a keen eye for metaphor, especially the way metaphors of sound and sight operate together within the methods of liberal theory itself, which in turn have been incorporated into the speech genres of policy analysis and professional ethics.

As long as we read modern liberal theory analytically, constructively, or archaeologically, we will have a difficult time not depreciating its significance as political education. The metaphor of analytic reading favors "right reckoning" over noncognitive learning. The architectural metaphor prefers moral learning to affective learning. The archaeological metaphor values historical understanding over technique. All three are sight-based metaphors that strive to eliminate political distance and deny differences that cannot be seen. In their haste to span these distances and transcend sometimes subtle textural differences, they miss the significance of intonation and reduce political education to some form of conditioning or training.

Why are liberal theorists in such a hurry? The answer is to be found in their Emersonian ambivalence toward power and their reluctance to confront their own participation in political education. Liberal theorists from Mill to Rawls have been haunted by a grotesque Emersonian image, and it is this ideal, even more than their faith in political socialization, that has affected how liberal theorists have understood their own mediating work.

Even though they reject Emerson's transcendentalism, modern liberal theorists have continued to see the world around them in terms of a disembodied self-reliance. "Standing on the bare ground,—my head bathed by the blithe air and uplifted into infinite space,—all mean egotism vanishes. I become a transparent eyeball; I am nothing; I see all; the currents of the Universal Being circulate through me; I am part or parcel of God."[89] From this detached, visual perspective that strives for self-transparency, the task of political education is tainted and corrupting. Unlike Plato's use of the metaphor of philosophy as seeing, which grounds his theory of *paideia*, the Emersonian visual ideal depreciates political education. For the Emersonian theorist all mean egotism vanishes in the act of seeing because it is projected onto others, making their political education a problem foisted on political theorists by the unenlightened other and not their paramount task. For the theorist who is "part or parcel of God," the notion of liberal theory as political education is perverse. Nothing of any lasting value, he suggests, is to be gained in conversations with others. "Conversation is a game of circles. . . . Good as is discourse, silence is better, and shames it."[90] Conversations are just one of the circles thought traces, but they are too ephemeral, Emerson suggests, and the distance we must travel within this circle reflects the imperfect understanding conversation provides. The smaller the circle the better, and so for Emerson "the eye is the first circle."[91]

To understand contemporary liberal theory's practical influence as a form of political education, we must put aside this one-eyed Emersonian ideal ("I am nothing; I see all") so that we can also listen to how contemporary liberal theory's familiar cadences and tones orient political clients and consumers toward the expert authorities of a more humanistic corporatism.

My reading of modern liberal theory, unlike more familiar readings that accept liberal theory's own Emersonian ego ideal, depends on the metaphor of listening rather than the sight-based metaphors of analyzing, rebuilding, or excavating liberal theory. I want to listen to the stylized Socratic conversations, dialogues, and arguments that philosophically minded liberal theorists have initiated and entered. Rather than see how they hold together, I want to register what it has sounded like when they have tried, sometimes successfully, to mediate between competing expert authorities, clients, and consumers and to seek out humane compromises within the boundaries of a mixed corporatist and pluralist society.

Analyzing liberal theories into their constituent parts, rebuilding them from the ground up, and unearthing their evolutionary past all tell us quite

[89] Ralph Waldo Emerson, *Nature*, in *Complete Works of Ralph Waldo Emerson*, ed. Joel Myerson (New York: AMS Press, 1979), 1:10. (Hereafter cited as *CW.*)

[90] Ralph Waldo Emerson, "Circles", in *CW*, 2:310.

[91] Ibid., p. 305.

a bit, but they do not tell us much about modern liberal theory as a form of political education that mediates expert authority and orients the trust of political clients and consumers. Specifically, they do not tell us whether its tone is commanding or reassuring, judgmental or inviting, confident or hesitant, distant or caring. How does the voice of contemporary liberal theory encourage or permit political clients to trust the authority of experts in some cases and to trust their own judgment as skeptical consumers in others? This is not the question we ask when we are analyzing, reconstructing, or excavating liberal theory. It requires that the reader make distinctions not visible to the "mind's eye." When we listen with this question in mind, we begin to hear how modern liberal theory prepares clients and consumers as well as policymakers for compromise and competition by rehearsing them for the subtle and often painful exchanges that hierarchical expert authority relations depend on. It is the voice of modern liberal theory—or more accurately, how these theories impart a range of voices against the background of Manichean images—that accounts for their significance as a form of political education.

This is where liberal theory's synesthetic use of orienting metaphors becomes important. Visual images, recall, just like philosophical arguments, have "dialogical overtones." To hear liberal theory means being able to picture it up against a larger theoretical and practical narrative. In Maurice Merleau-Ponty's words, "Speech always comes into play against a background of speech; it is always only a fold in the immense fabric of language."[92] If we listen without Emersonian disdain to modern liberal theory within the conversations of policy analysts, ethicists, bureaucratic experts, and their clients and consumers, then we may be able to hear its mediating power more clearly. As we understand who is doing the talking, we will also be able to interpret more clearly the flood of images that have engulfed the politics of policymaking.

The relation between liberal theory and the politics of policymaking is metaphorical, then, in a dual sense. The generative metaphor of politics as policymaking (politics understood and engaged in as a process that integrates consumer demands and client trust through humane expert intervention) depends for its attractiveness on liberal theory as political education. Politics as policymaking is a visual as well as a vocal process. To understand how voices are modulated against the background of Manichean images, we have to attend to the orienting power of liberal theory itself. That is, we have to be sensitive to the way the methods of reasoning in liberal theory orient us toward the generative metaphor of politics

---

[92] Maurice Merleau-Ponty, "Indirect Languages and the Voices of Silences," in *Signs*, trans. Richard C. McCleary (Evanston, Ill.: Northwestern University Press, 1964), p. 42.

as policymaking. In Kant and Mill the orienting metaphors are visual and sedentary, despite the voracious visual appetites of both and Mill's periodic bursts of street-level political energy. They encourage the reader to step back and see the differences between self and other, public and private, political and aesthetic. In Rawls the orienting metaphors are mixed. He invites readers to see liberal theory as another player in the policymaking game, but he also enables us to hear some accents and internal voices more clearly than others once the "veil of ignorance" has been drawn.

We are not accustomed to thinking about policymaking as a political metaphor like the body politic. We also do not think about how we read liberal theory in terms of metaphors of engagement that orient clients, consumers, and experts toward power as spectators, referees, players, and interlocutors. The practical importance of liberal theory for the modern problem of political education has depended no less on our uncritical acceptance of its orienting metaphors than on our acceptance of its generative metaphors.

# CHAPTER THREE

# Liberal Theorists
# and Their Ideals

A complex Socratic ideal of citizenship accented by a Weberian "matter-of-factness" has often guided and sometimes shadowed liberal theorists as they have come to terms with expert authority. To illustrate how this ideal works in practice, I examine one typical policymaking arena where the familiar voice of expert authority can be heard: the college classroom. The picture of the classroom I present is intentionally idealized to reveal how the speech genres of policy analysis and professional ethics are supposed to work to sustain trust in expert authority, helped when necessary by more finely articulated methods of practical reason like those developed by Mill and Rawls.

In the closing section I suggest how ideals outside the liberal tradition can be enlisted to formulate an alternative, more democratic conception of political education. What is needed is not a solution to the modern problem of liberal political education, which presumably would teach clients and consumers when to trust and when to distrust expert authority with fewer risks,[1] but rather a conception of political education that emphasizes the poise needed to cope with the frustrations of democratic political experience in terms other than conscience and risk. Democratic theory's contribution to this political education, which I discuss in part 3, would be analogous to the role liberal theory as political education has played under humanistic corporatism. It would orient citizens toward power so as to replace the modern problem of political education with a more democratic problem: how citizens can share their experiences with power and thus be more poised in facing beguiling and intimidating images and more aware of the overtones of authority in their own voices.

[1] See Diego Gambetta, ed., *Trust: Making and Breaking Cooperative Relations* (New York: Blackwell, 1988).

## Socratic Dialogue

Modern liberal theorists generally have endorsed democratic institutions and practices so long as they have respected individual conscience.[2] The inspiration for this instrumental view of politics and the centrality of conscience is the modern liberal reinterpretation of the Platonic Socrates, both the substance of his views and his methods of getting them across. Liberal theorists have been drawn to this account of Socrates as the symbol of disciplined conscience in order to avoid solipsism on one side and obeisance to authority on the other.

Bruce Ackerman claims to apply this Socratic discipline to the policy problems that arise in a liberal society. In *Social Justice in the Liberal State* Ackerman fashions a series of Socratic exchanges in order to defend the thesis that the liberal state is the best political arrangement for protecting conscientious Socratic conversation and its participants. His derivation of the powers of the liberal state from a hypothetical dialogue that is only formally constrained by principles of consistency and rationality is open to criticism on logical grounds. More revealing are Ackerman's comments on the Socratic inspiration for his theory. In discussing the centrality of dialogue for both liberal society and liberal theory, he says that "despite the very different sympathies and arguments that different dialogues require, all liberal philosophers will be marked with the same Socratic spirit—for they all will use dialogue to lead their partners to see the virtue of professing a certain kind of political ignorance."[3] But according to Ackerman, it is not just the Socratic insistence on honesty that inspires liberal theorists and should guide the liberal state:

> Socrates . . . stands as the emblem on the liberal standard. This is so not only because his death stands as the paradigmatic political wrong, but because his life stands as the paradigmatic ground of political right—in its insistence that *all* people submit to questioning about the things they hold dearest; that *each of us* contemplate the possibility that our moral vision may be distorted; that *all* of us accept the discipline of dialogue and restrain the temptation to destroy those whom we cannot convince. (p. 348; emphasis added)

It is wrong for any state to persecute its citizens for their beliefs, and it is right for citizens to question one another about their beliefs, no matter how deep their differences. But—and this is the crucial point—a Socratic

[2] William N. Nelson, *On Justifying Democracy* (London: Routledge and Kegan Paul, 1980).

[3] Bruce A. Ackerman, *Social Justice in the Liberal State* (New Haven: Yale University Press, 1980), p. 360.

discipline of dialogue should restrain all citizens from destroying those they cannot convince. This exercise of individual restraint, then, is a model for the exercise of state power. In a liberal society, according to Ackerman, this means that neither the state nor its citizens should give in to the temptation to destroy. In this way, the liberal state guarantees an environment within which Socratic dialogue can continue.

In a later essay, Ackerman elaborates this notion of an exemplary self-discipline. He suggests that Socratic dialogue may be too much in matters of personal morality where some "key decisions are made in silence."[4] But on matters of public morality, Socratic dialogue remains an imperative as long as it is limited by a formal "principle of restraint."

> When you and I learn that we disagree about one or another dimension of the moral truth, we should not search for some common value that will trump this disagreement; nor should we try to translate it into some putatively neutral framework; nor should we seek to transcend it by talking about how some unearthly creature might resolve it. We should simply say *nothing at all* about this disagreement and put the moral ideals that divide us off the conversational agenda of the liberal state. In restraining ourselves in this way, we need not lose the chance to talk to one another about our deepest moral disagreements in countless other, more private, contexts. We simply recognize that, while these ongoing debates continue, we will gain nothing of value by falsely asserting the political community is of one mind on deeply contested matters. (Ibid., p. 16)

A liberal Socratic dialogue, Ackerman says, should not permit one side to marshal the power of the political community behind one or another dimension of the moral truth. In order to keep the majoritarian liberal state out of conflicts in which divisive issues are raised, liberals have an obligation not to answer in public. The original Socratic discipline of raising questions remains limited by how much the respondent can understand, but there also must be a self-imposed limit on the kinds of answers one can give on matters that have been placed on the conversational agenda of the liberal state.

The revealing thing about Ackerman's derivation of the liberal state is the political purpose to which he wants to put Socratic discipline. He urges us to model limited government on Socratic self-discipline. Just as individual Socratic citizens qua citizens should remain silent on morally divisive issues, so too should the state and its officials. It is not enough that they resist the temptation to destroy the opposition. If the goal of liberal politics is to arrive at morally neutral policies rather than to con-

---

[4] Bruce Ackerman, "Why Dialogue?" *Journal of Philosophy* 86 (January 1989): 6.

duct morally charged debates, then Ackerman's version of Socratic discipline is precisely the discipline policymakers must have. Citizens in their private lives can speak their minds, so long as they do not destroy one another, but those who draw up the political agenda based on their reading of public issues and needs must exercise additional restraint. Socratic silence represents the virtue of political neutrality: the liberal state maintains its neutrality when its policymakers refuse to speak their minds on morally divisive issues.

Michael Walzer argues that Ackerman has missed the point of Socratic dialogue.[5] One cannot and should not try to derive institutional political principles from an idealized conception of dialogue. This does not mean that Socratic dialogue is not a politically relevant ideal, however. Walzer argues that Socrates was an exemplary social critic, operating within the walls of ancient Athens, calling attention to public and private hypocrisy at his own peril; he was not an exemplary policymaker. The value of Socrates today is not his implicit message about the need for political neutrality through restraint among policymakers when divisive moral conflicts arise, as Ackerman suggests. For Walzer, Socrates' life illustrates how important it is for social critics to be connected to the "shared understandings" of their own societies. If they are to call their fellow citizens to task, it must be by reminding them of the internal moral and political norms of their societies. To do this effectively, they must have an "intimate" feeling for, as well as knowledge of, these shared understandings, and they must be close enough to be heard. Unless they are connected, social critics will not be sensitive enough to the importance of place, and they will not be near enough to be heard by the people they are telling to "live up to their own ideals."[6] Socrates' great virtue was his ability to engage his intelocutors on their own ground and then call them to task in their own terms. He measured his critical distance "in inches."[7] The formalization of Socratic dialogue into a principled method of cross-examination obscures its social and historical content, which gave it its credibility.

If Ackerman's Socrates is the exemplary, neutral policymaker, Walzer's Socrates symbolizes the policymaker's alter ego, the prophetic social critic. Socrates' method of challenging others in a prophetic tone not only reminds them of their forgotten moral principles, it instills in them the right

[5] Michael Walzer, "A Critique of Philosophical Conversation," *Philosophical Forum* 21 (fall–winter 1989–90): 182–96.

[6] Michael Walzer, *The Company of Critics: Social Criticism and Political Commitment in the Twentieth Century* (New York: Basic Books, 1988), p. 188.

[7] Michael Walzer, *Interpretation and Social Criticism* (Cambridge: Harvard University Press, 1987), p. 61.

kind of ambivalence toward politics.[8] Socrates was not disengaged from politics in the conventional Athenian sense (*apragmon*), but he also was not an active citizen in the conventional Athenian sense.[9] His character, and the character he sought to cultivate in his students and interlocutors, was a special combination of civic responsibility and moral distance. He saw himself as a gadfly who could keep the demos from becoming lazy and weak through constant questioning, but he avoided public office. Because Athens and its laws provided the best environment for speaking out on public as well as private matters (*parrhesia*), he was indirectly committed to upholding the laws as long as obedience did not conflict with his primary duty to search for moral truth. By teaching others to question politicians just as they would question anyone else who claimed to know the truth, he sought to give them a critical distance from politics and those in power while they still remained within the radius of the laws.

This prophetic Socrates, then, is a partial model for the episodic, private citizen in the liberal tradition whose conscientious refusal can push the state to give an account of its actions and, by example, also can moderate mass political passions. Furthermore, this version of the Socratic ideal values politics but does not require full-time political activity from anyone, especially those capable of moral inquiry. Socrates served when he had to, but no more. When the demos acted wrongly from his perspective he resisted, just as he resisted when the Thirty Tyrants issued an unjust order. But he also refused to put the feelings of family and friends or the chance to philosophize in exile above respect for just laws. He was a private citizen in Ackerman's sense, a private seeker after moral truth and, at times, a citizen willing to risk challenging political power in the name of moral excellence.[10] It is this ambivalent political character that Walzer's liberal theory promotes.

As attractive as these Socratic ideals of neutrality and prophetic social criticism have been for liberal theorists, however, the Socratic method as a means to these ideals, not just a symbol of them, has proved even more irresistible. Gregory Vlastos has argued that the Socratic method explains the paradoxical allure of Socrates' life.

[8] J. Peter Euben describes this ambivalence by characterizing Socratic politics as "democratically aristocratic." See *The Tragedy of Political Theory* (Princeton: Princeton University Press, 1990), p. 208.

[9] L. B. Carter, *The Quiet Athenian* (Oxford: Clarendon Press, 1986), p. 185.

[10] For two accounts of episodic private citizenship and its defense in liberal theory, see Bruce Ackerman, *We the People*, vol. 1, *Foundations* (Cambridge: Harvard University Press, 1991), and George Kateb, *The Inner Ocean: Individualism and Democratic Culture* (Ithaca: Cornell University Press, 1992), chap. 1.

Socrates, according to Vlastos, believed that people had to have knowledge of the good in order to be good, that he himself did not have this knowledge, and that searching for it was what made life worth living. "Our soul is the only thing in us worth saving, and there is only one way to save it: to acquire knowledge."[11] But paradoxically, his relentless cross-examination of others does "not seem to fit this role" (ibid., p. 7). Socrates is forever shipwrecking the arguments of others, not salvaging them.

Is this any way to respect others? The way out of this practical paradox, according to Vlastos, is through the Socratic method itself.

> Why rank that method among the great achievements of humanity? Because it makes moral inquiry a common human enterprise, open to every man. Its practice calls for no adherence to a philosophical system, or mastery of a specialized technique, or acquisition of a technical vocabulary. It calls for common sense and common speech. . . . But while the Socratic method makes moral inquiry open to everyone, it makes it easy for no one. It calls not only for the highest degree of mental alertness of which anyone is capable, but also for moral qualities of a high order: sincerity, humility, courage. (p. 20)

What Socrates wants, for himself and his interlocutors, is further examination and questioning. He believes that his own views are as open to revision as those of his interlocutors. Thus the Socratic method represents the high demands moral inquiry places on human character and the long distance we all still have to travel in this common search. To adopt this method, Vlastos concludes, is to "give wholehearted assent to Socrates' vision of man as a mature, responsible being, claiming to the fullest extent his freedom to make his own choice between right and wrong, not only in action, but in judgment" (p. 21).

Vlastos capsulized what many other liberal theorists have felt: the Socratic method is a procedural expression of liberal moral personality. It captures in procedural terms the conception of moral personality on which politics should rest. It not only symbolizes the moral virtues of sincerity, humility, and courage, as Vlastos says, it strives to foster them. If Vlastos is right, however, there is yet another Socratic paradox. Socrates' discipline and criticism suggest to Ackerman and Walzer a political frame of mind. For Ackerman, again, it is the disciplined restraint of the policymaker who knows when not to raise issues in public; for Walzer it is the social critic's ability to make the prophetic charge of political hypocrisy in a way exemplary for citizens. In contrast, Socrates' dialogical method suggests to Vlastos a very antipolitical frame of mind. For Vlastos, Socrates refuses

[11] Gregory Vlastos, "The Paradox of Socrates," in *The Philosophy of Socrates*, ed. Gregory Vlastos (Garden City, N.Y.: Doubleday, 1971), p. 7.

to play politics when moral questions are involved. Even at his own trial, he will not make the argument that could persuade the jury as a whole; he prefers to engage his accusers individually through dialogue, as he would his interlocutors. Socrates appears to believe that moral judgment and individual freedom cannot survive in the world of political persuasion and coercion, and he refuses to give up the former.[12] On Vlastos's interpretation, the Socratic method is deeply hostile to politics, not a model for policymakers or episodic citizens. With this question in mind (How can a man committed to an antipolitical method of philosophical reasoning serve as a model for both neutral policymakers and episodic citizens?), I want to take a closer look at the Socratic method.

The first two parts of the Socratic method, *elenchos* and *aporia*, work together to instill in Socrates' interlocutors humility and an appreciation of the challenge they face.[13] The *elenchos*, a method of refuting weak arguments or exposing unargued assumptions, is an ad hominem way of demonstrating the flaws in a particular person's beliefs.[14] By bringing his interlocutors face-to-face with internal inconsistencies and other weaknesses in their own beliefs, Socrates hoped to impress on them their own inability to give an adequate account of those beliefs. Coupled with this method of refutation was Socrates' ability to leave his interlocutors perplexed by cutting off the familiar passages through which they might retreat (*aporia*).

But this is only half the story. Socrates was also committed to building up the individual soul (*psyche*) of those he questioned. Just as he tailored the elenctic and aporetic parts of his method to the beliefs and personalities of individual interlocutors, he also tailored its constructive side to their particular potentials and predispositions.[15] In order to instill the desire to eliminate inconsistent beliefs, a respect for others who may be of some help, and compassion for those who may need help themselves, Socrates had to demonstrate the sensitivity of a midwife in eliciting sincere cooperation.

The maieutic side of the Socratic method is best seen in his handling of the young slave in the *Meno*. There he gradually led the slave from false

---

[12] This interpretation is made more explicit in a 1954 lecture on Socrates by Hannah Arendt, published posthumously as "Philosophy and Politics," *Social Research* 57, no. 1 (spring 1990): 73–103.

[13] I have taken the following four-part outline of the Socratic method from Laszlo Versenyi, *Socratic Humanism* (New Haven: Yale University Press, 1963), pp. 110–28.

[14] Vlastos has since offered several sophisticated accounts of the motivational logic of the *elenchos*. See "The Socratic Elenchus," in *Oxford Studies in Ancient Philosophy*, ed. Julia Annas (Oxford: Clarendon Press, 1983), 1:27–58, and "Socrates's Disavowal of Knowledge," *Philosophical Quarterly* 35 (January 1985): 1–31.

[15] See Henry Teloh, *Socratic Education in Plato's Early Dialogues* (Notre Dame: University of Notre Dame Press, 1986).

confidence to confusion to self-conscious perplexity and finally to a desire to understand. He describes this as questioning rather than teaching, and though it falls short of knowledge, which will require much more work on the slave's part, at the end of the questioning the slave can feel the force of the logos himself.[16] In the *Theaetetus* Plato has Socrates describe himself explicitly in this way, with one addition. Midwives not only help in "harvesting," they are also the most skilled "in selecting a pair whose marriage will produce the best children." Socrates claims he can recognize who can and who cannot benefit from Socratic dialogue. Some couples are better than others, and that is why Socrates admits to Theaetetus that he has, in fact, sent some students to Prodicus, a Sophist, rather than take them on himself.[17] Similarly, in the *Meno* the slave must know Greek before Socrates can question him.

This precondition foreshadows the more complicated dynamic of the last feature of the Socratic method—irony. Even among those candidates Socrates chooses to question himself, further discrimination is necessary. Socrates uses irony to temper the humbling experience of the *elenchos* and the painful labor that Socratic midwifery oversees as appropriate to particular interlocutors. In some cases—for example, the famous exchanges with Thrasymachus and Callicles—his denial of knowledge has a sharp, combative edge. In other cases such as his exchange with Alcibiades in the *Symposium*,[18] he is more standoffish. In yet other cases—for example, in the *Crito*—his tone is patient and almost avuncular. Socratic irony is an attempt to bridge the gap between teacher and student without destroying the important differences between them. Although he wants his interlocutors to learn for themselves, he realizes that this is not literally possible. It is through self-conscious irony that Socrates tries to lead others without either transparently pretending not to know more than they do or lording it over them. He uses irony to uncover the flaws in others' beliefs and arguments without discouraging them. By giving them the sense that he honestly shares in their perplexity, he provides encouragement through solidarity.[19]

Irony is at once the most essential and most controversial part of the Socratic method. It can degenerate into duplicity, sarcasm, and manipu-

[16] Plato, *Protagoras and Meno*, trans. W. K. C. Guthrie (Harmondsworth, Eng.: Penguin, 1976), 84B, p. 135.

[17] Plato, *Theaetetus*, trans. F. M. Cornford, in *Plato: The Collected Dialogues*, ed. Edith Hamilton and Huntington Cairns (New York: Pantheon, 1966), 149a–151c, pp. 854–56.

[18] This is the case Vlastos focuses on in his defense of Socratic irony against the blunt charge that it is merely manipulation. See *Socrates, Ironist and Moral Philosopher* (Ithaca: Cornell University Press, 1991), pp. 21–44.

[19] See Mill, *Autobiography*, in *The Collected Works of John Stuart Mill*, ed. John M. Robson (Toronto: University of Toronto Press, 1963–91), 1:23–24.

lation, but there seems to be no easy alternative as long as teachers know more than their students but need the students' cooperation and initiative, not their obedience. Socratic teachers must have some idea in advance of the answers to their questions, which otherwise could not be formulated in comprehensible ways. But if students think dialogue is only a game of hide-and-seek, the compassion, mutual respect, and seriousness of the enterprise will be jeopardized.[20]

This sketch of the Socratic method seems to support Vlastos's general claim that Socratic dialogue is a shared moral enterprise, not a political activity defined by the art of rhetoric. But it also turns out to be consistent with the interpretation of Socrates offered by Ackerman and Walzer, despite their claims for Socrates' political relevance, if we locate the Socratic method within the context of neocorporatism. In Ackerman's case, Socratic dialogue is a model for the kind of conversation that policymakers structure for political consumers. This is not rhetoric and persuasion, but risk analysis and advice. The Socratic policymaker must tell political consumers what they need to know in order to weigh the risks on both sides themselves. In Walzer's case, Socratic dialogue is possible only between members of the same ethical community, when it is delivered in a professional yet not unfamiliar voice. It cannot be sustained in a society in which ethnic, religious, and other deep-seated differences exist. Ackerman's and Walzer's appropriations of Socratic dialogue are not inconsistent with Vlastos's interpretation of the Socratic method. When applied to politics, the Socratic method in the fourfold sense just described limits the negotiations between policymakers and their customers to manageable problems and renders prophetic social criticism acceptable to clients by phrasing it in a familiar, steady professional voice. The Socratic method is not broad enough to bring a culturally and racially diverse people together as a political society, but it can operate within the confined space of some policymaking arenas to serve the ends that Ackerman and Walzer as well as Vlastos want. In the next section I examine one such policymaking arena, the college classroom, to illustrate the relation between the liberal ideal of Socratic dialogue and the power of expert authorities.

## Weberian Matter-of-Factness

As teachers and students in the modern university search for their respective voices as experts and as clients or consumers, they also try to mini-

---

[20] For two classic opposing views of Socratic irony, see Paul Friedlander, *Plato: An Introduction*, trans. Hans Meyeroff (Princeton: Princeton University Press, 1969), 1:137-70, and Richard Robinson, *Plato's Earlier Dialectic*, 2d ed. (Oxford: Clarendon Press, 1984), pp. 7-20.

mize controversial political disagreements. This is what Weber wanted, and it is also what liberal theory's Socratic discipline attempts to realize. Ethical disagreements should be reduced to matters of fact whenever possible. When they cannot, then a special matter-of-fact tone has to be used to moderate the disagreement.

College teachers, at either public or nominally private institutions, enjoy the status many other professionals enjoy within a mixed corporatist and pluralist society because of the de facto indispensability of a college degree for full membership within this mixed political economy. They are gatekeepers, but not just for their own professions. In the following discussion I will focus initially on the social practice of clientism and not the imagery of consumerism. This does not mean that visuals are not important in the college classroom or that consumerism is insignificant in this arena. In discussing the breakdown of trust I will emphasize the central role that consumerism and policy analysis play. My purpose is to illustrate how the liberal version of Socratic dialogue works within the Weberian setting of a typical policymaking arena, and how skeptical trust in expert authority depends on Weberian matter-of-factness as well as on the liberal Socratic virtues and methods. In its precise mix of clientism and consumerism the college classroom is not a typical policymaking arena: there may be no such thing. What is typical is the way Socratic methods and a Weberian demeanor are deployed to stabilize the social practices of clientism and consumerism when standard forms of policy analysis and professional ethics fail.

Weber's own views on the relation between science and politics strengthen the assumption that this is indeed a typical policymaking arena in which voice and vision combine to constitute expert authority. Weber described the Socratic method, in passing, as a way of "putting the screws upon somebody so that he could not come out without admitting either that he knew nothing or that this and nothing else was truth, the *eternal* truth that never would vanish as the doings of the blind men vanish." [21] This comment should not be read as a rejection of Socratic humanism. On the contrary, Weber's arguments for value neutrality and his attempts to preserve the prophetic voice of the teacher without letting it become demagogic parallel the concerns of Ackerman and Walzer. Furthermore, his belief that policymaking arenas like this should be free from political coercion anticipates Vlastos's characterization of Socratic dialogue. The teacher-student relationship I will describe illustrates how the liberal version of the Socratic ideal, despite Weber's caustic remark, has gained

[21] Max Weber, "Science as a Vocation," in *From Max Weber: Essays in Sociology*, ed. Hans H. Gerth and C. Wright Mills (New York: Oxford University Press, 1958), p. 141.

greater credibility within a Weberian model for conscientious, responsible, and therefore trustworthy policymaking.

Weber is credited by liberal theorists with having recognized the unavoidable economic and political pressures on modern research and teaching universities and how these pressures affect the authority experts in the classroom can exercise. He did not think it would be possible to practice "science as a vocation" without frontally addressing the political and economic origins of these pressures. For the ethic of the scientist and the ethic of the political leader to be successful, according to Weber, they must make sense out of those things they have in common. The scientist must have the right technical training and the moral discipline to confront others with the "inconvenient" facts about the "ultimate meaning" of their conduct.[22] The scientist must be able to tell students, other scholars, and patrons where they are headed and predict the unintended as well as intended consequences their actions will have for their lives as meaningful wholes. At the same time the temptation to use this knowledge to persuade captive student audiences must be resisted.

The Weberian political leader must be able to speak with the voice of an exemplary prophet, not loudly but quietly with a depth of conviction and "matter-of-factness" that impresses the audience with the gravity of the subject and the speaker's responsibility to it. The same must be true for the scientist in the classroom. Methodology, the purification ritual of social science, can convey this matter-of-fact conviction, but the tone of the prophet's speech seems to be more important. It is "genuinely human and moving" to be in the presence of a politician who believes in his or her work, as Luther did, as if it were a religious vocation[23] but who also recognizes that "a genuine community" can be built only through intimate, exemplary work, that is, "in pianissimo."[24] The same pessimistic but heroic character must be the "ideal interest" of the scientist. According to Weber, science, like politics, is vulnerable to demagoguery, and the only salvation for the scientist is through inner restraint.[25]

Weber's analogy between science and politics is weak at both ends. Although individual scientists may certainly indulge in demagoguery, to the extent that they do so they are hardly practicing science. More important, his characterization of democratic politics' vulnerability to the same kind of prophetic demagoguery is simply a pejorative way of describ-

[22] Ibid., p. 151.

[23] Max Weber, "Politics as a Vocation," in *From Max Weber: Essays in Sociology*, p. 127.

[24] Weber, "Science as a Vocation," p. 155.

[25] On the common theme of vocation in Weber's two famous essays, see Sheldon S. Wolin, "Max Weber: Legitimation, Method, and the Politics of Theory," *Political Theory* 9 (August 1981): 401–24.

ing the unavoidable need for persuasion in democratic politics. Liberalism tends to use Weber's account of the relation between science and politics as an argument for insulating science from demagogic abuses of political power. Instead, the disanalogy should alert us to the way Weber's aversion to democratic politics has colored his account of science. Keeping science free of demagoguery makes sense only if you accept Weber's character- ization of political persuasion and if you believe that science as a whole is vulnerable to this abuse of power. Weber wants to keep prophetic teachers from becoming demagogic politicians. In the name of this alleged danger, he constructs an idealized account of value freedom and self-restrained prophecy in the classroom, and these professional ethics are supposed to govern the classroom as a policymaking arena. The expert authority of teachers, then, is legitimate when these antipolitical norms are followed.

But liberal theorists have not made this objection to Weber's parallel misunderstanding of science and politics. Their objections have focused on his failure to ground liberal politics on an adequate moral foundation and on his tendency to flirt with charismatic authority at the same time that he denounced demagoguery. They have for the most part accepted the interpretation of his view that idealizes scholarship as a heroic enter- prise for passionate yet self-restrained individuals. If we follow this liberal separation of politics and science into the college classroom, a college teacher is ideally someone the students trust to grade them fairly, to lead them through new and difficult material, and finally to involve them in that material in a passionate but responsible way. Grading fairly, leading carefully, and involving wholeheartedly all require a mastery of the subject matter, and when students can no longer assume that practical mastery, then the teacher's authority dissipates. This is as true of the authority to grade as of the authority to lead and involve. The college teacher's ex- pert authority can be replaced by coercive measures to preserve order and issue final grades or by persuasive measures to preserve cordiality, but these measures cannot achieve the same ends as expert authority. They may bring higher test scores and rising enrollments, but they cannot lead to fair grades, careful exploration, and excitement about the subject.

Take grading, the primary form of diagnostic knowledge in the Weber- ian college classroom. A college teacher's authority is not simply a func- tion of the power to assign grades. Grades are supposed to be part of the process of learning. If they were simply exit scores, teachers would not be so concerned to justify them to students. They must show students how well they have understood the material thus far, and also where they should go from there. They are both diagnostic instruments and forms of treatment. They should not be punitive policing exercises, but at the same time, grades should not lull students into a false confidence that they are naturally going to progress regardless of their efforts. If testing and grading are done in a forward-looking as well as backward-looking way, students gradually trust the teacher's fairness. This depends on attitudes and sensibilities, not just the accurate collection of raw scores. Teachers must give good reasons for the grades they give, but more important, they must find a way to grade that students can hear. For many students, too many detailed comments and criticisms are just as deafening as none at all. Students have to be encouraged to discuss the evaluation of their work by restating their arguments or rehearsing their proofs, comparing this with what they originally did and then taking a second look at the teacher's grade and comments. In other words, students have to be implicated in their own grading, and only then will they be willing to listen to suggestions about the next step. If this sounds utopian, it is because teachers have little time to do this kind of grading. For most, grading is primarily an exchange and the least rewarding part of the job, psychologically and economically. It puts them in an adversarial relationship with students, and very rarely are teachers evaluated on the quality of their grades.

Trust in expert authority in the Weberian classroom also depends on leading, primarily based on inferences drawn from assessments of what students know and where they are headed. Here too a practical mastery of the subject is a necessary but not sufficient condition for gaining students' trust. The key to leading students so they come to trust the teacher is providing them with a feeling of continuity. They must have a sense of where they have been and a belief that it is connected to where they are going. The teacher must provide reports of future turns in the road, dangers, resources, and refuges. Reading lists and syllabi, like roughly drawn maps, can help in this regard. But ultimately this continuity must be conveyed through classroom discussions. The way the teacher brings old material forward and introduces new material or intimates the place of material yet to come in discussion will determine whether students feel confident that they are on the right road. How it sounds to the student will determine how it looks. And how it sounds is more than a matter of reassuring students that they will someday be able to use what they have just learned. They have to take part in putting things together, making new connections, and building the bridges that connect past and future work.

Like grading fairly, leading well is hard: it takes Socratic discipline. The pressures on teachers to get through the material are great, and the incentives for students to follow blindly in hopes that that is all it will take to get a good grade are even greater. Leading can easily degenerate into leading by the nose. When it does, the teacher no longer has authority as an expert. When a student who has been led by the nose either stumbles or is dissatisfied, it becomes clear that all the teacher can do at that point is push or make friends. In other words, discussion can be trivial if its only goal is to force students to pay attention for the moment. But if it is an invitation to explore subterranean connections within the material, it gives them trust in the teacher as a fallible yet trustworthy guide.

The third aspect of a college teacher's authority derives from the process of involving students in the material in a passionate yet responsible way. Only after students have had a chance to talk through their grades and have come to trust the teacher as a guide are they able to invest something of themselves in the work. Involvement is not, Weber argued, "sterile excitation."[26] Whether it is capturing the beauty of a pastoral scene in a sonnet or conserving fossil fuels, the teacher must somehow convey to students that these are valued endeavors that require dedication. With this passion comes pride of ownership. Involved students understand that they have created and objectified something of themselves in their work. They are involved in what they have done because it represents them. It bears their signature, and they should take responsibility for it. This again is part of what Weber meant by an ethic of responsibility.

Involving students in this way requires an exemplary activity in the classroom that not all well-meaning teachers can master. It indeed may be something like a gift. Through a combination of passion and self-restraint, but without proselytizing or bullying, the teacher may be able to convey the depth of the material. This kind of "matter-of-factness" is the greatest asset of teachers whose authority students trust in this way. As Michael Oakeshott has noted, voice is what is most distinctive of the exemplary Socratic teacher in this Weberian context.

> Learning, then, is acquiring the ability to feel and to think, and the pupil will never acquire these abilities unless he has learned to listen for them and to recognize them in the conduct and utterances of others.
>     . . . It is implanted unobtrusively in the manner in which information is conveyed, in a tone of voice, in the gesture which accompanies instruction, in asides and oblique utterances, and by example. . . . It is a habit of listening for an individual intelligence at work in every utterance that may be acquired by imitating a teacher who has this habit.[27]

The teacher's unobtrusive manner of speaking sets the tone for trust in this context and it is this habit that students learn as they become trusted and trusting parties to this enterprise. The same is true for clients and professionals in other street-level policymaking arenas.

[26] Weber, "Politics as a Vocation," p. 115.
[27] Michael Oakeshott, "Learning and Teaching," in *The Voice of Liberal Learning: Michael Oakeshott*, ed. Timothy Fuller (New Haven: Yale University Press, 1989), pp. 61–62.

The erosion of trust in expert authority that occurs in the college classroom also applies to other policymaking arenas in modern liberal societies. The failure of college teachers to sustain trust in their interpretation of students' needs follows a common pattern that is neatly framed within the confines of the classroom but not peculiar to it. The same dynamics are present in the welfare office, the legal services office, and the offices of most other policymakers. In the most degenerate cases, the clients of these professionals and government officials are subjected to a combination of sanctimonious posturing and self-serving interpretations by experts who may be unsure of their ability to exercise authority responsibly. The intelligence of ordinary citizens may be insulted by the managers of housing policy no less than by managers of foreign policy. The honest mistakes and desperation of legal services clients, welfare recipients, and students are too quickly dismissed as instances of deceit, fraud, and laziness.

To detect this, we have to hear the voices of teachers and students, benefits recipients and caseworkers, clients and lawyers, patients and doctors, and neighborhood residents and planners. Their voices tell us whether there is trust based on a liberal Socratic dialogue or simply a show of trust. Their voices tell us whether the irony in the expert's voice is designed to bring clients and consumers along or to steer them one way or another. Their voices tell us whether the performance is merely enthralling or if the conversation enables clients and consumers to hear voices other than their own familiar ones.

The problem with detecting these coercive dialogical overtones is that the teacher's voice is self-consciously matter-of-fact, and students are encouraged to speak with the same Weberian accent. The ethic of responsibility that Weber believed this tone of voice served actually is an ethic of protective coloration. In an unstable environment where consumer skepticism erodes client loyalty, the expert retreats behind an administrative shield. Eyes glaze over, and the voice of authority barely fluctuates as it rehearses the facts. Don't reveal too much, don't give anything away, and don't create the impression that problems can be solved through compassion. These guidelines for the policymaker are followed in a matter-of-fact voice so that the student/client/consumer does not take anything personally and thus has no grounds for a personal appeal.

The Weberian ethic of responsibility, in practice, proves too harsh. It does not stabilize policymaking at the street level and sometimes makes matters worse. At this point more complex methods like those developed by Mill and Rawls take on practical significance. Their philosophical methods dampen, mute, and arrange the sounds of trust and expert authority within these policymaking arenas so that a liberal Socratic dialogue can continue within the boundaries of policy analysis and professional ethics. They do not replace matter-of-factness, but they can mitigate its divisive effects.

## Objections to the Socratic Ideal

To clarify my criticism of the Socratic ideal in liberal theory and its Weberian construction of trust in expert authority, I want to comment on several objections to Socratic political theory and distinguish them from my own argument.

*Political Inadequacy.* According to the criticism of political inadequacy, Socratic political theory undervalues political participation. Private citizenship, according to this objection, is not a viable moral stance because it does not value political activity and appreciate its special moral demands as well as its rewards. Socratic political education does this by underestimating the difficulties of sustaining an episodic moral commitment to political activity. Private citizens who are capable of coming forward when necessary to say no to state power in an exemplary way are indeed the exceptional heroes of representative government. These sacrifices are not restricted to civil disobedience. They include episodic, but less dramatic, involvement in local political issues from picketing to recall elections. What makes the episodic private citizen an inadequate political model is the unpredictable and unfinished nature of political activity. For the episodic private citizen, moving in and out of politics, knowing that political outcomes are temporary compromises worked out in ambiguous language yet getting involved anyway gets harder and harder. The private citizen may be able to make a moral stand in the exceptional case, but moral stands tend to weather poorly in politics. The real difficulty that a private citizen faces is not mustering the courage or energy for the first moral stand, but coming back a second or third time after seeing either how little has changed as a result of that first effort or how different the outcome was from what was expected. Episodic private citizenship breeds political cynicism.

I am sympathetic to this objection. Moral conscience and even moral outrage may have an important place in politics, especially liberal politics, where individual freedom functions as a crucial counterweight to gross abuses of political power. But when resistance to the politics of policymaking takes the form of conscientious objection or civil disobedience, it seems misplaced and ineffective. Withholding a portion of one's income taxes to protest the failure of environmental policymaking does not have the same ring as withholding "war taxes." Socratic acts of individual conscience can be effective when their targets and goals are well defined. But when the target is a street-level bureaucrat or a planning board, Socratic citizenship may be difficult to sustain. To the extent that Socratic political education focuses on dramatic acts of conscience, it may be politically inadequate, although still important in exceptional cases.

*Political Bias.* Socratic political theory, to the extent that it is true to Socrates' own understanding of the relative merits of democratic and oligarchic political systems, has been charged with being biased against democracy.[28] It places a premium on the linguistic skills of the rich and well educated. On this view, Socrates was more concerned with educating the opponents of democratic Athens than its defenders, and his own behavior was a cause for concern among the democrats. His conception of a life worth living was based on the value of intellectual exchange, and he had very little confidence that the demos or their leaders were very interested in this. One could argue that by extension, early liberal theorists have shown the same class preferences in their conceptions of moral and political education, especially Hobbes and Locke. Mill and Rawls have qualified their democratic principles in much less drastic ways, but a Socratic bias against democracy remains. Mill's ingenious voting schemes are hard to explain away, and Rawls, as evidenced by his "Aristotelian principle," seems to prefer the intellectual challenges Socrates relished to a game of checkers.[29]

I am much less sympathetic to this objection. It oversimplifies Socrates' own project,[30] and it ignores the commitment to political equality that modern liberal theorists do have. Yet one danger that this objection does raise for liberal theorists committed to a Socratic method can be approached through a question: How will Socratic critics support themselves in a liberal democratic society? Socrates took a vow of poverty; he was not a paid tutor for the sons of the rich, nor was he a kept man in the way intellectuals have so often been kept by private and public patrons. To make their views known as Socratic critics in modern liberal society, liberal theorists must have some institutional base. It may be a university position, a syndicated column, or a position as a research associate. Whatever it is, it will affect the range of political issues that modern Socratic critics can and will want to address, and in many cases, whatever their base, they simply will not have the resources to address some issues. In other

---

[28] Ellen Meiksins Wood and Neal Wood, *Class Ideology and Ancient Political Theory: Socrates, Plato, and Aristotle in Social Context* (New York: Oxford University Press, 1978), and I. F. Stone, *The Trial of Socrates* (Boston: Little, Brown, 1988).

[29] John Rawls, *A Theory of Justice* (Cambridge: Harvard University Press, 1971), pp. 424–33.

[30] Gregory Vlastos, "The Historical Socrates and Athenian Democracy," *Political Theory* 11 (November 1983): 495–516.

cases cruder institutional biases may limit the range of their political criticism. This may not always result in an antidemocratic bias, but the danger of institutional political bias is one that liberal theorists cannot ignore.

*Political Immaturity.* Political immaturity is one of the oldest criticisms of Socratic political theory. It was first made by Socrates' harshest Platonic interlocutors, Thrasymachus and Callicles. Although the Socratic method may be an appropriate way of disciplining a young mind, supposedly it is inappropriate as an introduction to political discourse. To the extent that older men like Socrates persist in using it, they make political fools of themselves. Their fine distinctions and elaborate analogies distract us from the harsh and fairly straightforward realities of power and injustice. Modern liberal theorists, still fascinated by logical fictions such as the state of nature and abstract theories of moral development, over-intellectualize politics. They construct useless philosophical conventions when they should be paying attention to natural tendencies, and they mistake self-serving political conventions for natural patterns of domination. They may not have the class biases of earlier liberal theorists, but they have uncritically adopted their apolitical philosophical style because they lack practical political experience.

This criticism misses the mark. Socrates did raise fundamental questions about the nature of political authority and obligation in Athens. He challenged the existing political institutions by voicing these questions in the marketplace, outside the established institutions. He may have been stubbornly philosophical, but he was not speaking a language that had no political purchase. In Peter Euben's words, Socrates "may have been trying . . . to reconstitute public life in moral terms outside the formal channels of the 'state,' seeking in his dialogues both the improvement of his fellow citizens and offering philosophical dialogue as a paradigm for how 'political' institutions might function."[31] Socratic dialogue is not inherently politically immature.

*Ephemerality.* Ephemerality is the criticism that Nietzsche levels against Socrates in *Twilight of the Idols.* According to Nietzsche, the Socratic method or "dialectic" is not just a pathetic slave morality, it is a "merciless tool" that can render opponents helpless by forcing them to think of themselves as idiots. "He makes one furious and helpless at the same time." Why did Athenians succumb to this? Why didn't they resist? Again according to Nietzsche, Socrates appeared to Athenians as a "physician,

---

[31] Euben, *Tragedy of Political Theory,* p. 209.

a savior" who could rescue them from "degeneration." "Everywhere their instincts were in anarchy," and the Socratic agon promised them a cure.

But then Nietzsche pulls back. The Socratic method may not be quite as potent as it first appears or as those directly under its spell believe. "One chooses dialectic only when one has no other means. One knows that one arouses mistrust with it, that it is not very persuasive. Nothing is easier to erase than a dialectical effect: the experience of every meeting at which there are speeches proves this." [32] The Socratic method is more than a procedure for discovering or constructing the truth: it is an act of power. It creates a determinate set of moral and political dispositions in which "mistrust" eventually overtakes feelings of helplessness and anger. "Dialectic" is a mediating social practice whose effects quickly wear off. When used as a technique for political education it will have only ephemeral results.

One problem with this criticism is that it incorrectly compares the Socratic method to speechmaking. In fact, one of the recurrent themes in Plato's dialogues is Socrates' resistance to speechmaking or long uninterrupted speeches (*macrologia*) and his clearly stated preference for less public exchanges in the form of questions and answers (*braxologia*).[33] Socrates considers speechmaking a rhetorical art that sophists trade in, and in both the *Gorgias* and *Protagoras* he makes it clear he wants nothing to do with it. Although it may be appropriate for law courts, where votes are taken on the merits of opposing arguments, it is not the appropriate way to search for truth. Second, precisely because the Socratic method is more personal, Socrates believes it will have a more lasting and not just a better effect than a public speech.

This Socratic rejoinder to the Nietzschean attack is unconvincing. In the case of the Platonic Socrates, at any rate, there are very few successful cases of "dialectic." The exchange with Meno's young slave is one, and the exchange with Crito in the *Crito* possibly is another. But both these examples are weak. Socrates' questioning of the slave deals with a mathematical problem, and only with difficulty can it be extended to moral and political education. Furthermore, in a sense it is really Meno Socrates is talking to, and the slave is simply an object on which Socrates is conducting an experiment. The dialectic is directed at reshaping not the political dispositions or emotions of the slave, but indirectly those of Meno, and on this score it fails. Similarly, Socrates' exchange with Crito becomes a

32 Friedrich Nietzsche, "Twilight of the Idols," in *The Portable Nietzsche*, ed. Walter Kaufmann (New York: Viking Press, 1968), p. 476.

33 See H. L. Hudson-Williams, "Conventional Forms of Debate and the Melian Dialogue," *American Journal of Philology* 71 (April 1950): 156–69, for a clear exposition of this distinction in another context.

dialogue with himself. Crito becomes a passive listener, and though he accepts the conclusion drawn by "the Laws" that Socrates should not attempt to escape, Crito has understood very little during the dialogue, and ultimately Socrates must appeal to his sense of filial gratitude to persuade him to identify with the offspring of "the Laws." Crito does not join Socrates in a common search for moral or political truth.

The Socratic method is not a tyranny, however. In the form it takes in the college classroom and in other policymaking arenas it can be resisted, and often it is by consumers, clients, and even disgruntled policymakers themselves who sense the limits of policy analysis and professional ethics. Effective resistance depends in part on a democratic political education that prepares citizens to read the sights and sounds of humanistic corporatism through speech genres other than policy analysis and professional ethics. Citizens need a more sensitive ear and a more discerning eye than liberal theory has given them if they are to hear the language of power that informs trust in expert authority and to see through the spectacular images of modern politics. The power relations that exist between clients, consumers, and policymakers are not adequately captured by humane regulative principles of client autonomy, consumer sovereignty, and professional responsibility.

The next section concludes part 1 of my argument with a brief description of the elements of a democratic political education that would prepare citizens to criticize the social practices of humanistic corporatism. Later, in part 3, I suggest how democratic political theory could contribute to this project of political education.

## Democratic Political Education

The ability to interpret trust in expert authority critically depends on a familiarity with political life itself. This ability to make political judgments comes from the experiences of political achievement, disappointment, uncertainty, ruthlessness, and exhilaration. Politicians learn it by struggling with the rhetoric of their own leaders and the attacks of the opposition. Citizens learn it when causes, not just friends, are betrayed, but they also learn how to make political judgments when they have lived through unexpected moments of populist engagement and enthusiasm. They learn political judgment under duress. Picking up on these rhythms, dissonances, and tempos of power can be done only by citizens who have had some direct acquaintance with political life.

Power, then, is the first concern of political judgment; teaching citizens how to keep up with power's double-edged and ever-changing form is the theoretical task of a democratic political education. Unlike beauty and moral conscience, power is not something that strikes our aesthetic imagination or awakens a deep, mysterious feeling of respect. To liken power to a great work of art or an inspiring moral character is to miss its protean nature. Therefore to liken political judgment to aesthetic or moral judgment is to miss the way power can carry us along, diverting our attention, lulling us into complacency, and then, without warning, can galvanize us. Political judgment in the modern context is the ability to hear the muted voices of power within the nexus of trust and expert authority before the tone becomes too reassuring and before the blinding spectacles of consumerist politics distract citizens from these dialogues. But to flesh out this conception of political judgment and make its relation to democratic political education clearer, we have to consider its most important antecedents.

In the opening passages of the *History of the Peloponnesian War*, the "Archaeology," Thucydides presents an overview of Athenian power. The tensions and dissonances are surprising and palpable, especially to a modern reader accustomed to scientific language. The first surprise is that Athenian naval power and the tribute it has amassed depended in part on the infertility of the Athenian soil. Because it is unattractive in this regard, Athens has not suffered numerous invasions. It has been able to develop a coherent collective identity precisely because of this weakness in its own resources.[34] Thucydides extends this argument by suggesting that without periods of quiet and tranquillity, a political society becomes weak. Constant movement, continuous activity and expansion, undercuts collective identity. Without a name, without a way of identifying itself as a distinct people, a political society, no matter how blessed with material and military resources, will not be powerful; and maintaining this political identity requires time to deliberate collectively over common purposes. Stable political power is not a set of forces in equilibrium, checking and balancing each other. Power depends on shared self-understandings, discussed and debated in times and places that are protected from alluring spectacles of action and that can then limit and direct military and material resources.

After Thucydides retraces the development of the Athenian empire in the first half of the fifth century, we hear how these shared understandings first articulated by Pericles are corrupted. We listen as Pericles' words of restraint, compromise, and praise for Athens's "daring and deliberation" (2.40, p. 105) gradually lose their meaning. This happens first in Corcyra, where death "raged in every shape" (3.81, p. 188) and citizens butchered

---

[34] Thucydides, *The Peloponnesian War*, ed. John H. Finley Jr. (New York: Modern Library, 1951), 1.2, p. 4.

one another for private gain as well as out of treason. This stasis, fueled by passion, envy, and the lust for power, made it impossible to regain control over events. They were literally running their course, and the words that might have channeled them were forced to "change their ordinary meaning and to take that which was now given them" (3.82, p. 189).

The speeches that follow the revolution in Corcyra cannot escape this fate. The speakers use justice and freedom as self-serving tags or drop them completely with no regrets. The famous obstinate remarks of the Athenians at Melos epitomize this attitude (5.90, p. 331), but they had been foreshadowed in the sarcastic comments of the Athenian warmonger Cleon, who ridiculed those Athenians who thought it necessary to deliberate long over the decimation of Mytilene (3.38, p. 164). Politics is driven by the increasing speed of the action, and the corruption of speech accelerates this pace. Pericles earlier recognized that the empire had become a tyranny (2.64, p. 118), but the language he used to bolster the failing Athenian will, at least according to Thucydides, was not yet hollow. The sacrifices made by dead Athenian soldiers, Pericles reminded his audience, were made in the name of democratic ideals, however imperfectly realized.

After Melos Athenian power can no longer be disciplined by language. This loss affects the structure of power itself. Allowed to multiply and expand, it becomes even more self-destructive. Thucydides makes the point historically when he interrupts the action after the massacre on Melos to provide a second "Archaeology," this time of Sicily, the future site of Athens's fateful defeat. The structure of power he presented in the first "Archaeology" no longer fits the world. Where Athenian power had once depended on a common name, Sicily has become an island of numerous Hellenes and barbarians capable of thwarting the Athenians. As the Sicilian expedition begins and Alcibiades dominates the action, what it means to be an Athenian, a Spartan, or a Persian becomes obscure. As he moves from one camp to the next, it becomes clear that Alcibiades is not the only one who has lost his political identity. Just as Pericles was emblematic of Athens before the plague, Alcibiades represents the volatility, ruthlessness, and unpredictability of power when it is not anchored to a collective identity.

Thucydides emphasizes the importance of speech and deliberation for containing the imperial impulses of a democracy. Citizens must be alert to the danger of trusting too much in the judgments of their leaders. Most leaders will lack the self-restraint of Pericles. Citizens must be wary of supporting parties in seemingly distant lands for the sake of strategic or material interests. And if they finally resist the temptation to follow an Alcibiades, whose daring and skill are beyond question, they may ironically bring ruin on themselves by forsaking the one leader who could salvage their cause (6.15, pp. 346–47).

Thucydides underscores the need to learn these lessons from the inside out. His narrative, and the speeches within it, give the reader a feel for the chaotic pace of war and for the way lust for power and fear of power corrupt speech and political judgment. It is one thing to know that words like *justice* can be used self-servingly. It is another to hear this in the flow of political life and find a voice that enables one to articulate what is happening. Speech fails in the Peloponnesian War, but the history of speech and action may enable the readers of the *History* to avoid similar tragedies.[35]

If citizens cannot recognize the voice of the demagogue in circumstances that make it tempting to deny his seductive power over them, and if they cannot also recognize the lust and fear of power in their own voices, then formulas and principles of justice will be of little help. The *History* gives us a chance to hear these voices in advance.

I am not suggesting that a modern democratic education must include reading Thucydides or that Weber is right after all and demagoguery is a value-neutral way of describing democratic political rhetoric. But modern democratic education must cultivate an awareness of the different voices that emerge in a democratic society under stress, and Thucydides comes to terms with this multivoicedness. The important point is that political voices carry. They echo over long distances, and they reverberate in unpredictable ways within the psyches of citizens and subjects. Thucydides does not tell us how to judge the effects of strong voices, terrifying silences, and blinding images. Judging such effects and then acting on these judgments presupposes the kind of historical knowledge Thucydides values, but it must include something more. Aristotle called this "something more" practical wisdom, *phronesis.*

Aristotle, like Thucydides, realized that political education involves more than cognitive learning: "Knowing about excellence or virtue is not enough,[36] including the excellences and virtues of the citizen, if power is to be disciplined by justice. To come to an effective shared understanding of the meanings of power and justice, where justice is not a sham, "the soul of the listener must first have been conditioned by habits to the right kind of likes and dislikes, just as land ⟨must be cultivated before it is able⟩ to foster the seed."[37] In the case of politics, this spadework orients indi-

[35] Cynthia Farrar, *The Origins of Democratic Thinking: The Invention of Politics in Classical Athens* (Cambridge: Cambridge University Press, 1988), chap. 5.

[36] Aristotle, *Nicomachean Ethics*, trans. Martin Ostwald (Indianapolis: Bobbs-Merrill, 1979), 1179b1, p. 295.

[37] Ibid., 1179b25, p. 296.

viduals toward each other as fellow citizens. Only then, after they experience their life together as a polis, as a collective enterprise, is it possible to settle their differences politically based on competing interests and shared understandings of the just exercise of power.

At the beginning of book 8 of the *Politics* Aristotle summarizes the distinct features of a political education capable of orienting citizens toward their life together as a polis.

> The citizens of a state should always be educated to suit the constitution of their state. The type of character appropriate to a constitution is the power which continues to sustain it, as it is also the force which originally creates it. . . . In the second place every capacity, and every art, requires as a condition of its exercise some measure of previous training and some amount of preliminary habituation. Men must therefore be trained and habituated before they can do acts of goodness, as members of a state should do.[38]

First, according to Aristotle, the attitudes, knowledge, and practical reasoning appropriate for politics are acquired as part of a process of character development specific to the way of life or "constitution" (*politeia*) of one's society. Second, this political character, not just territory, material resources, or even the dynamics of public speech, is what accounts for the power of a society.

Thucydides alludes to the role of character in his assessments of individual leaders and the propensities of city-states in general.[39] Aristotle is more systematic: political character draws on moral virtues such as justice and friendship as well as on the intellectual virtue of *phronesis*.[40] Political character is not simply a dominant attitude like heroic pride, deceit, or fearfulness. Political character involves listening to the world with a particular sensitivity to power, doing so as a member of a political community, with all the ties, grudges, and suspicions that entails, and doing this listening so regularly that it becomes almost second nature.

Aristotle was a much more acute observer of moral character than of political character.[41] And from a democratic perspective, his claim that a constitution determines the ideal character of its citizens is especially sus-

---

[38] Aristotle, *Politics of Aristotle*, 1337a11, p. 332.

[39] See, for example, the Corinthian characterization of both Athenians and Spartans just before the outbreak of the war, 1.68–71, pp. 38–41.

[40] See Aristotle, *Nicomachean Ethics*, 1144b30, p. 172: "Our discussion, then, has made it clear that it is impossible to be good in the full sense of the word without practical wisdom or to be a man of practical wisdom without moral excellence or virtue."

[41] I am indebted to Sheldon Wolin for first suggesting this interpretation of Aristotle. See Nancy Sherman, *The Fabric of Character: Aristotle's Theory of Virtue* (Oxford: Clarendon Press, 1989).

pect given his conception of a constitution as rule by a particular class. Even though his fragmentary account of democracy is at odds with his conception of a political constitution, however, and even though he developed a conception of practical wisdom as a virtue of those faced with personal dilemmas, he grounded this form of practical reason in an account of character appropriate to democratic politics.

Without the right character, political principles—even limited, contingent ones—do not adequately orient citizens toward the exercise of political power and the interplay of power and justice. In Aristotle's language, citizens without political character will not be able to identify the potential conflicts and problems that are only beginning to take root. They must share certain habits of perception and certain emotional predispositions toward power and justice, and only then will they have the character and practical wisdom to respond to the images and sounds of power in a timely way.

What, then, are the habits of political perception and the emotional predispositions that democratic citizens must develop as part of a shared common life if they are to have an ear for power in the current context? Aristotle has of late become a favorite of moral philosophers who are dissatisfied with seemingly arid, rigid Kantian and utilitarian orthodoxies. These neo-Aristotelians who favor an ethics of virtues over an ethics of rules and principles cover a wide spectrum. Some, like Alasdair MacIntyre, argue that we must identify the substantive moral ends that particular social practices should aim at in order to rebuild moral virtues. Others, like Martha Nussbaum, have emphasized the dramatic quality of moral life and the need to follow Sophoclean and Aristotelian advice if we are going to balance on "the razor's edge." This revival of Aristotle's moral and aesthetic theories, however, has not produced an Aristotelian account of political judgment that democratic citizens could adapt. The problem, I think, is with Aristotle.

First, his conception of politics, the activity of ruling and being ruled, is too narrow. Aristotle did not simply overlook political judgment; there is no need for a rich theory of political judgment within this conception of politics as ruling. Aristotelian rulers must know how to interpret general laws to fit particular cases, when to issue decrees rather than press for new laws, and when to follow the spirit of the laws rather than the letter. They must on occasion be prudent and merciful. In general, they must know how to rule wisely in order to preserve the constitution of the city. But the strength of character and the practical wisdom necessary for ruling in this way do not amount to political judgment as I have described it. Political judgment—that combination of character and practical wisdom that prepares citizens to perceive power relations and respond to them justly together—is not the judgment of rulers, it is the judgment of participants. Aristotle acknowledges cases in which deliberation by the many may be preferable to decisions made by the few, but this is because the rules the many would choose would be better rules in those circumstances. That the process of compromise and deliberation shared by the many would make citizens more attentive to the rhythms and dissonances of political power is not of particular interest to Aristotle. The best preparation for ruling, according to him, is being a subject. These are the two political stations— rulers and subjects—in Aristotle's political universe. Because citizenship is a matter of ruling and being ruled in turn, there is no need to address the character and practical wisdom of citizens who are never either rulers or ruled.

In addition to Aristotle's antidemocratic taste for ruling and being ruled, his account of shared deliberation is skewed because of the strong assumption of homogeneity among citizens. The kind of practical wisdom he attributes to citizens is adequate only because his polis excludes those who do not share the same cultural tradition. In a multicultural society like a modern democracy, where justice is never *the* principle of distribution but a set of competing and contested principles, Aristotelian judgments based on a common understanding of a shared tradition are fantastic and dangerous. Power is too protean and justice too contested in a modern democracy for them to be ordered by Aristotelian judgments that presuppose such a high level of homogeneity.

Aristotle's value to contemporary "virtue ethics" has been considerable, but it would be a mistake to reconstruct his political theory as a democratic theory. For this reason I want to turn to several modern political theorists who have been concerned with political judgment as I understand it. Their views are Aristotelian in a very general sense, but it is not their compatibility with Aristotle that makes them useful.

John Dewey was concerned with the growth of moral judgment in both formal and informal educational settings. For Dewey, moral judgment was not just a desirable component of political action. Moral judgments in politics should also be self-critical: "Judgments about values are judgments about the conditions and the results of experienced objects; judgments about that which should regulate the formation of our desires, affections and enjoyments." [42] He believed that education should be designed to reconstruct experience in order to critically monitor and evaluate our likes and dislikes. Furthermore, the best environment for this reconstruction of experience is a participatory democracy.

[42] John Dewey, *The Quest for Certainty: A Study of the Relation of Knowledge and Action* (New York: G. P. Putnam's Sons, 1960), p. 265.

Democracy as compared with other ways of life is the sole way of living which believes wholeheartedly in the process of experience as end and as means; as that which is capable of generating the science which is the sole dependable authority for the direction of further experience and which releases emotions, needs, and desires so as to call into being the things that have not existed in the past. For every way of life that fails in its democracy limits the contacts, the exchanges, the communications, the interactions by which experience is steadied while it is also enlarged and enriched. The task of this release and enrichment is one that has to be carried on day by day. Since it is one that can have no end till experience itself comes to an end, the task of democracy is forever that of the creation of a freer and more humane experience in which all share and to which all contribute.[43]

Clearly, Dewey thought education not only should enable us to critically reassess existing wants and needs, but also should pay an innovative, experimental role in releasing new emotions, needs, and desires. Dewey had no patience for education as a preparation for a remote future or the recapitulation of the past. In a democratic society "education . . . gives individuals a personal interest in social relationships and control, and the habits of mind which secure social changes without introducing disorder."[44] It is through this kind of education, be it in a legislature, a school, or some other policymaking arena, that one learns the value of order, mutual respect, self-control, and also the creative confidence and skill to reorder likes and dislikes.

According to Dewey, a democratic political education must not ignore the way emotions, desires, and preferences perpetuate these social practices and spawn their own justifications. Emotions, desires, and preferences must be the object of self-critical reflection. Power is not simply a matter of external arrangements; it works its way into our character. This insight, however, has to be combined with an appreciation of the importance of concrete experiences of power for a democratic political education. Despite his own practical engagement in politics and his many practical suggestions,[45] Dewey's analysis of power and political education is highly abstract. Commenting on Dewey's proposals for industrial democracy in *Democracy and Education*, Robert Westbrook observes, "What remained absent . . . was anything resembling a *political* strategy for the redistribution of power Dewey proposed. He remained wedded to moral

43 John Dewey, "Creative Democracy—the Task before Us," quoted in Richard J. Bernstein, *Praxis and Action* (Philadelphia: University of Pennsylvania Press, 1971), pp. 223–24.

44 John Dewey, *Democracy and Education* (New York: Macmillan, 1916), p. 115.

45 See Robert B. Westbrook, *John Dewey and American Democracy* (Ithaca: Cornell University Press, 1991). I am indebted to Donald Koch for useful discussion on this topic.

exhortation as the sole means to ends that required democratic politics. . . . Thus, though he now argued that industrial democracy necessitated structural changes in the distribution of power in the workplace, he had yet to envision a politics commensurate with this radical vision."[46] Dewey never formulated a conception of democratic political judgment to advance his practical aims; however, the conservative British political theorist Michael Oakeshott has a view of political education that partially remedies this problem. More than Dewey, Oakeshott's conception of political education emphasizes the particularity of political judgment and the limits the dynamics of power place on moral exhortation.

Oakeshott's famous essay "Political Education," originally delivered in 1951, begins with a summary statement of the reigning skepticism toward the idea of political education: "The expression 'political education' has fallen on evil days; in the wilful and disingenuous corruption of language which is characteristic of our time it has acquired a sinister meaning. In places other than this, it is associated with that softening of the mind, by force, by alarm, or by the hypnotism of the endless repetition of what was scarcely worth saying once, by means of which whole populations have been reduced to submission."[47] But Oakeshott was also a critic of more abstract forms of political philosophy because of their deductive methods of theorizing and ahistorical views of politics. A conception of political education from this perspective, he argued, was bound to be as ineffective as the Marxist conception had been harmful.

According to Oakeshott, politics is neither naked interest group bargaining nor ideological discipline. Politics is "the activity of attending to the general arrangements" of a society. It is a "flow of sympathy" for a community's traditional customs and patterns of life. Political education sustains this tradition, but it "is not merely a matter of coming to understand a tradition, it is learning how to participate in a conversation: it is at once the initiation into an inheritance in which we have a life interest, and the exploration of its intimations."[48]

Politics, because of the kind of knowledge it requires, can be sustained only by placing active, discursive political education at its center. Political knowledge cannot be distilled from survey data or deduced from regulative principles and then transmitted to entering citizens. Political knowledge is local and often tacit. It is acquired gradually—it is a feel for the body politic that begins in early socialization, expands through academic historical and comparative studies, and matures in practical political work

[46] Ibid., p. 179.

[47] Michael Oakeshott, "Political Education," in his *Rationalism in Politics and Other Essays* (New York: Methuen, 1981), p. 112.

[48] Ibid., pp. 112, 126, 129.

itself. These are the conversations Oakeshott recommends to us, if we are to understand and advance our political traditions.[49]

Oakeshott excludes from this political conversation what he calls the history of political ideas. Abstract ideas, like Mill's notion of representative government that is designed to fit any society that has reached the requisite stage of "civilization," are of little value in political education. The history of political philosophy, argues Oakeshott, can add to our political education, but it is not a storehouse of practical "doctrines and systems" to be plundered. It is an "explanatory" history of the limits and "incoherencies philosophers have detected in common ways of thinking and the manner of solutions they have proposed." Studying political philosophy helps us monitor our "ways of thinking" so we do not trap ourselves in the same old ways. At the most, it can remove "some of the crookedness in our thinking."[50]

When Oakeshott says that the history of political philosophy is explanatory, not practical, he is warning us not to look for shortcuts. The exploration of our political traditions comes slowly. Like politics itself, political education is "the strong and slow boring of hard boards."[51] It takes time to dislodge established needs and the emotions that bind us uncritically to them. Intimations are audible only to those immersed in a tradition, and even then they are muted and often interrupted. There are no abstract ideas that can guide the imposition of political order or justice, because they cannot be imposed from outside. All the history of political philosophy can do is make available a set of examples in which past intimations were either recognized and extended or misunderstood and lost. Not everyone has to study the history of political philosophy in order for a community to give its citizens a political education. But some should, so that their political "ways of thinking" allow them to get straight to the point.

Oakeshott emphasizes the need to think of politics as an interpretive activity, hostile to sweeping deductions. Politics, he claims, occurs on the ground, one step at a time, with a lot of backing and filling. By characterizing the history of political theory as nothing more than an explanatory history, Oakeshott has minimized political theory's own potential to inform and organize the rallying cries of opposing groups.[52]

This is the burden of Sheldon Wolin's argument in *Politics and Vision: Continuity and Innovation in Western Political Thought.* The Western tradi-

---

[49] Ibid., p. 132.

[50] Ibid., p. 130.

[51] Weber, "Politics as a Vocation," p. 128.

[52] See Walzer, *Interpretation and Social Criticism*, pp. 28–29, for a brief discussion of Oakeshott's exclusion of arguments over abstract values from political conversation.

tion of political theory, according to Wolin, cannot be abstracted from the wider political traditions of the West. Sometimes in response to severe political disorder, a theory has helped to reshape the way citizens see themselves and their political life. Hobbes, Wolin argues, wrote this kind of "epic" theory.[53] Sometimes the shift is more gradual and the effects are more cumulative. Sometimes the results are a renewal of political vitality, but more recently theory has depreciated politics. Political theory, like all social practices, cannot be reduced to a set of necessary and sufficient defining conditions. The tradition does have boundaries set by its concern with those things that political communities historically have held in common, but they are permeable as well as movable.

Reflecting on his own interpretation of the theoretical tradition, Wolin makes the connection to political education explicit: "Since the history of political philosophy is . . . an intellectual development wherein successive thinkers have added new dimensions to the analysis and understanding of politics, an inquiry into that development is not so much a venture in antiquarianism as a form of political education."[54] Learning how the tradition of political thought has been interpreted and has evolved enables a reader to see what modern politics devalues and what "the political" could yet mean. In Wolin's lexicon "the political" refers to those things a people holds in common (participation, membership, a shared sense of justice, and a shared feeling of collective responsibility) as well as those things on which the coercive force of the community can be brought to bear. It is "the political" as well as politics as a process for sustaining "the political" that political education takes as its proper subject. Whether political theories are "epic" in their approach to this task and or are less dramatic (for example, modern organizational theory), they are always prompted by actual political problems and seek to reinterpret the political in response to these political problems, issues, and conflicts.

But though Wolin seems willing to consider modern organizational theory from Lenin to Herbert Simon as one type of political theory that has operated as a social practice, even though it narrows rather than enriches our understanding of the political, he implies that genuine political theory must take seriously what Michael Polanyi calls tacit political knowledge. This is knowledge that is resistant to quantification and scientific manipulation. It is the nuanced, ambiguous knowledge of history, art, and religion out of which our language of the political in its detail is drawn. It is sometimes contradictory, often ironic, and rarely unbiased,

[53] Sheldon S. Wolin, *Hobbes and the Epic Tradition of Political Theory* (Los Angeles: William Andrews Clark Memorial Library, University of California, 1970).

[54] Sheldon S. Wolin, *Politics and Vision: Continuity and Innovation in Western Political Thought* (Boston: Little, Brown, 1960), p. 27.

which is what has made modern social science so hostile to it.[55] This tension in Wolin's interpretation of political theorizing (organizational theory is hardly sensitive to tacit political knowledge) leads to a gap in his account of liberal theory. On the one hand, some liberal theorists like Locke and Smith are attentive to tacit political knowledge and therefore merit careful interpretation even though they have cut back the boundaries of "the political."[56] There seems to be little doubt that these theories have been effective social practices. On the other hand, Wolin treats more philosophically minded liberals like Kant, Mill, and Rawls in a much more cursory way. They are merely moralists who are unconcerned with the tacit political knowledge of their societies: "Yet there remained a hopelessly unreal quality about Mill's principles of liberty, one which has the effect of reducing them to mere preaching, even if of a highly commendable kind. For when it is asked, how are these principles to be enforced? Mill could give no answer because his own argument had compromised the integrity of the only means possible, namely government."[57] Mill's aversion to politics allegedly reduces his thought to harmless compassion. By extension, Rawls offers us even less in the way of a creative account of institutional political reform. He urges us to provide all people with some form of property beyond their own labor power, he calls for a functional separation of political institutions for the purpose of economic management, and he believes that a reinvigoration of the party system through campaign finance reform and other measures will restore competition.[58] But there is no urgent need for liberal societies to build new political institutions that would bring the majority of their citizens, the party of nonvoters, into public life. Perhaps it is because Locke recognized the need for political theory to address institution building in a creative way that Wolin finds him more deserving of membership in the tradition than the apolitical Kantians and utilitarians who have inherited the liberal mantle.

[55] Sheldon S. Wolin, "Political Theory as a Vocation," in *Machiavelli and the Nature of Political Thought*, ed. Martin Fleisher (New York: Atheneum, 1972), pp. 23–75.

[56] According to Wolin, Locke is not just the father of liberalism's apolitical view of membership (*Politics and Vision*, pp. 286–351). Locke initiated the modern interest group approach to political analysis that American pluralists have mistaken for reality ("The American Pluralist Conception of Politics," in *Ethics in Hard Times*, ed. Arthur Caplan and Daniel Callahan [New York: Plenum Press, 1981], pp. 217–59), and his distinction between "federative power" and "executive power" prefigures today's welfare state way of thinking ("Democracy and the Welfare State: The Political and Theoretical Connections between Staatsräson and Wohlfahrtstaaträson," *Political Theory* 15 [November 1987]: 487). But Wolin has also argued that there is a Lockean conception of revolution that contemporary democrats should embrace, an enthusiasm and flair for building new political institutions and not just rejecting the old ("Revolutionary Action Today," *Democracy* 2 [fall 1982]: 17–28).

[57] Wolin, *Politics and Vision*, p. 349.

[58] Rawls, *Theory of Justice*, pp. 258–83, 221–28.

At least that is one way of explaining his endorsement of Locke's theory of revolution despite his criticism of Locke's own devaluation of the theoretical vocation as "underlaboring."

A critical reading of the liberal tradition and its relation to political education must pay more attention than Wolin has to the relation between philosophy and politics in the liberal tradition; and Wolin, in fact, admits this.[59] His critique of Locke and organizational theory tells only part of the story, and as expert authority and corporatism have expanded, there is more to be told. Kant, Mill, and Rawls may not have packed the epic punch Hobbes and Locke did, and they may not have had as sharp an impact on the language of politics as have organizational theory and the economics profession. But Mill and Rawls have found ways to mediate the professionalized conflicts within nineteenth- and twentieth-century capitalist democracies, and this has given liberal theory a new importance as a form of political education.

[59] See Shelden S. Wolin "History and Theory: Methodism Redivivus," in *Tradition, Interpretation, and Science: Political Theory and the American Academy,* ed. John S. Nelson (Albany: SUNY Press, 1986), p. 64.

PART II

TRADITION

# CHAPTER FOUR

# From Hobbesian Geometry
# to Kantian Casuistry

Both Hobbes and Kant recognized the political need to transform human character in order to meet the challenges of emerging liberal political orders. Hobbes's visually oriented geometric method, I argue, addresses the danger posed by "masterless men" and other slightly less dangerous characters possessed by the passion of "vain-glory." I contrast this geometric method of political education with Kant's method of casuistry, which is designed to meet a different political need: material and psychological independence.

Hobbes acknowledged the political power of speech as well as geometric method, but his account of speech reduced words to either "wise men's counters" or "the money of fools." Unless speech could be purged of its ambiguities and misleading metaphors, Hobbes argued, human beings would continue to thrash about, "entangled in words, as a bird in lime twigs, the more [they] struggle the more belimed." [1] Whereas Hobbes dreamed of rebuilding out of this expurgated material a Tower of Babel from which the entire commonwealth could be surveyed, Kant argued that such a misbegotten project would lead only to greater disharmony.

> We have found, indeed, that although we had contemplated building a tower which should reach to the heavens, the supply of materials suffices only for a dwelling-house, just sufficiently commodious for our business on the level of experience, and just sufficiently high to allow of our overlooking it. The bold undertaking that we had designed is thus bound to fail through lack of material—not to mention the babel of tongues, which inevitably gives rise to disputes among the workers in regard to the plan to be followed, and which

[1] Thomas Hobbes, *Leviathan*, in *The English Works of Thomas Hobbes*, ed. William Molesworth, 11 vols. (London: J. Bohn, 1839–45), 3:23. (Hereafter cited as *EW*.)

must end by scattering them over all the world, leaving each to erect a separate building for himself, according to his own design.[2]

To avoid disputes among workers, Kant designed a method of moral casuistry that involves them more effectively than does Hobbesian geometry in the project of moral and political construction on the "level of experience." Kant believed that "in philosophy the geometrician can by his own method build only so many houses of cards."[3] Kantian moral casuistry is not a solipsistic method of self-reflection, but its aversion to power restricts it to individual encounters between "independent" property owners.

The main purpose of this chapter is to contrast Hobbes's sight-based approach to the traditional problem of liberal political education with Kant's casuistic approach that anticipates the importance of voice for the modern problem of trust in expert authority. Just as the traditional problem of liberal political education has not vanished but persists alongside the modern problem, so Hobbesian geometry continues to fascinate political theorists and philosophers who yearn for a crystalline power structure. Kantian moral casuistry, however, has proved more important for normative policy analysts and applied ethicists who do not have Hobbes's keen eye for power.

## Hobbes's Place in the Liberal Tradition

Chronologically, Hobbes and Kant mark the beginning and end of the classical liberal tradition. This opposition is mirrored in the conclusions they reached. Though neither trusted democracy, Hobbes's absolutism, his preference for monarchy, and his weak commitment to individual rights stand in sharp contrast to Kant's republicanism with its separation of powers and qualified rights of property, participation, and expression.

There is also a vast distance between the underlying assumptions of their political theories. Hobbes rejected the notion that some conception of a summum bonum must serve as the moral foundation for political society. For Hobbes, the "good" is simply the object of one's appetite or desire. He tried to resist deriving political principles from a moral ideal of a person, defining "dignity" as "the public worth of a man which . . . is set on him by the commonwealth."[4] Instead, Hobbesian political order

---

[2] Immanuel Kant, *Critique of Pure Reason*, trans. Norman Kemp Smith (New York: St. Martin's Press, 1969), p. 573.

[3] Ibid., p. 585.

[4] Hobbes, *Leviathan*, pp. 85, 41, 76.

rests on the need for welfare and security; there are no deeper human needs steady enough to build a commonwealth on. Kant, of course, disgreed: with the right kind of moral training in the right kind of republican political society, individuals are capable of respecting each other as "ends in themselves." For Kant there is nothing cynical or politically irrelevant about such mutual respect or "dignity." Political order makes striving for "purity of heart" a real possibility, and so individuals have as much of a moral obligation to advance republican political order as to respect the individual dignity of other persons.[5]

Given these dramatic differences, including Hobbes within the liberal tradition requires strong justification. Hobbes may have anticipated some of the concerns of classical liberals, beginning with Locke, about the rule of law, but the combination of moral relativism, realism in foreign affairs, and monarchy at home suggests that he stands outside the liberal tradition.

Most efforts to portray Hobbes as one of the founders of liberalism have recognized this presumption. To overcome it, they have emphasized the primacy of the individual right of self-preservation,[6] the selection of relative market value as the measure of human worth,[7] and the devaluation of politics into a system of administrative rules.[8] These are the substantive themes that commentators have argued link Hobbes, despite himself, to Locke and later liberal theorists.

Another argument for including Hobbes's political theory within the liberal tradition has been made by Jürgen Habermas. Rather than emphasizing these substantive themes, Habermas has argued that Hobbes's resolutive-compositive method, with which the theorist first resolves political society into its constituent parts, repairs the broken ones, and then puts them back together, is what makes Hobbes "the real founder of Liberalism."[9] Habermas acknowledges that Hobbes's assumptions about the instrumental purpose of government, the legal protection of property, and formal equality under the law indicate a commitment to liberal ideals. But more fundamentally, argues Habermas, Hobbes's resolutive-compositive method is anathema to genuine political practice, and this is the main legacy Hobbes has left to succeeding liberal theorists. Because

---

[5] Immanuel Kant, *The Doctrine of Virtue*, part 2 of *The Metaphysics of Morals*, trans. Mary J. Gregor (Philadelphia: University of Pennsylvania Press, 1964), pp. 44–47.

[6] Leo Strauss, *Natural Right and History* (Chicago: University of Chicago Press, 1974), chap. 5.

[7] C. B. Macpherson, *The Political Theory of Possessive Individualism* (Oxford: Oxford University Press, 1962), chap. 2.

[8] Sheldon S. Wolin, *Politics and Vision* (Boston: Little, Brown, 1960), chap. 8.

[9] Jürgen Habermas, *Theory and Practice*, trans. John Viertel (Boston: Beacon Press, 1973), p. 67.

Hobbes "abstracts away from the distinction between controlling and acting," his theory cannot be adopted by "the mass of citizens." Hobbes addresses himself to people not in terms of the world as they see it, but in terms of a world he hopes to control through the "solitary and silent act" of technical manipulation.[10] The original covenant, on the other hand, is a social act that people choose because it speaks to their needs as they see them and offers them a solution in a social language they share. According to Habermas, the covenant is anomalous in Hobbes's technocratic system. For all the respect liberalism pays to individual liberty, at its core it is an authoritarian ideology whose meager legitimacy derives from the reputation of modern science.

I want to pursue the political significance of Hobbes's method, but with an emphasis on geometry, not Hobbes's resolutive-compositive method. Scholars have long debated the relative importance of these two methods in Hobbes's corpus. One thing seems clear: Hobbes did not always follow his own methodological advice. My interest is in the power of his geometric method to transform the passions of unruly citizens. Unlike Habermas, I am less interested in indicting Hobbes as an authoritarian liberal than in understanding how his geometric method addresses the traditional liberal problem of political education and its limitations as a means of transforming our "wild" passions.[11]

Hobbes believed that to address the problem of political education the theorist had to reshape the "artificer" of political society as well as redirect its "matter."[12] This meant transforming "masterless" and "vain-glorious" men into petty egocentrists so they could then see their common enterprise as a competitive race. Ultimately his geometric method falls short of this, even if we read it sympathetically. It lacks precisely the kind of self-conscious discipline that Kant's moral casuistry was designed to encourage.

## Hobbes's Geometric Method

In *De Cive* Hobbes's praise of geometry reaches its peak: "Whatsoever things they are in which this present age doth differ from the rude simpleness of antiquity, we must acknowledge to be a debt which we owe to geometry." And, Hobbes continues, if "moral philosophers" adopt this

---

[10] Ibid., pp. 76, 73, 75.

[11] I rely on Albert O. Hirschman, *The Passions and the Interests* (Princeton: Princeton University Press, 1977), for the general distinction between wild and tame passions.

[12] Hobbes, *Leviathan*, p. x.

method, the passions that drive men into war "would presently faint and languish." [13]

Geometric reasoning is analogous to arithmetic, according to Hobbes. Instead of adding and subtracting numbers, "geometricians teach the same in lines, figures . . . and the like." Similarly, "writers of politics add together pactions to find men's duties . . . in what matter soever there is place for addition and subtraction, there is also a place for reason; and where these have no place, there Reason has nothing at all to do." And so the "miserable condition of war" that impels us to consider life in Leviathan state is presented as an "inference made from the passions." The argument for the laws of nature that Hobbes recommends as "dictates of reason" [14] that will lead us out of this "condition" (and be codified in Leviathan state) is summarized as a "subtle" deduction. [15]

One way to construe this argument is as a form of rational convergence. [16] If you desire a life of felicity and security, if you only assume that other people are narrowly egoistic, if you assume that there is a rough intellectual and physical equality among people, and if you believe there are only two possible worlds—a warlike state of nature and a peaceful Leviathan state, then it makes sense to obey a Leviathan state that is capable of deterring other people from breaking their promises to you and depriving you of what is yours. Because, Hobbes suggests, everyone holds these views of others, obedience to a Leviathan state is assured. Only fools will try to get away with anything. [17] The problem with this argument from rational convergence is that people cannot be both "matter in motion" and the "artificers" or "makers" of a Leviathan state. It involves something like what Habermas calls a performative contradiction: You cannot make an agreement with others if one of the premises that you (and they) accept is that the other person is only "matter in motion."

In addition to this interpretation of Hobbes's theory—stressing the justification of Leviathan state there is another that is equally supported by textual evidence which addresses the problem of political education.

---

[13] Thomas Hobbes, *De Cive*, in *EW*, 2:iv. But in *Leviathan* Hobbes slips in this strong reservation: "Good counsel comes not by lot, nor by inheritance; and therefore there is no more reason to expect good advice from the rich, or noble, in matter of state, than in delineating the dimensions of a fortress; unless we shall think there needs no method in the study of politics (as there does in the study of geometry), but only to be lookers on; which is not so. For the politics is the harder study of the two" (*EW*, 3:340).

[14] Hobbes, *Leviathan*, pp. 30, 153, 114, 147.

[15] Ibid., p. 144. Also see Thomas A. Spragens, *The Irony of Liberal Reason* (Chicago: University of Chicago Press, 1981), p. 31.

[16] I have taken the idea of rational convergence from Thomas Nagel, *Equality and Partiality* (New York: Oxford University Press, 1991).

[17] Hobbes, *Leviathan*, p. 133.

Some people, according to Hobbes, have to be prepared for this appeal to their material interests, especially those he called "masterless" and "vainglorious" men who do not define their interests in terms of the goods Leviathan state promises—that is, security and a life that gradually "advances[s] to delectation."[18] These people will have to undergo a transformation before Babel can be rebuilt. To see why Hobbes thought this was so, we have to examine more closely the mentality and conduct he thought stood in the way of Leviathan state. Then we can turn to his theoretical response and its limitations.

Hobbes believed the first problem facing any political society is that some people are too proud to be ruled by others. They are masterless men who have a driving desire to hold dominion over others. To them life is a battle, not a race in which they must continually "out-go the next before" and "to forsake the course, is to die."[19] This is why Hobbes says that civil war is nothing but the "dissolute condition of masterless men," and Leviathan state goes on record against these "children of pride" by prohibiting pride under the "ninth law of nature."[20]

The masterless man was a familiar historical as well as literary figure in Hobbes's day. Hobbes was not writing only in response to his own civil war. In the Netherlands, Scotland, Germany, Switzerland, France, and Italy disorder had been no less severe during the past century, and he believed this was the result of a passionate drive for personal power over others. Luther, the Machiavellian princes, and Cromwell were just the most famous of this breed. At the heart of every masterless man, from the displaced peasants who had lost their land through enclosure to the aristocracy to Cromwell himself, was the proud belief that by nature he was his own man: "Here I stand, I can do no other."

One complex example of this mentality is in Shakespeare's *Richard II*. In power, but well aware of his enemies, Richard still holds fast to the belief that nature itself will protect him.

> This earth shall have a feeling, and these stones
> Prove armed soldiers, ere her native king
> Shall falter under foul rebellion's arms.
>
> (3.2)

Then after his allies have deserted him, Richard seems to recognize his own "vain conceit" (3.2). His natural defenses have failed him, and for a brief moment he sees that his power is waning. This fleeting introspective

[18] Hobbes, *De Cive*, p. 168.
[19] Thomas Hobbes, *Of Human Nature: The Fundamental Elements of Policy*, in *EW*, 4:53.
[20] Hobbes, *Leviathan*, pp. 170, 307, 141, 254.

moment passes, however, for when he is brought face-to-face with Henry, his pride again gets the better of him.

> Swell'st thou, proud heart? I'll give thee scope to beat,
> Since foes have scope to beat both thee and me.
>
> (3.3)

It is the fate of masterless men to be ruled by their own "vain conceit," to take comfort in the false belief that nature supports them, and eventually to have their "glory, like a shooting star / Fall to the base earth from the firmament" (2.4).

The proud pursuit of political glory, as Machiavelli knew, depends on manipulating appearance and thus the perceptions of others. The Machiavellian prince lived in the realm of sheer appearance and "effectual truth." His glory came from his triumphs over others. Hobbes reinterprets glory in a psychological way in order to gain more control over it.[21] Glory, for Hobbes, "hath as its cause, that the spirits, because they feel that the things they say and do are approved, rise from the heart to the face as witness of the good opinion conceived of themselves."[22] Glory is the "exultation of the mind."[23] In Hobbes's hands the act of triumph is overshadowed by the feeling of "precedence."

Once glory is identified with the desire for precedence, it must then be channeled toward divisible, material goods rather than hierarchical political offices. According to Hobbes, citizens of Leviathan state must learn to settle for a "commodious" life. Anyone, Hobbes assumes, can occupy the office of the sovereign, so he hopes no one will want it badly. Once in office the sovereign will have nothing to fear and so will not have any interest in abusing its powers. The "felicity" citizens of Leviathan state pursue will be material, not political.

But this does not entirely solve the problem. Materialists can become greedy and quarrelsome. To avoid this, Hobbes believed, vanity had to be held in check. Hobbes distinguished vainglory from the favored personality of the petty egocentrist. The egocentric pursuit of felicity is self-absorbed; vainglory is a state of madness. In Leviathan state it is only "the next before" whom we must outgo, not everyone else. Pascal, in one of his *Pensées*, captures this pettiness that Hobbes prefers over vainglory": "We are so presumptuous that we should like to be known all over the world,

---

21 Robert Denoon Cumming, *Human Nature and History* (Chicago: University of Chicago Press, 1969), 2:45–48.

22 Thomas Hobbes, *De Homine*, trans. in *Man and Citizen*, ed. Bernard Gert (Garden City, N.Y.: Doubleday, 1972), p. 58.

23 Hobbes, *Leviathan*, p. 45.

even by people who will only come when we are no more. Such is our vanity that the good opinion of half a dozen of the people around us gives us pleasure and satisfaction."[24]

Vainglory is what drives people to lose sight of their own modest place in society. Hobbes mentions the "one that preached in Cheapside from a cart here, instead of a pulpit, that he himself was Christ, which was spiritual pride or madness" to illustrate vainglory.[25] It is true that because they are unable to capture political power, the vainglorious will seek a life of "ease and sensual delight." But Hobbes makes it clear that unlike the petty, industrious entrepreneur whose tunnel vision leaves him satisfied with the kind words of a few close friends, the vainglorious man is not "fit"[26] for the society of others at all. Vainglorious men frustrated with politics take refuge in materialism, but vainglory still leads to the same ungovernable temperament as glory. Like their more successful political brothers, their desire for precedence makes it impossible for the vainglorious to establish a society that is either "great or lasting."[27] In their own way, they also want "to be known all over the world" and will not settle for less.

## Hobbes and Political Education

Hobbes begins and ends *Leviathan* by calling on the university to promote his "moral and civil science."[28] He denounces the "insignificant speech" of the "Schoolmen" but tells us this should not be taken as a "disproving" judgment against the university's "office" in the commonwealth. *Leviathan* is precisely the kind of "discourse" that "may be profitably printed, and more profitably taught in the Universities." What makes *Leviathan* so deserving of this official position is that it provides the "clear and exact method" necessary for ending civil war. Civil war arises when "men know not the causes of neither war nor peace."[29] Give them a method for tracing out the consequences of alternative hypothetical states of affairs, and they will learn how to avoid civil war.

Although Hobbes relies on this argument to educate aristocrats and clergymen and on a "civil decalogue" that simplifies the duties of citi-

---

[24] Blaise Pascal, *Pensées*, trans. A. J. Krailsheimer (London: Penguin, 1966), p. 60. See Michael Walzer, *Spheres of Justice* (New York: Basic Books, 1983), p. 255 for a similar interpretation of this passage, to which I am indebted.

[25] Thomas Hobbes, *Human Nature*, in *EW*, 4:41.

[26] Hobbes, *De Cive*, p. 2.

[27] Ibid., p. 6.

[28] Hobbes, *Leviathan*, pp. 170, 3, 713.

[29] Quoted in Habermas, *Theory and Practice*, p. 72.

zens for the "vulgar" so that they can get on with the relatively peaceful business of procuring a "commodious living,"[30] there is more involved in political education, especially that of masterless and vainglorious men, and Hobbes knows it. For citizens already inclined to work hard and mind their own business, daily assemblies in which they are reminded of their civic duties may be enough.[31] But for masterless and vainglorious men, neither drill nor abstract demonstrations of self-interest will do.

In the passage in which Hobbes introduces his adaptation of the Ten Commandments, he says that the sovereign has an obligation to teach citizens "the grounds or reasons of those his essential rights." These grounds or reasons must be "diligently, and truly taught."[32] Just as it is not enough to intimidate citizens into obeying, it is not enough, as Hobbes argues elsewhere, for those citizens capable of careful reasoning to merely "parrot" or memorize the rules of order, if they truly are to understand them and be moved by them.[33] They must understand these rules in the sense that they must know why they must not "dispute the Sovereign power."[34] Pledging themselves to live by the rules without this level of understanding will not ensure obedience, nor will it be enough to simply walk them through the requisite deductions. "Evidence is to truth, as sap to the tree, which so far as it creepeth along with the body and branches, keepeth them alive; where it forsaketh them, they die; for this evidence, which is meaning with our words, is the life of truth."[35] Teaching people inclined to lust after political power or to endlessly compare themselves with others that their well-being depends on giving up politics and "precellence" is no simple matter. It involves teaching them the grounds or evidence for their views. Otherwise, as Mill argued in *On Liberty*, their beliefs will lose their meaning and be of little value for the purposes of action.

But it is one thing to say that political education has to be more than rote memorization and quite another to say that learning how to read the evidence for obeying Leviathan state will reorder your passions. What is it about truly learning the grounds and reasons of sovereign authority that orients citizens toward a life of competitive racing and reshapes their character so that glory and vainglory will be supplanted by the egocentrism of the petty entrepreneur?

---

[30] Sheldon S. Wolin, *Hobbes and the Epic Tradition of Political Theory* (Los Angeles: William Clark Memorial Library, University of California Press, 1970), p. 47, and "Hobbes and the Culture of Despotism," in *Thomas Hobbes and Political Theory*, ed. Mary G. Deitz (Lawrence: University Press of Kansas, 1990), p. 31.

[31] Hobbes, *Leviathan*, p. 328.

[32] Ibid., p. 323.

[33] Hobbes, *Human Nature*, p. 28.

[34] Hobbes, *Leviathan*, pp. 327–28.

[35] Hobbes, *Human Nature*, p. 28.

Like terms in geometry, the basic terms of political life in Leviathan state must be clearly defined, and initial assumptions must be noncontroversial. In *Leviathan* we are told that the first move is actually one of naming, and the crucial names are those given to the passions. It is important not to exaggerate Hobbes's nominalism, however. Words may be only "wise men's counters," but names signify "the nature of that we conceive, and this "be the same" for all persons.[36] The naming of the passions and self-examination must proceed hand in hand. The problem, according to Hobbes, is that some people are likely to choose names that are colored by a prejudice or interest of their own. To avoid this, names—especially the names of the passions—must signify only "their nature" and not the "nature, disposition and interest of the speaker." This is what Hobbes means by the "apt imposing of names." The "true grounds of ratiocination" can never include words like justice, cruelty, gravity, and stupidity, whose "signification" is "inconstant" in this sense.[37] These are not the basic terms of political life of Leviathan state; they are too easily slanted, and the temptation to use self-serving definitions is too great.

Once the initial process of self-examination and naming has occurred so that the real nature of the human passions themselves is captured, the next step is to plot the directions of persons moved by these passions. Hobbes begins with the smallest movements, "endeavors," and tracks them not just as single particles but as vectors that extend in two directions. The passions of competition, diffidence, and glory[38] lead to recurrent conflict and disagreements; other passions tend to mitigate the problems of a life of constant movement and resistance. People remain "matter in motion," never fully confident of preserving themselves and their possessions, but something can be done to slow them down and lower their sights. Hobbes tells us they can become "fit for society not by nature but by education."[39]

To be fit, Hobbes argues in *De Homine*, is to have the right "dispositions and manners," which in turn depends on a variety of factors including bodily constitution, experience, self-image, luck, habit, and most of all the teachings of those in authority. "Good dispositions are those suitable for entering civil society; and good manners (that is, moral virtues) are those whereby what was entered upon can be preserved."[40] It is the aim of Hobbes's "moral and civil science" to create "good dispositions" and preserve them. In *Leviathan* Hobbes puts the point in terms of passions rather than dispositions and manners: "Appetites of particular things, proceed

[36] Hobbes, *Leviathan*, p. 28.
[37] Ibid., pp. 35, 29.
[38] Ibid., p. 112.
[39] Hobbes, *De Cive*, p. 2.
[40] Hobbes, *De Homine*, p. 70.

from experience, and trial of their effects upon themselves of other men," and "the difference of passions proceedeth partly from the different constitution of the body, and partly from different education."[41] Dispositions and manners appear to be socialized and civilized forms of action, often dictated by authority, but their springs, the passions, are also amenable to education.

To improve dispositions and manners, at least partially, through a transformation of the passions, Hobbes must first juxtapose the wilder passions of colliding masterless men and those run ragged by their own vainglory against the passions that "incline men to peace," which are "fear of death; desire of such things as are necessary to commodious living; and a hope by their industry to attain them."[42] One way to create an attachment to the passions of "industry," then, would be through a geometric meditation that might loosen the grip of the former. Hobbes never explicitly takes this step, but his theory of language suggests one way to construct such a self-formative comparison.

Hobbes thought speech and method distinguished human beings from other animals, and he described the original covenant as the creation of "an artificial animal."[43] This nearly blasphemous covenant concludes an even bolder linguistic act of self-creation. The geometric argument of *Leviathan* begins with the human act of naming human passions, but it contains an important presupposition. According to Hobbes, rebellious men lost the names God gave them and were reduced to a "diversity of tongues." Neither their sheer numbers nor their social nature could save them from this. Only speech and method can restore and preserve political order.[44] By reminding us of this peculiar linguistic power, Hobbes's theory suggests that we can reconstruct ourselves with geometric precision.

This is still not enough, however. Even if we grant that the passions can be tamed and good dispositions can be created, it is not clear why Hobbesian, linguistically self-made men would favor their tame passions and mind their own business. What's in it for them? Only if we attribute to them a more self-conscious form of reasoning and an interest in their own integrity as continuous persons over time, which Hobbes never did, can we motivate them to this degree.

Here is one way these persons might think about themselves. If they check Hobbes's account of the passions against their own personal experience, as he urges us to do,[45] they may find that they are no longer haunted

---

[41] Hobbes, *Leviathan*, pp. 40, 61.
[42] Ibid., p. 116.
[43] Ibid., pp. ix–x.
[44] Ibid., pp. x, 19, 155–56, 16.
[45] Ibid., p. xi.

by doubts about their own ability to act freely in a previously mysterious world. They can look back on their lives to see where they have gone wrong on their own and where they have been misled by "insignificant speech." They may be able to see one path they could have traveled, leading back into their past and extending into the future that had not been visible to them before. This new self that is revealed no longer is caught between the drive for glory and the pitfalls of vanity. From the point of view of this newly formed self, which still understands its life as the vector sum of "matter in motion," the antinomy of liberty and dominion is replaced by liberty and necessity—and necessity, according to Hobbes, is not inconsistent with voluntary motion.[46] Life finally begins to make sense, and wilder passions lose their attraction.

I will return to the contemporary versions of this Hobbesian internal dialogue later, but let me note in passing that it amounts to a one-person game in which one is trying to outguess and outmaneuver oneself. These prospective citizens of Leviathan state are using their reason as more than a scout or spy. They are critically reflecting on the past uses of reason and retracing their own steps to see where they have gone wrong. The mere absence of "external impediments"[47] would no longer be enough to make them free, for freedom would depend on reason's ability to reconstruct its own history so that wilder passions could be abandoned. With the recognition of this new historical self through the proper use of speech and method, there may come a desire to preserve this newfound continuity in their past and future lives. For persons who are forever in "perpetual motion,"[48] wild passions might be less attractive because they lead to unpredictable collisions where the laws are silent.[49] Alternatively, passions that lead to methodical, industrious behavior might be more attractive. They could enable this new self-made private citizen to continue to build a modest, familiar environment. Having found themselves in this geometric sense, these self-reflective Hobbesian citizens might be unwilling to give it up for something as unpredictable as "glory" or "precellence." It might make more sense to run slowly between the "Hedges" they themselves have erected out of contracts and covenants.[50]

Their understanding of where they have come from is still remarkably linear, however, and their confidence rests on a strange, pre-Freudian view

[46] Ibid., p. 198; see also "Of Liberty and Necessity," in *EW*, 4:239–78.
[47] Hobbes, *Leviathan*, p. 116.
[48] Hobbes, *De Homine*, p. 54.
[49] Hobbes, *Leviathan*, p. 65.
[50] Ibid., p. 335. Hobbes relied on building metaphors several times, for example, ibid., pp. 325, 340.

of living and thinking. Even this Hobbesian thought experiment is devoid of play, fantasy, and most important, political judgment. If Hobbes's moral geometry can be used as a form of political education to tame wild passions and fit people for political order, it is a political order in which the traditional problem of political education never really arises with full force. Hobbesian citizens, even at their most self-reflective, may know how to reconcile freedom and necessity, but they do not have the judgment to balance private loves and affections against public duties. Because public and private life are so artificially and radically separated under Leviathan state, the need for the judgment that balancing requires never arises. Moral geometry may enable Hobbesian citizens to fit themselves to Leviathan state by cutting a path back and forth between past and future, but it does not help them find a home in a political world in which definitions, axioms, and proofs in a geometric sense fail to hold. As Kant said, "In philosophy the geometrician can by his method build only so many houses of cards."[51]

## Kant's Political Project

To reconstruct Hobbesian political theory as political education, we first had to be clear about the problem Hobbes was addressing. Whereas Hobbes wanted to end civil war, Kant's political objective was to overcome German political, economic, and intellectual stagnation. Just as Hume had roused him, Kant hoped to rouse the German middle class and other civil servants like himself. Political fragmentation among the German states had to be overcome, and individual rights, especially the rights to private property and speech, had to be placed on a firmer footing if Germany was to catch up politically with France and economically with England. Religious prejudices had to be dispelled and a new basis for citizenship established. Kant called this new basis "independence."

Every man who has the right to vote on this legislation is termed a *citizen* (*citoyen*, i.e., a *citizen* of the *state*, not of a city or borough, a *bourgeois*). The only necessary qualification, aside from the *natural* one of not being a child or a woman, is that he be *his own master (sui iuris)*: that he own some sort of property—among which may be counted any skill, craft, fine art, or science that supports him. That is to say that whenever he needs to acquire things from others in order to live, he will acquire them only by *disposing* of what is *his own*, not by allowing others to use his services, so that he will not, in the

---

51 Kant, *Critique of Pure Reason*, p. 585.

proper sense of the word, be anyone's servant but the community's. (Emphasis in original)[52]

This was obviously no small task, but Kant believed that intellectuals had a key role to play in getting people, "the reading public" in particular, to think for themselves rather than blindly trusting the wisdom of books, pastors, high public officials, and other professionals. Kant believed that human history was in the long run progressive, but in Germany progress required the intervention of intellectuals who could teach people to demand new rights, aggressively exploit them, and strengthen themselves politically at the same time. A German nation-state and a vigorous middle class both had to be built. Stagnation and a regressive political identity had to be overcome, and Kant believed this meant teaching people to think critically about authoritative pronouncements about God, power, justice, and the law. Property, I argue, is at the center of Kant's ideal of independent thinking.

Whereas Hobbes struggled against the disruptive passions and interests of masterless men, the madness of vainglorious men, the obscurantism of the Schoolmen, and the simplemindedness of the common lawyers, Kant focused on a parochial middle class and a wide range of defensive civil servants, including university intellectuals, and the deferential way they interpreted their freedom and social responsibility. Kant's major contribution to the liberal tradition, I argue, is the philosophical method that he urges the educated middle class, civil servants, and "scholarly" intellectuals to adopt so that they can begin to think for themselves and meet the political problems of the day. It is a method of compromise that is designed to overcome political and economic stagnation without risking the turmoil of the French Revolution that weighed so heavily on Kant's mind.

Kant's philosophical method, then, can be read as a practical response to the passions, manners, and dispositions of particular segments of German society; but unlike Hobbes's geometric method,[53] Kant's philosophical method was Socratic in several senses. Both before and after the writing of the three *Critiques*, according to Saner, Kant thought of his project in Socratic terms.

Such a polemicist wants truth. For truth's sake he must take the liberty to re-examine all past thought with factual arguments. To do this, he must "place

[52] Immanuel Kant, *On the Old Saw: That May Be Right in Theory but It Won't Work in Practice*, trans. E. B. Ashton (Philadelphia: University of Pennsylvania Press, 1974), pp. 63–64.

[53] Hobbes tried his hand at dialogue, but the result was flat and didactic. See *A Dialogue between a Philosopher and a Student of the Common Laws of England*, in *EW*, vol. 6, pp. B, B2, 4–160.

a certain noble confidence in his own powers," and in that confidence, aware of the possibility that he may be in error, he must dare to leave "the beaten path." Such self-confidence will not prevent him from recognizing flaws in his cognition, flaws which he himself cannot correct. . . . Calling for "limitless assent" to his thought is alien to him. He knows that letting himself be convinced takes as much merit as convincing others; for to allow oneself to be convinced may well presuppose a superior measure of renunciation and self-examination.[54]

First I want to take up the polemical essays, especially "What Is Enlightenment?" and "The Conflict of the Faculties." These will provide us with a historical view of Kant's practical philosophy as a form of political education. These occasional pieces are Socratic in two senses: they represent a challenge to those who claim to know the truth, and they cloak their own political character in a philosophical self-presentation. Then in the next section I turn to the more abstract philosophical work in which Kant adopts a subtler form of debate in order to rouse and prepare his audience without stampeding them.

In Prussia at the turn of the century mercantilism was the order of the day. Königsberg, Kant's home, along with the other Baltic cities of Danzig, Lübeck, and Stettin, was an important port, "though mostly through foreign initiatives."[55] The guild tradition, an obstacle to capitalist development because of the restrictions it placed on entry to the labor market, was especially strong in these old towns, which generally did not welcome the new large-scale industries. Where there were signs of development, as in Prussia, they were in large measure the result of Protestant immigrants from France, Italy, and Holland and the protective foreign trade policies of the Crown.[56]

But, Kant believed, absolutism, mercantilism, and the guild system reinforced a deeper intransigence rooted in religious identity. In "What Is Enlightenment?" Kant trained his sights on religious consciousness and its historical importance for Germany at the time. The religious views of middle-class Lutherans were a serious obstacle to political and economic development. Even in Prussia, where despots tended to be more benevolent and trade more vigorous than in the South, a steadfast Lutheranism dominated political and economic discourse, at least as Kant saw it.

To overcome this obstacle, Kant interpreted religion in a philosophical

---

54 Hans Saner, *Kant's Political Thought*, trans. E. B. Ashton (Chicago: University of Chicago Press, 1973), pp. 77–79 (footnotes omitted).

55 W. H. Bruford, *Germany in the Eighteenth Century: The Social Background of the Literary Revival* (Cambridge: Cambridge University Press, 1971), p. 168.

56 Ibid., pp. 171, 174.

way that would replace the religious ground of political membership with a moral ground. By reducing politics to a set of constitutional principles and individual rights and then grounding them in a conception of moral personality, Kant hoped that political conflicts could be handled by morally astute lawmakers and politicians. Once popularized, he thought that his critical philosophy could tame religious passions and redirect that energy along paths similar to those it had followed in France and England. That is, he hoped to reinterpret metaphysics, including religious doctrines, in universalistic moral terms in order to ease religious conflicts and loosen the grip of Lutheranism on the anticipated agents of political and economic change, the middle class. Simply branding religious faith irrational and calling for universal suffrage would be ineffective: old political identities had to be reinterpreted, and religion had to be incorporated into, not excluded from, the new moral and political universe. Religious toleration had to be established, which meant teaching believers that their faith was a private matter and that their public duty demanded they respect the beliefs of others, no matter how wrongheaded they seemed. If ever there was a traditional liberal balancing problem, this was one. But it was not an isolated problem in Kant's eyes because religion was at the center of the German political economy.

This is why Kant focuses on the historical importance of religious consciousness rather than universal suffrage or freedom of speech in "What Is Enlightenment?" even though the essay at first glance appears to be about academic freedom. He is not sanguine about the ability of "the public" in general to outgrow prejudice on its own, and he does not think a revolution will achieve a "true reform in the ways of thinking."[57] A better strategy is to permit intellectuals like himself, employed by the state, "the freedom to make public use of one's reason at every point." "By public use of one's reason, I understand the use which a person makes of it as a scholar before the reading public. Private use I call that which one may make of it in a particular civil post or office which is entrusted to him."[58] Kant himself had run afoul of state censorship on religious matters and hoped that by acquiescing in his "private" capacity as a lecturing professor employed by the state he would be allowed to publish his religious views for the reading public. He sought freedom not for the scholar as classroom teacher but for the intellectual as public conscience. Kant was not as concerned with fighting state censorship in the classroom as with bringing his "moral faith" to a wider audience. If he had to choose between the two, he had little doubt which was the more urgent task. The state could have

[57] Kant, "What Is Enlightenment?" in *On History*, ed. Lewis White Beck (Indianapolis: Bobbs-Merrill, 1963), p. 4.

[58] Ibid., p. 5.

its classroom, but Kant would not be the unwitting servant of a backward religious political identity. Kant was not thinking only of himself. Other civil servants like soldiers and clergymen should also enjoy the free "public use" of their reason, and it should extend to the middle class as well, since their "economic activities were a privilege granted to them by the state."[59]

Hannah Arendt has argued that Kant's project was Socratic. She quotes a letter he wrote in 1783 in which he said, "Every philosophical work must be susceptible of popularity; if not, it probably conceals nonsense beneath a fog of seeming sophistication."[60] Kant, she infers, neither took cover "behind the protective walls of a school" nor retreated to harmless "speculative thought." He wanted to subject both dogmatic and skeptical orthodoxies to criticism and to challenge people who claimed to know how to give an account of the grounds for their assertions or who claimed such an account was impossible. This kind of Socratic philosophizing, Arendt argues, is necessary if people are to be freed from their old ways of thinking. "As the midwife helps the child to come to light to be inspected, so Socrates brings to light the implications to be inspected. (That is what Kant did when he complained about progress: he extracted the implications of this concept."[61] Arendt believed that Kant's Socratic political philosophy is to be found in *The Critique of Judgment*, not in either his occasional political writings or his practical philosophy. I think she misses something here, and in the next section I say more about how Kant's practical philosophy operates as a form of political education. But before I get to that, more needs to be said about the Socratic character of the popular essays Arendt tends to depreciate.

The Socratic character of Kant's occasional political writings is not to be found only in their maieutic function. What we see in these essays is a subtle form of political intervention reminiscent of the Socratic denial of political ambition. Kant was deeply engaged in politics, and though John Laursen is right to see a "subversive" element in these essays, there are also elements of compromise and mediation. "What Is Enlightenment?" is the most aggressive of these pieces, but it is by no means the whole story.

In "The Conflict of the Faculties" Kant argues that philosophers should be allowed to speak about the teachings of the three "higher faculties" (theology, jurisprudence, and medicine). Furthermore, freedom of speech for the higher faculties can be legitimately restricted because of the close connection between these subjects and the interests and affairs of the

[59] John Christian Laursen, "The Subversive Kant: The Vocabulary of 'Public' and 'Publicity,'" *Political Theory* 14 (November 1986): 589.

[60] Hannah Arendt, *Lectures on Kant's Political Philosophy*, ed. Ronald Beiner (Sussex: Harvester Press, 1982), pp. 38–39.

[61] Ibid., p. 41.

nation. According to Howard Williams, "Priests, judges and doctors carry out in their day to day work the concepts and doctrines that are taught in their places of learning. So, according to Kant, the manner in which these three vocations interpret their disciplines is of intimate concern to the state, and as a consequence the State has every right to supervise the teaching of these subjects."[62] In contrast, Kant claims, the subject matter of philosophy ultimately is truth. Censoring philosophers makes the pursuit of truth and the instruction of the people impossible.

There are two important qualifications in this essay, published in 1798, not long after Kant had antagonized Frederick William II with *Religion within the Limits of Reason Alone*. First, Kant no longer feels compelled or able to defend the freedom of all scholars in the public use of their reason. He acknowledges the dangers the "higher faculties" may pose to the state if they are allowed to go uncensored. Second, he recommends philosophy, the "lower faculty," to the state as a check on the higher faculties and an overseer of their views. The state, he says, has nothing to fear from philosophers, whose work is generally inaccessible to the public, and it has much to gain by enlisting them in the control of other intellectuals.[63] This retreat is mirrored in Kant's ingratiating suggestion in *Perpetual Peace* that philosophers should serve quietly as advisers to rulers on matters of war and peace and that subjects are never justified in rebelling, no matter how despotic the goverment.[64]

Kant clearly understood the political importance of what we now refer to as the three classic professions. This is a continuing theme in later liberal theory, but very few liberal theorists have been so self-conscious or forthcoming about the need to mediate professional authority. In these occasional essays, we can see how Kant attempted to position philosophy with respect to the state as well as the "higher" faculties in order to advance the progress of the Enlightenment as he understood it.

Now that we have a rough sense of what Kant was trying to do, who the other actors were, and how important a new way of thinking was to him, let us turn to his practical philosophy. It is here that Kant addresses those among the reading public who are in a position to rethink their practical views from the ground up. The key to understanding Kant's practical philosophy as a form of political education with the same goals as his occasional polemical essays is his method of moral casuistry.

[62] Howard Williams, *Kant's Political Philosophy* (New York: St. Martin's Press, 1983), p. 153.

[63] Immanuel Kant, *The Conflict of the Faculties*, trans. Mary J. Gregor (Lincoln: University of Nebraska Press, 1992).

[64] Immanuel Kant, *Perpetual Peace*, in *On History*, pp. 115, 130,

## Kant's Method of Moral Casuistry

Since Pascal's blistering attack on the Jesuits in *The Provincial Letters*, casuistry has been a term of opprobrium. I will use it in a nonpejorative sense to describe Kant's method of practical reasoning generally, not just the dialogue and catechism between teachers and students he describes at the end of *The Doctrine of Virtue*.

How Kant's practical philosophy should be characterized as a whole has been a matter of continuing controversy. Rawls's reinterpretation of Kant as a "constructivist" rather than a "rational intuitionist" is largely responsible for keeping this issue alive in recent years. Although constructivism captures the antidogmatic intent of Kant's critique of rationalism,[65] I think it understates the unifying political purpose of his critical philosophy as a whole. Rationalism, as practiced by Descartes and Hobbes, was to Kant a form of political dogmatism because it erected a "tribunal" of reason that simply could not be sustained by reason alone. Principles of cognition and principles of moral and political conduct rest on more modest foundations: they must be rebuilt regularly in a consensual way in order to carry the weight of new cases and problems as they arise. This is the thrust of Rawls's notion of reflective equilibrium, which is the centerpiece in his Kantian constructivism understood as an alternative to dogmatic rational intuitionism. Casuistry, then, as I will use the term, emphasizes the way first principles and more determinate maxims are balanced among a small plurality of persons with only the modest cognitive and moral resources Kant believes they have. As Onora O'Neill stresses, Kant really meant it when he said that "we should be able at the same time to show the unity of practical and theoretical reason in a common principle, since in the end there can only be one and the same reason, which must be differentiated solely in its application."[66] That common principle is the categorical imperative, Kant's answer to the traditional problem of liberal political education: if citizens want to speak and act with one another with some assurance that their individual rights will be respected, then they must act in accordance with the categorical imperative. Demonstrating the cognitive as well as practical significance of the categorical imperative is the difficult task O'Neill has set for herself, and I will return to her argument below.

---

[65] Onora O'Neill, "Constructivisms in Ethics," in her *Constructions of Reason: Explorations of Kant's Practical Philosophy* (Cambridge: Cambridge University Press, 1989), pp. 206–18, and Thomas E. Hill Jr., "Kantian Constructivism in Ethics," *Ethics* 99 (July 1989): 752–70.

[66] O'Neill quotes this line from *The Groundwork of the Metaphysic of Morals* (4:391) at the end of her essay "Reason and Politics in the Kantian Enterprise," in *Constructions of Reason*, p. 27. I have benefited greatly from her reading of Kant.

My goal in this section is somewhat different and derivative of O'Neill's interpretation of Kant. If we accept O'Neill's thesis that the categorical imperative unites Kant's accounts of theoretical and practical reason, what more can we say about its casuistic political content? Does Kant tell us anything more about how this modest consensus—O'Neill likens it to agreeing on how to build a cottage rather than a tower—that reason and its resources make possible can actually be built?

To amplify the casuistic political content of the categorical imperative, we have to move slowly from Kant's seemingly apolitical arguments about moral personhood to his more explicit political discussions of republican government and individual political rights. Kant often makes very abstract, sometimes unconvincing, logical connections between these various levels of practical philosophy. My purpose will be to interpret some of these connections keeping in mind the traditional problem of liberal political education, as Kant phrased it, not to improve on his logic or shore up the moral base of the theory. But we have to begin with the moral base.

Kant's view of how moral personhood can ground liberal political institutions and practices is that it must be done procedurally. What makes liberal political institutions and practices moral is that they would be chosen by moral persons. In other words, moral persons would choose political institutions and practices that respect and encourage respect for the worth of each individual as a free and equal person—and, Kant argued, "republican" institutions and practices do this best. Neither individual moral worth nor republican institutions and practices can be fashioned according to metaphysical truths. They must be constructed by actual persons working within their own political traditions, asking themselves what they would have agreed to in an original contract. This is what Rawls is getting at when he argues that the original position is a procedural expression of the Kantian notions of autonomy and the categorical imperative.[67]

Kant's version of the traditional problem of liberal political education follows directly from this proceduralism. If you can show moral persons how their moral dignity and autonomy depend on support for republican institutions and practices, then they may be able to balance public duties and private life. Kant was not very confident that they in fact would be able to manage this balancing act, and his practical philosophy reflects this doubt. His practical philosophy pulls in several directions. In this section I want to distinguish between the teleological bent in Kant's practical philosophy that threatens to make political education superfluous and the general method of moral casuistry whose purpose is to engage people in

---

[67] Rawls, *Theory of Justice*, p. 256.

their own political education on an intimate scale, and that rests on the constructivist and procedural assumptions Kant makes about philosophy as a whole.

Kant seemed to be perennially tempted by a teleology that severs the connection between moral autonomy and political responsibility. His famous comment in *Perpetual Peace*, which I noted earlier, on how easy it might be to create political order even for a "race of devils" is the product of this teleological faith: "The problem of organizing a state however hard it may seem, can be solved even for a race of devils if only they are intelligent. The problem is: 'Given a multitude of rational beings requiring universal laws for their preservation, but each of whom is secretly inclined to exempt himself from them, to establish a constitution in such a way that, although their private intentions conflict, they check each other, with the result that their public conduct is the same as if they had no such intentions.'" This is a familiar notion to contemporary pluralists. Through institutional designs like the separation of powers, "man is forced to be a good citizen even if not a morally good person." [68] In Madison's terms, men need not be "angels" to be good citizens in a good society. And, we might ask, if they do not have to be angels, why, as citizens, do they have to know how to deliberate as free and equal rational persons?

The competence citizens need to bargain effectively, pursue their own interests, and understand the laws of a republican government will be the product of competition and conflict, not moral respect and harmony.

> Without those in themselves unamiable characteristics of unsociability from whence opposition springs—characteristics each man must find in his own selfish pretensions—all talents would remain hidden, unborn in an Arcadian shepherd's life, with all its concord, contentment, and mutual affection. Men, good-natured as the sheep they herd, would hardly reach a higher worth than their beasts; they would not fill the empty place in creation by achieving their end, which is rational nature. Thanks be to Nature, then, for the incompatibility, for heartless competitive vanity, for the insatiable desire to possess and to rule.[69]

These teleogical views obviate the need for any liberal political education, morally grounded or not.

Offsetting this, however, is Kant's equally strong tendency to praise a different kind of individual initiative and independence of mind. Kant be-

---

[68] Kant, *Perpetual Peace*, p. 112.

[69] Immanuel Kant, "Idea for a Universal History from a Cosmopolitan Point of View," in *On History*, p. 15.

lieved individuals could still think for themselves. In the first *Critique* he argues that "there is in man a power of self-determination, independently of any coercion through sensuous impulses." The basis for this claim is not historical: "That our reason has causality, or at least that we represent it to ourselves as having causality, is evident from the imperatives which in matters of conduct we impose as rules upon our own active powers."[70] Much like Marx, Kant believed human freedom exists within a world that constrains individual choices and growth but does not destroy them.[71] In order to recognize the weight of history and act within the political spaces it provides, he believed a strong moral character was essential, one that relied on determination, practice, and material independence. Kant's view of history need not be read as a form of strong determinism, but unfortunately it sometimes sounds as if he thought it could substitute for political education.

Now to the method of moral casuistry. Alongside this ambivalence toward history is Kant's endorsement of moral casuistry, a philosophical method oriented toward the kind of political character transformation he calls for in his polemical essays. Recall his injunction that citizens should think for themselves. Kant did not leave it at that. He had a very detailed conception of what this entailed, how it could be accomplished, and what changes in political character might result.

In the *Critique of Judgment* Kant explains what it means to think for oneself in terms of "maxims" of "common human understanding." People who think for themselves must also put themselves in the position of others and think consistently.[72] According to O'Neill, together these maxims constitute a form of self-discipline. In fact, she claims, they are a procedural representation of the categorial imperative in the sense that in testing the underlying principles of individual action according to it, one must not take anything "on authority" but rather must see things from others' point of view. To do this is to fashion one's own view in light of how others would see it and then struggle to make one's new, revised view as consistent as possible with one's earlier views. In O'Neill's words,

> The only route by which we can vindicate certain ways of thinking and acting, and claim that those ways have authority, is by considering how we must discipline our thinking if we are to think or act at all. This disciplining leads us

[70] Kant, *Critique of Pure Reason*, pp. 465, 472.
[71] Lucien Goldmann, *Immanuel Kant*, trans. Robert Black (London: New Left Books, 1971), pp. 136–45.
[72] Immanuel Kant, *Critique of Judgment*, trans. J. H. Bernard (New York: Hafner, 1974), p. 136.

not to algorithms of reason, but to certain constraints on all thinking, communication and interaction among any plurality. In particular we are led to the principle of rejecting thought, action or communication that is guided by principles that others cannot adopt, and so to the Categorical Imperative.[73]

O'Neill claims that the *Critique of Pure Reason*, not just Kant's overt practical philosophy, is guided by this procedural requirement. If we test the way we think about the world, as well as the way we act in it, by the categorical imperative, we will be able to build a modest "home" on the "level of experience" with others who share with us resources such as the categories of understanding and certain intuitions. The categorical imperative suggests a set of self-disciplining maxims that shape the political as well as the moral character of those who use them. They include the maxims of "common understanding" (*sensus communis*) that O'Neill emphasizes, and also the maxims of justice we find elsewhere in Kant's political philosophy. The following argument is an attempt to expand the moral self-discipline represented by the categorical imperative so that we can see the tacit political content O'Neill calls attention to more clearly. In other words, in learning to think cooperatively for themselves on "the level of experience" Kantian citizens acquire a certain political recognition as well as a view of themselves as moral persons.

Character for Kant is not an internal state or even a set of dispositions. It is a self-reflective, self-disciplining activity, and he expresses this view in his practical philosophy as well as in the polemical essays we have surveyed. In the second *Critique* Kant does not identify the "maxim of the will," what is "absolutely good or evil," with a formal proposition or even some internal state of mind. It is a "manner of acting" that does not appear full-blown but develops slowly over time.[74] "The man who adopts this purity into his maxim is indeed not yet holy by reason of this act (for there is a great gap between the maxim and the deed). Still he is upon the road of endless progress towards holiness. When the firm resolve to do one's duty has become habitual, it is also called the virtue of conformity to law; such conformity is virtue's empirical character . . . virtue in this sense is won little by little and, for some men requires long practice."[75] Moral autonomy depends on long practice aimed at building a habitual commitment to the

73 Onora O'Neill, "Reason and Politics in the Kantian Enterprise," in *Constructions of Reason*, p. 27.

74 Immanuel Kant, *Critique of Practical Reason*, trans. Lewis White Beck (New York: Liberal Arts Press, 1956), p. 62.

75 Immanuel Kant, *Religion within the Limits of Reason Alone*, trans. T. M. Greene and H. H. Hudson (New York: Harper Torchbooks, 1960), p. 142.

categorical imperative. The purity of heart that acting from duty signifies is a process of striving to make the moral law a sufficient incentive for acting in ways consistent with individual autonomy. As one commentator has said, "Striving of that type is not striving *for* purity of heart; it *is* purity of heart."[76] It is a habitual manner of acting that is won little by little.

But this manner is primarily a habit of the mind, not a habit of the heart. According to Kant, human beings, unlike other animals, need both harsh physical discipline and a disciplining moral education. The fault lies with reason itself. If human beings were simply pleasure seekers, instinct would suffice. Since they are not, they must rely on their rational faculties, which, though imperfect, can be improved. Instinct neither needs nor is receptive to such improvement. Toward the close of his short essay on education Kant has this to say about the culmination of this process of improvement: "Morality is a matter of character. *Sustine et abstine* (endure and abstain), such is the preparation for a wise moderation. The first step towards this formation of a good character is to put our passions on one side. We must take care that our desires and inclinations do not become passions, by learning to go without those things that are denied us." And, "Our ultimate aim is the formation of character. Character consists in the firm pursuit to accomplish something, and then also in the actual accomplishing of it."[77] Moderation, effectiveness, resolve, and really the repression of Hobbesian feelings of "felicity" that might come from "those things that are denied us"—these seem to be the constituent elements of a disciplined moral character. Kant argues that any substantive religious teaching should be postponed until this kind of moral character has had time to take root. In fact, religion is simply "morality applied to the knowledge of God." With even more daring he adds, "If religion is not united to morality, it becomes merely an endeavor to win favor."[78]

Kantian moral character is not something we can simply counsel others to adopt like a policy or program. A good will comes from acting in a very specific kind of examined and cautious way for the sake of the categorical imperative. Moral education, the process of mutual examination and tutelage, is the only way to acquire this habit of mind. Like Aristotle, Kant believes morality depends on certain habits of mind and on choosing an exemplary role model. Unlike Aristotle, however, Kant wants ethics to be

---

[76] Paul Dietrichson, "What Kant Means by 'Acting from Duty,'" in *Kant: A Collection of Critical Essays*, ed. Robert Paul Wolff (London: University of Notre Dame Press, 1967), p. 321.

[77] Immanuel Kant, *Education*, trans. Annette Churton (Ann Arbor: University of Michigan Press, 1960), pp. 97, 98.

[78] Ibid., p. 111.

a theoretical discipline that aims at exactness, and this criterion has important implications for his understanding of political education.

In the closing sections of the second *Critique* Kant suggests how one might learn to be moved by the maxims of practical reason and thus enjoy self-respect and merit the respect of others: "Certainly it cannot be denied that in order to bring either an as yet uneducated or degraded mind into the path of the morally good, some preparatory guidance is needed to attract it by a view of its own advantage or to frighten it by fear of harm. As soon as this machinery, these leading strings, have had some effect, the pure moral motive must be brought to mind."[79] As Kant sees it, fear and self-interest can be replaced as practical motives through a method of moral argument. This is a method to which we are naturally and directly drawn without the help of political institutions. One can easily confirm this, Kant contends, by our irrepressible interest in debating the various sides of any moral problem. Kant puts it this way: "Now of all arguments there are none which excite more ready participation by those who are otherwise soon bored with all subtle thinking, or which are more likely to bring a certain liveliness into company, than one about the moral worth of this or that action from which the character of some person is to be made out."[80] Moral casuistry moves to capitalize on this readiness to participate in debate and argument. We are naturally interested in controversial moral problems, and in the casuistic process of disentangling questions of moral worth from other issues, moral character begins to form.

Moral casuistry, at its best, creates a new habit of mind; and it does this systematically.

> The method therefore takes the following course. The first step is to make judging according to moral laws a natural occupation which accompanies our own observations of those of others, and to make it, as it were, a habit. We must sharpen these judgments by first asking whether the action is objectively in accordance with the moral law, and if so, with which one; by this, heed to the law which merely gives a principle of obligation is distinguished from one which is in fact obligatory. . . . For instance, we distinguish between the law of that which the needs of men require of me from that which their rights demand, the latter prescribing essential duties while the former assigns nonessential duties. This teaches how to distinguish between the different duties which come together in an action. The second point to which attention must be directed is the question as to whether the action also is done (subjectively) for the sake of the moral law, and thus not only is morally correct as a deed,

[79] Kant, *Critique of Practical Reason*, p. 156.
[80] Ibid., p. 157.

but also has moral worth as a disposition because of the maxim from which it was done.[81]

Kant's method of moral argument contains three steps. First, we are to examine an action to see if it can be consistently willed as a universal law of nature. Second, we are to break the action down into its constituent parts based on the distinction between perfect and imperfect duties. Finally, we must decide whether it is morally worthy as well as morally correct: Was it done for the sake of duty by someone who might have acted otherwise? By learning how to parse our arguments *with others* in this threefold way, we acquire the habit of respecting individual autonomy and, Kant hopes, the desire to uphold the institutions needed to promote autonomy.

In *The Metaphysics of Morals* Kant sketches this cooperative learning process. As in the second *Critique*, one begins with exposure to moral problems: our natural response is to construct arguments that rely on self-interest and later on reasons drawn from our views about rights and duties. This exposure allows for imitation, and "to the as yet unformed human being, imitation is what first determines him to embrace the maxims that he afterwards makes his own."[82]

In some cases imitation is short-lived. Two other approaches are then called on. When dealing with a "mere audience,"[83] the doctrine of virtue can be delivered in a lecture. The other, more interesting approach is divided into the method of dialogue and the method of catechism. Using the former method, the teacher addresses questions to the student's reason, while catechism involves memory only. Catechism is more appropriate to the "untrained pupil," while dialogue seems to be the highest level of moral education.

> For if the teacher wants to question his pupil's reason he must do this in a dialogue in which the teacher and pupil reciprocally question and answer each other. The teacher, by his questions guides the pupil's thinking merely by presenting him with situations in which his disposition for concepts will develop (the teacher is the midwife of the pupil's thoughts). The pupil, who thus sees that he is able to think for himself, provides, by his questions about obscurities or doubts in the propositions admitted, occasion for the teacher to learn how to question skillfully, according to the saying *docendo discimus.* — (For logic has not yet taken sufficiently to heart its task of furnishing us with rules as to the appropriate way of searching for things: that is to say, logic

---

[81] Ibid., p. 163.

[82] Immanuel Kant, *The Doctrine of Virtue*, trans. Mary J. Gregor (Philadelphia: University of Pennsylvania Press, 1964), p. 152.

[83] Ibid., p. 150.

should not limit itself to giving rules for determinant judgments but should also provide rules for preparatory judgments (*iudicia praevia*), by which one is led to conceptions.[84]

Both teacher and student learn in this dialogue, and what they learn is more than simply a set of "rules for determinant judgments." They learn how to recognize each other on a moral ground where having and making an argument depends on respecting humanity as an end in itself.

The evasive part of this passage is the sentence, "The teacher, by his questions guides the pupil's thinking merely by presenting him with situations in which his dispositions for certain concepts will develop." We immediately wonder which situations will be chosen. If the dialogue is to work, the student will be asked to make arguments that take as their point of departure humanity as an end in itself. That is, arguments that are not just self-consistent but rely on principles that all free and equal persons could choose without giving up their equal freedom.

Yet moral casuistry understood in this narrow sense still falls short as a method of political education. The respect we owe others as interlocutors tells us very little about the respect we owe most people with whom we have a much more distant, abstract political relationship. It is at this point that we must widen our understanding of Kant's method of moral reasoning and bring out the political character of the categorical imperative and the related principle of justice.

Many past and present critics of Kant's practical philosophy have claimed that his formalism makes his practical philosophy virtually impractical. Hegel thought Kant was foolish to suggest that substantive ethical and political rules could ever be derived from the strictly formal value of universalizability. It amounts only to "the preaching of duty for duty's sake," and only when additional content is added is "the specification of particular duties" possible.[85] Roberto Unger has repeated this criticism and traced Kant's mistake to his metaphysics: ethics must be formal, and therefore empty, as long as its central concept, freedom, is possible only outside the phenomenal world of temporally ordered, causally related events.[86] Robert Paul Wolff has said the same.[87]

There is no denying that Kant would have welcomed a demonstration of the synthetic, a priori connection between a good will and rational agency.

[84] Ibid.

[85] G. W. F. Hegel, *The Philosophy of Right*, trans. T. M. Knox (London: Oxford University Press, 1967), p. 89.

[86] Roberto M. Unger, *Knowledge and Politics* (New York: Free Press, 1975), chaps. 2 and 3.

[87] Robert Paul Wolff, *The Autonomy of Reason* (New York: Harper Torchbooks, 1973), pp. 66–68.

The perplexing third chapter of the *Groundwork of the Metaphysic of Morals* is an attempt to demonstrate this. There Kant struggles with the problem of showing that the proposition "An absolutely good will is one whose maxim can always have as its content itself considered as a universal law"[88] is true without relying on experience or the meanings of "rational agency" and "the good will." The proposed synthetic connection is to be made through the "positive concept" of freedom. If Kant could have shown that this synthetic proposition was known to be true a priori, he would have strengthened his belief in the unity of practical and synthetic reason. Without this connection particular moral rules, the (assertoric) hypothetical imperatives of "republican" citizenship, and the categorical imperative itself can be true only empirically or by virtue of linguistic convention.

Although the *Groundwork* fails to establish a synthetic a priori connection between rational agency and a good will, it does point to a conception of the moral ground of practical philosophy that is less formal than the "mere legislative form of maxims." The categorical imperative is phrased in a number of ways in the *Groundwork;* the first and most familiar is, "Act only on that maxim through which you can at the same time will that it should become a universal law."[89] It is formal in the sense that the requirements it places on the maxims of our actions are consistency and impartiality. But Kant gives us several other versions of the categorical imperative that expand these formal requirements. They indicate the substance or "matter" of this principle—and every principle, Kant tells us, must have a matter as well as a form, even the supreme principle of morality.[90]

Two of the alternative formulas of the categorical imperative obliquely refer to the content or matter of that principle as the ends of moral virtue and self-mastery. Though these are unconditioned objective ends, according to Kant, they are still not the "determining ground" of a good will. The same is true of the objective but conditioned ends of happiness and security, though for different reasons. The categorical imperative and its political mate, the universal principle of justice, are ostensibly defined independent of these ends. In fact, both conditioned and unconditioned ends influence the structure of the regulative moral rules in Kant's doctrine.

This can be seen in the second and third versions of the categorical imperative: "Act as if the maxim of your action were to become a universal law of nature." And, "Act in such a way that you always treat humanity,

---

[88] Immanuel Kant, *Groundwork of the Metaphysic of Morals*, trans. H. J. Paton (New York: Harper Torchbooks, 1960), p. 115.

[89] Ibid., p. 88.

[90] Ibid., p. 103.

whether in your own person, or in the person of any other, never simply as a means, but always at the same time as an end."[91] The second version is clearly an expansion of the original formula. Its significance is belied by the casualness with which Kant appends the phrase "of nature." As Murphy notes, Kant has quietly added substance to the formal values of impartiality and consistency.[92] The maxims of moral conduct we should strive to take into our hearts must be consistent with human nature. The third version of the categorical imperative tells us that this means the maxims of our actions should not treat persons simply as means, but always at the same time as an end. To be treated this way would be to be used toward an end one did not share in.[93] An impartial maxim, then, would be one that treated those persons as equals with a capacity to share in certain ends.

But as an imperative for imperfectly rational agents, the categorical imperative by itself cannot fully regulate conduct. Individuals cognizant of and moved by the value of humanity as an end in itself may still constrain each other's self-legislative freedom simply because making choices means acting with and on other things in the world, including other people. An authority, then, must be established that will keep these imperfectly rational agents from undermining each other's self-legislative power as they search the world for those things that will enable them to develop their talents and skills. In other words, they have to know what property is and how to hold it. They have to learn to recognize and respect themselves and others as property holders. This is the more distant and abstract form of social responsibility Kant wants his fellow citizens to feel. To bring them around, Kant argues, they must become citizens under a republican government.

A republican "form of government" is one in which the executive power is separated from the legislative power, but Kant also firmly believes that vesting sovereign power in all of the people necessarily leads to despotism. In a democracy it is impossible to keep the people who make the laws from also executing them. When they do both, they will exempt themselves from laws so regularly that they will make a travesty of the rule of law itself. It is possible to have a republican form of government only by having a representative "form of sovereignty." And, Kant suggests, although representative democracy meets this standard, the fewer representatives the better. The best republican government would be a monarchical one in

[91] Ibid., pp. 89, 96.

[92] Jeffrie G. Murphy, *Kant: The Philosophy of Right* (New York: St. Martin's Press, 1970), chaps. 2 and 3.

[93] See Hardy E. Jones, *Kant's Principle of Personality* (Madison: University of Wisconsin Press, 1971), chap. 2.

which it would be easier to keep an eye on the exercise of executive power than if there were more than one person in the executive. The important thing, Kant argues, is not the form of sovereignty, but the form of government, and that should be republican.[94] Understood as a process, then, republican government is not important because it permits citizen participation in legislative and executive politics. This should be minimal. It is a process of law-abiding acquisition of property that enables citizens to develop their talents and skills and think independently about themselves and the power of government.

Not only is republican government according to Kant, the form most likely to protect individual rights of property and also individual rights of speech and the press, it is "the ultimate end of all public right and the only condition under which each person receives his due peremptorily."[95] This is more than an instrumental justification of the republican state. The hypothetical consensual basis of republican government is not a way of acknowledging de facto political authority when it effectively protects prior or natural rights. Republican governments are legitimate governments that would have been consented to because they enable otherwise self-centered casuists to realize that they must respect the legal property rights of others if they are to have the independence to develop their own talents and skills and know how to act on reasons they give to themselves.

Republican government is not just a hollow shell within which independent, free, and equal citizens dispose of their property as they wish. Like the language of moral agency, it is no exaggeration to say, republican government is a method of conceptualizing and initiating a system of reciprocal social cooperation that, Kant argues, fosters adequate respect among fellow citizens. Why is this? The answer lies, I suggest, in the legalistic way Kant conceives of the relationship between citizens. The method of reasoning that enables them to respect one another involves thinking of oneself as a free, equal, and now independent person, where independence refers to a legal frame of mind that defines the kind of social cooperation Kant assumes is best suited to republican political processes. To see how deeply embedded this legalism is in Kant's political theory and how important the notion of material independence is, we have to make sense out of the set of postulates and principles he ostensibly derives from practical reason. In truth, the derivation is simply a confession of the legalistic way Kant conceives of a politics of *Recht*.

In part 1 of *The Metaphysics of Morals* Kant introduces a new principle, the "universal principle of justice": "Act externally in such a way that the

94 Williams, *Kant's Political Philosophy*, pp. 173–77.
95 Immanuel Kant, *The Metaphysical Elements of Justice*, trans. John Ladd (Indianapolis: Bobbs-Merrill, 1965), p. 113.

free use of your will is compatible with the freedom of everyone according to a universal law."[96] Like the categorical imperative, this principle has three distinguishable elements. Consistency and impartiality are contained in the notion of universal compatibility. They apply directly to actions, not to maxims as they did in the categorical imperative. But here there is no end comparable to humanity as an end in itself. Kant tells us that duties of justice, unlike duties of virtue, are without ends. They are negative duties because justice is merely the "aggregate of those conditions under which the will of one person can be conjoined with the will of another in accordance with a universal law of freedom" (p. 34). The third element seemingly is quite unlike humanity as an end in itself: the very idea of external freedom requires a coercive political authority. This is the third element in the "universal principle of justice." Because some freedoms can be "hindrances" to others, there must be a mechanism to guarantee external freedom, since it is a practical, not just theoretical, concept.

Kant then supplements this principle and the coercive authority it logically entails with a further explication of the concept of justice. As Ladd observes in a footnote to his translation (p. 37 n. 3), this is a difficult passage that relies on strained analogies to physics and geometry and bears little fruit. The next move is to identify a "juridical postulate of practical reason" that will bring out the social implications of the concept of justice.

Kant asserts that "it is possible to have any and every external object of my will as my property" (p. 52), implying that like his other postulates of practical reason, this one also must be true unless we are willing to abandon an important part of what we ordinarily consider our humanity. But in this case we would have to give up our use of the concept of justice if we denied this postulate. In other words, we would have to abandon the idea that we could act on our own without denying others the same right. Then once we accept this postulate, Kant claims, we must accept another obligation in addition to the obligation to respect the coercive authority that protects us from "hindrances" to our freedom. We now have an obligation to respect the intelligible property of others (p. 53). Simply respecting their external freedom would be a sham if we did not respect their right to acquire the things they need to think independently and develop their own talents and skills as they see fit.

Intelligible property is property we own even when we do not physically possess it. We possess it "externally." Since not everything beyond our grasp is "externally" ours, something more must be said about what we can and do possess: "A thing is externally mine if it is such that any prevention of my use of it would constitute an injury to me even if it is not in

---

[96] Ibid., p. 35.

my possession (that is, I am not the holder of the object)" (p. 55). We have a right to expect that others will not interfere with our external property because when we, as self-legislative persons, say, " 'this external object is mine' . . . an obligation is imposed on everyone else to refrain from using the object, an obligation that one would not otherwise have had" (p. 62).

Thus property rights of this sort are the basis of social responsibility as well as cooperation in the ideal Kantian polity. They are universal because they express a formal connection between persons that is embodied in their possessions when they use them to realize their talents and skills. This kind of "having" does not depend on arbitrary differences between people such as hereditary status, race, or religion (p. 62). When property is only provisionally held, Kant argues, not only do we have a duty to respect its ownership, we have a duty to strengthen that ownership through the establishment of a coercive authority. Property is not just secured by a republican government; it is the frame of reference through which we understand our obligations to our fellow citizens. For Hobbes, political obligations are incurred only to the sovereign authority. For Kant they are more than that—they pervade the polity along the lines of independent ownership.

Finally, contracts are the mechanism for preserving and developing external property. They express our freedom and equality, and they cannot be used to abdicate our material and mental independence once we have it: "No one can bind himself by a contract to the kind of dependency through which he ceases to be a person, for he can make a contract only insofar as he is a person" (p. 98).

This interpretation of Kant avoids two common misunderstandings. First, Kant is not the uncritical defender of individual conscience who believed that other people are just furniture in my world because only I can know my own heart and act according to its dictates. We depend on others for legal recognition and cooperation. Without them our possessions, a necessary condition for meaningful autonomy, would be insecure. Second, Kant's concern with intelligible possessions and divisible goods is not a selfish defense of private property. He worried that as market relations grew we could lose sight of the fact that people have a "dignity" as well as a "price."[97] He hoped that a system of "independent" property relations could be the basis of mutual respect, reciprocity, and republican politics. His legalistic arguments were an attempt to widen the scope of moral casuistry. We should be ready to ask not just what any human being would do when faced with a particular moral dilemma, but what our fellow republican citizens—independent property owners—would do when faced with a

[97] Kant, *Groundwork*, p. 102.

common political problem. Kant thought the best way to achieve this end was to show people, his "reading public" in particular, how to recast their own lives through a casuistic method of practical reasoning.

To summarize, Kantian moral casuistry is a method of self-reflective discipline in which learning to think consistently for oneself includes incorporating the views of other independent persons. By conducting arguments with one another in the language of the categorical imperative and Kant's universal principle of justice, we will gradually acquire the cast of mind that fits us for a responsible and law-abiding life under a republican government. Kantian language may be cumbersome, but its objective is quite plain: accustoming individuals whose property rights may conflict to settle their differences with dignity and willingness to accept the republican state's interpretation of the law.

What Kantian moral casuistry fosters, I argue in the next section, is a particular kind of political deafness among independent citizens who know and respect each other only on the basis of their telltale property rights. On the one hand, Kantian moral casuistry encourages an intimacy between individuals engaged in arguments over their competing property claims (which may extend to their persons and jobs as well as their land and capital). On the other hand, using property ownership, no matter how broadly defined, as the basis of political membership or recognition invites the kind of administrative and professional mediation that I have suggested may alienate citizens from democratic politics. That argument still remains to be made, but in the closing section of this chapter I suggest briefly how the Hobbesian and Kantian philosophical methods of political education I have described continue to operate in the current context.

## Geometry and Casuistry Today

At the beginning of this chapter I said that Hobbes posed the traditional problem of liberal political education in terms of the need to dislodge the passions, dispositions, and manners of masterless and vainglorious men so that tamer passions could take over under reason's guidance. His own geometric method is not quite up to this task, but with some revisions we can see how individuals with the potential for being masterless and vainglorious might reconsider these passions that drive them to war. The revisions, I argued, depend on attributing to these persons a more self-reflective concern about maintaining continuity between their past and future selves.

This is not, however, the way twentieth-century Hobbesians have tried to solve the problem.[98] In fact, some have simply dismissed the problem of character entirely and argued that what is needed is a more meticulous account of the conflicts between rational, self-interested individuals to show that the conflicts can (or cannot) be resolved by an agreement on obedience to an absolutist Hobbesian sovereign. Character transformation plays no role in their game-theoretic reformulations of Hobbesian moral geometry. If people think the way Hobbes says they think, know what he says they know, and face what he says they face, will they or won't they reach the agreement he says they will reach?[99]

At the opposite extreme, other interpreters of Hobbes have argued that his geometric inferences and deductions do not go through because the real problem in Hobbes is one of transforming human passions, and he provides no solution. He may urge his readers to adhere to religious commands or commit themselves to a new secular morality of industry and ambition, but he does not give them a method for inculcating and acting on these virtues.

My own view is that these allegedly opposing tendencies in Hobbes are connected. Hobbes's rudimentary game theory, understood as something like a "one-person" iterated game, might well have an effect on the passions, manners, and dispositions of those who play it. If we think of Hobbes's theory as an invitation to reflect individually on our opposing sets of wild and tame passions within the artificial environment of an iterated, cooperative one-person game, then gradually our wilder passions may become dislodged for the sake of something like the continuity of the self. Shifting back and forth at random between wild and tame passions may be an effective strategy in a competitive, $n$-person game of chicken, at least within limits: it may force one's opponent to play very conservatively. But Hobbes is not asking us to play chicken with ourselves—we would always lose. Rather, he is asking us to try on these opposing tendencies and take a look at what life would be like "in" them. The attractiveness of the tame passions and their associated manners and dispositions is that they would give our lives greater continuity and offer some hope that human freedom is not impossible in a world tightly organized according to scientific laws of motion.

Game theory originally had a similar transformative intention.[100] Real games, even competitive ones, depend on some level of civility and mutual

[98] See Jean Hampton, *Hobbes and the Social Contract Tradition* (New York: Cambridge University Press, 1986), for a thorough treatment of Hobbes and some of the secondary literature from a game-theoretic perspective.

[99] For example, David Gauthier, *Morals by Agreement* (Oxford: Clarendon Press, 1986).

[100] I owe this point to John Wallace.

respect. If the dynamics of these games can be understood, it might be possible to transpose them onto other less cooperative activities. If economic exchanges and political bargains can be made more like games, perhaps the playfulness, the willingness to experiment, and the spirit of good sportsmanship can also be carried over. This original intention, I think, has been lost as game theory has become more mathematically sophisticated, but something like it is visible in Hobbes. The Hobbesian state of nature is an artificial game in which players try out new forms of power with the stakes temporarily reduced. They experiment with themselves to see how they would fare under new conditions and what it would feel like. This one-person game, like geometry, temporarily abstracts from their actual circumstances, but it is designed to have the same practical value as geometry. It points us in what Hobbes thought was the right direction.

Having said this, however, let me repeat that this kind of Hobbesian thought experiment does not strike me as an adequate democratic conception of political theory as political education. It is too iconoclastic. It does not teach us how to cooperate with others. Kant's method of moral casuistry, as it has resurfaced in contemporary professional ethics, is not subject to this criticism. To close, I mention the very different limitations of this new variety of moral casuistry as a philosophical method of political education.

In their defense of casuistic moral reasoning, Albert Jonsen and Stephen Toulmin are prepared to make room for Kant and, it seems, even Rawls.[101] This is surprising after they have suggested that the few people who do favor casuistic moral reasoning—for example, Sissela Bok and Michael Walzer—are not recognized members of the "guild" of moral philosophy.[102]

Jonsen and Toulmin confess that their interest in casuistry is not purely historical even though their analysis is primarily so. Their interest is a product of work they have done in medical ethics where, they say, it is readily apparent that the crude reliance on universal abstract principles of morality in complex cases is unhelpful and sometimes damaging. Medical ethicists, they argue, have developed a legitimate way of working *with* moral rules and principles, not from them. Their casuistry is not simply a matter of clever applications of general principles to particular cases, but rather entails creative interpretations of particular moral dilemmas aided, when possible, by general rules but never hamstrung by them. The casu-

---

[101] Albert R. Jonsen and Stephen Toulmin, *The Abuse of Casuistry: A History of Moral Reasoning* (Berkeley and Los Angeles: University of California Press, 1988), pp. 285–93.

[102] Ibid., pp. 13–14.

istry of medical ethics, they argue, is Aristotelian: it is not an exact science but depends on a healthy dose of *phronesis*.[103]

Medical ethics, from their perspective, is almost a natural form of moral reasoning because of the parallels between medicine and morals. If we pay attention to the inherent uncertainties of medical practice, we can begin to appreciate similar problems in moral philosophy. When we combine the two in medical ethics, we come about as close as possible to achieving a moral practice. "In both fields the best we can do is appraise the particular situation in which we find ourselves with the highest degree of clinical perceptiveness we can bring to the situation. But our judgments are always made at particular times, on the basis of the given facts and observations, and so are often 'timely' and 'context dependent.' They remain, that is, substantive and practical, with all the fallibility and revisability that these terms imply."[104] If this is so, then what could Kantian reasoning have in common with moral casuistry?

Before they defend Kant as a casuist, Jonsen and Toulmin take us on a long tour of religious casuistry. The villain in their story, surprisingly, is not Pascal. It is also not some generic Kantian or utilitarian rationalism. It is Henry Sidgwick. With the exception of pragmatism, English-speaking moral philosophy has been dominated since the late nineteenth century by Sidgwick's narrow view that individual cases are "relevant" only to the extent that they provide occasions for probing or testing "matters of general theoretical doctrine."[105] Neither Kant beforehand nor Rawls after him is committed to such a narrow view.

Kant, according to Jonsen and Toulmin, was more interested in the "boundaries" between law, morality, and science than in any purely theoretical subject. Furthermore, he believed these boundaries shifted over time and that it was necessary to rely on a case-by-case analysis ("casuistical digressions") in order to get the cases right—and for Kant this included getting the boundaries right. The universalistic tone in his practical philosophy was rhetorical, another sign of his belief that moral philosophy had to be tailored to one's specific audience.[106] Rawls is a harder case. According to Jonsen and Toulmin, Rawls's historically specific commitment to compensatory justice is what makes his theory a form of moral casuistry. Rawls's arguments for redressing past wrongs and closing the gap created by differences in historical social positions as well as natural endowments, which he considers arbitary from a moral point of view, are aimed at the racial inequalities in constitutional democracies like the

103 Ibid., p. 37.
104 Ibid., p. 45.
105 Ibid., p. 281.
106 Ibid., pp. 286–88.

United States. *A Theory of Justice* does not pretend to apply universally to all problems of justice; it addresses only impersonal institutional ones, and only those whose history makes compensatory justice relevant.[107]

This reading of moral casuistry illustrates how modern medical ethicists naturally incorporate Kantian moral casuistry. Jonsen and Toulmin defend moral casuistry as a reasonable method for making sense of hard cases. Medical ethicists and physicians, they say, are seeing things through the same conceptual lens, and it is one that has a distinguished history in moral philosophy, despite the efforts of Sidgwick and his followers. Furthermore, it is one that is flexible and humane, giving recognition both to professionals and to those who depend on them. Kant is indeed a good model for this kind of moral casuistry. As I have argued, the Kantian method centered on the categorical imperative is more than a system of enlightened pedagogy. It is a method for cultivating mutual respect and consensus within these intimate encounters, even if it structures these encounters in more abstract terms like informed consent and due process.

Jonsen's and Toulmin's attempt to implicate Rawls in this tradition of moral casuistry, however, underscores the limits of the Kantian moral casuistry they favor. Kantian moral casuistry is perfectly suited to the intimate encounters between, say, independent patients with rights of privacy and autonomy and doctors with wider responsibilities to provide health care to the entire community. But squeezing Rawls into this casuistic model ignores the wider scope of his theory. The mediation that the original position and reflective equilibrium seek to promote is not within particular encounters between professionals and their clients and patients. Rawls's methods of practical reason have found a receptive audience among professionals, but not because they provide them with clinical tools for reaching patients and clients and making sense to them. Rawls's method, unlike the Kantian method of moral casuistry, is pitched at a more general political level. It is a method for those citizens aware of their roles as patients, clients, consumers, and policymakers but not confined to one or another of them. Unlike Kantian moral casuistry, Rawls's method provides these individuals with a way to think about the authority relations that bind them together from a particular political perspective—the perspective of humane citizens in a neocorporatist society.

Rawls himself has resisted the lure of game theory, arguing that it takes initial endowments and other contingent facts as given, whereas it is the aim of justice as fairness to subject these background conditions and individual preferences to critical moral scrutiny.[108] Gradually, he has also

---

[107] Ibid., pp. 292–93.
[108] John Rawls, *A Theory of Justice* (Cambridge: Harvard University Press, 1971), p. 134 n. 10. Also see Brian Barry, *Theories of Justice* (Berkeley and Los Angeles: University of

distanced himself from Kant's practical philosophy because it is a comprehensive moral theory, not a political theory. Rawls is right that his methods of practical reason are quite different from Hobbesian geometry and Kantian casuistry, but not simply because they are more critical and less dogmatic. Rawlsian methods, I argue, are better suited to the problem of political education as it has been structured in modern, neocorporatist liberal societies, where policy analysis and professional ethics mediate conflicts between clients, consumers, and policymakers to a degree Kant could not have anticipated.

---

California Press, 1989), pp. 50–85. For Rawls's own reflections on his turn away from game theory, see "John Rawls: For the Record," interview by Samuel R. Aybar, Joshua D. Harlan, and Won J. Lee, *Harvard Review of Philosophy* (spring 1991): 38–47.

# CHAPTER FIVE

# John Stuart Mill
# Representing Progress

In one of his early polemical exchanges, Kant found himself in a battle in which one issue was whether he, "the Little Socrates of Königsberg," or Johann Georg Hamann, "the Wizard of the North," was right about the power of the Socratic method. Hamann contended that philosophers of the *Aufklärung* had misread their favorite patron saint: Socrates was not the first apostle of rationality but rather an inspired genius whose confession of ignorance and *daimone* revealed the power of his faith and divine inspiration, not his reason. Only Socratic faith in providence, not rational analysis, could reconcile us to this world of suffering. Reason, Hamann argued, when it addressed larger questions, invariably produced foolish talk about the best of all possible worlds.

Kant, of course, acknowledged the suffering and injustice around him, but he fiercely objected to the idea that Socratic reason could not uncover the logic of providence. Kant optimistically held that deeper, providential reasons will eventually ensure that evil is punished and suffering compensated. Socratic analysis, he argued, could bring these reasons to light. At this time in his life, 1759, Kant expressed little doubt that these strong religious beliefs could be rationally accounted for and that Leibniz's best of all possible worlds was indeed upon us.[1]

Kant soon tempered this youthful optimism, and in the process he gave his own stamp to the Socratic method. John Stuart Mill went through a similar transformation. He initially confronted injustice and suffering with a Socratic optimism handed down from his father and Jeremy Bentham. Then, like Kant, he gradually developed a more cautious interpretive stance toward power. In Mill's case, however, this change involved a

[1] See Frederick C. Beiser, *The Fate of Reason: German Philosophy from Kant to Fichte* (Cambridge: Harvard University Press, 1987), chap. 1.

novel Platonic conception of "a man as a progressive being" and an even more novel autobiographical presentation of his own exemplary evolution from a Socratic to a Platonic theorist.[2] In this chapter I examine this "progressive" ideal of self-development in Mill's political theory, how Mill's method of political emulation differs from Kant's moral casuistry, and the limits of emulation as a visual form of democratic political education.

## Power and Progress

Mill was neither as philosophically broad nor as systematic as Kant. He sought to reconcile his liberal understanding of freedom and toleration with the rising tide of democracy.[3] It was a theoretical project driven more by his ambivalence toward democratic political participation and economic equality than by a philosopher's need for consistency. Mill met the challenge that democratic politics posed for classical liberalism by fashioning a method of reasoning more subtle psychologically and less teleological historically than Kant's critical philosophy. As Mill himself noted, however, both Kant and he believed that the "formation of our characters" was vital for political as well as cultural progress.[4]

Raised to be a utilitarian reformer, Mill became increasingly dissatisfied with the universalistic Benthamite program of investigation, legislation, and inspection. A Panopticon world may have represented progress to Bentham, but it was not an unqualified improvement in Mill's eyes. Maximizing the happiness of the greatest number, measured in units of pleasure and pain, was too ahistorical a principle and too simplistic a psychological program. Mill's sympathy for others, his respect for excellence, his appreciation of poetry and art, and his qualified belief in the educative value

---

[2] Mill's early writings are sometimes characterized as more Platonic than his later ones because of the drift away from elitism and toward an evolutionary brand of socialism. Graeme Duncan, in *Marx and Mill* (London: Cambridge University Press, 1977), p. 259, suggests that the shift is not significant and that Mill's theory in general should be thought of as democratic Platonism. Dennis Thompson argues that Mill became increasingly interested in balancing competence with participation and that his concrete proposals in *Considerations on Representative Government* reflect this turn away from faith in the political need for a Platonic elite. See Dennis Thompson, *John Stuart Mill and Representative Government* (Princeton: Princeton University Press, 1976). I use the terms *Socratic* and *Platonic* to refer not to Mill's attitude toward democracy but rather to his views on his own methods of political theorizing.

[3] Here I follow Amy Gutmann, *Liberal Equality* (Cambridge: Cambridge University Press, 1980), p. 13.

[4] John Stuart Mill, "On the Freedom of the Will," quoted in Bernard Semmel, *John Stuart Mill and the Pursuit of Virtue* (New Haven: Yale University Press, 1984), p. 50. See Janice Carlisle, *John Stuart Mill and the Writing of Character* (Athens: University of Georgia Press, 1991).

of political participation made accurate felicific calculations impossible. Instead of searching for an abstract method to reduce these diverse concerns to a single measure, Mill combined his commitments to utilitarian principles of aggregate well-being and these other values under a characterological notion of humanistic progress. "I regard utility as the ultimate appeal on all ethical questions, but it must be utility in the largest sense, grounded on the permanent interests of a man as a progressive being." [5]

There are three elements in Mill's ideal of a progressive being. The first involves historical consciousness, the second expertise in political economy, and the third a composite quality of moral courage, poetic inspiration, and heroic grandeur.

For Mill "a progressive being" is first someone who consciously and freely acts in a progressive way within the laws of historical development, as hazy as they may be at times. A progressive person must have a practical grasp of the openings provided by the politics and history of his or her culture. In his review of Tocqueville's *Democracy in America* Mill wrote that "man cannot turn back the rivers to their source; but it rests with himself whether they shall fertilize or lay waste his fields." [6] The laws of historical development that Mill thought defined social necessity are like rivers that can be diverted but never drained. Which way they run depends in part on how property is regulated, knowledge disseminated, and participation gradually introduced. [7]

The second element in Mill's ideal of a progressive being is expertise in political economy and respect for those who possess it. Mill believed that production in capitalist society was governed by natural laws that professional political economists could uncover. Principles of distribution, then, should be arranged in light of these laws of production so that the pursuit of equity does not frustrate the desire for maximizing the social product. Progress depends on sound economic policymaking, primarily done by government administrators and periodically checked by elected representatives.

Third, progressive persons have the power to motivate and inspire, by their example, moral courage and originality. Citizens in a liberal democracy have to be motivated to respect the liberties of others as if they were their own, to participate in representative institutions, and to trust well-

---

[5] John Stuart Mill, *On Liberty*, in *The Collected Works of John Stuart Mill*, ed. John M. Robson (Toronto: University of Toronto Press, 1963–91), 18:224. (Hereafter cited as *CW*.)

[6] Quoted in John M. Robson, *The Improvement of Mankind* (London: Routledge and Kegan Paul, 1968), p. 183.

[7] Mill did not think that historical laws of development were properties of organic wholes: "Human beings in society have not properties but those of individual man"; from *A System of Logic*, quoted in John Stuart Mill, *Autobiography*, in *CW*, 1:233.

trained experts. Instruction, even Kantian instruction, is not enough to instill these sentiments: they have to be inspired. As Mill noted, commenting on Plato, "The love of virtue, and every other noble feeling, is not communicated by reasoning but caught by inspiration or sympathy from those who already have it; and its nurse and foster-mother is Admiration." [8]

The interests of a progressive being do not systematize Mill's work, nor do they improve the logic of his arguments. They also do not amount to a first principle from which other principles of liberty, reciprocity, and contribution are deduced or against which policies and states of affairs can be judged: they are much too indeterminate. Yet, this ideal of a progressive being is the key to understanding how Mill's political theory has functioned as a form of political education, and this, I believe, has been more important than any particular philosophic argument or policy recommendation he made. In presenting himself as a person cognizant of his own progress, Mill hoped to shed light on the direction of future progress.

Where Hobbes sought to come to terms with the power of masterless and vainglorious men and Kant's confrontation with the narrower legal power of the state led him to prepare more independent citizens, for Mill the task of political education was to build a political character that could resist the social power of the majority. According to Mill, neither Hobbesian geometry nor Kantian casuistry could meet this peculiarly democratic challenge. He sought to advance his ideal of a progressive being through a method of political emulation capable of insulating liberal citizens against the danger of conformity and equipping them to play a limited role in representative government.

In other words, Mill did not just attach his ideal to hedonistic utilitarianism to advance an abstract moral perfectionism. A progressive being, for Mill, is above all someone aware of the "spirit of the age"[9] and capable of taking full advantage of the rivers of change. Mill's own *Autobiography* is an attempt to represent this kind of evocative portrait of poetic genius, liberal individuality, and economic expertise to guide democratic practices in an age when he thinks the most threatening form of power is the "tyranny of the majority." [10]

[8] John Stuart Mill, "Comment on Plato's *Gorgias*," in *Mill's Ethical Writings*, ed. J. B. Schneewind (New York: Collier, 1965), p. 76.

[9] John Stuart Mill, "The Spirit of the Age," in *CW*, 22:227.

[10] On the "tyranny of the majority" see, for example, Mill, *On Liberty*, in *CW*, 18:219, and "Bentham," in *CW*, 10:128. The *Autobiography* has been grist for many. I have benefited from Robert Denoon Cumming, *Human Nature and History: A Study of the Development of Liberal Political Thought*, 2 vols. (Chicago: University of Chicago Press, 1969), which reads Mill's other writings through the lens of the *Autobiography*. Also, Eldon J. Eisenach, "Mill's *Autobiography* as Political Theory," *History of Political Thought* 8 (spring 1987): 111–29; Alan Ryan, "Sense and Sensibility in Mill's Political Thought," in *A Cultivated Mind: Essays on*

My reconstruction of Mill's theory as political education is in two parts. First I discuss Mill's relation to Kantianism and Kant's casuistic method. More than Bentham, Coleridge, Comte, or Wordsworth, Kant was the foil against which Mill developed his own theoretical practice. Mill used and criticized the "one-eyed" arguments of these other writers,[11] but his relation to Kantianism was of a different sort. Despite the many complaints he leveled at Kant, Kant's method for establishing an ethical orientation toward power was the starting point of Mill's political theory as a form of political education. Second, I describe the two overlapping self-perceptions, a Socratic one and a Platonic one, embedded in the *Autobiography*. The self-reflective way Mill weaves them together is, I argue, what gives his political theory its significance as political education designed to hasten progress, as Mill understood it, in the face of stifling social conformity. The Socratic Mill is committed to liberal values of free speech, discussion, and debate. His Platonism complicates this commitment with a concern for both expertise in matters of political economy and the need for heroic, inspirational grandeur. The presentation of these two self-perceptions in the *Autobiography* is what translates Mill's ambivalence toward democratic politics into a theoretical form of political education.

The tension between Socrates and Plato in "the life" also weakens his theory as a form of democratic political education. Mill would like his readers to develop the character they need to meet the challenges of majoritarian democracy through their own debates, discussions, and expert policymaking. He fears that without a model like himself that incorporates the best of both Socrates and Plato, they will be swept away by the current. Mill presents himself to his readers as an example of a life worth living: one of character, principle, humility, and engagement. He would like citizens to listen carefully to each other, but the method he designs to teach them this skill is primarily visual. He hopes to show his readers what it feels like to look back on a life well lived, but the feelings he wants to awaken are monotonic.

## Kantianism

Mill's critique of Kant was based on his belief that Kant was a rational intuitionist. I argued against this interpretation of Kant in the preceding

---

*J. S. Mill Presented to John M. Robson*, ed. Michael Laine (Toronto: University of Toronto Press, 1991), pp. 121–38; and Elizabeth S. Anderson, "John Stuart Mill and Experiments in Living," *Ethics* 102 (October 1991): 4–26.

[11] Mill applied this tag to Bentham, in particular in the essay "Bentham," p. 115. Bentham, Mill argued, "failed in deriving light from other minds" (p. 112).

chapter, but to understand how Mill arrived at his own method of emulation we must see Kant through Mill's eyes.

In his essay on Coleridge, Mill rejected the Kantian "technical language" that divides the world into phenomena and noumena to be grasped by understanding and reason, respectively.[12] In "Theism" he made this more general objection to a priori metaphysics.

> I entertain a strong conviction that one of the two modes of argument is in its nature scientific, the other not only unscientific but condemned by science. The scientific argument is that which reasons from the facts and analogies of human experience as a geologist does when he draws conclusions respecting the physical composition of the heavenly bodies. This is the a posteriori method! . . . The mode of reasoning which I call unscientific, though in the opinion of some thinkers it is also a legitimate mode of scientific procedure, is that which infers external objective facts from ideas or convictions of our mind.[13]

Mill's objections to Kantianism as the preeminent unscientific doctrine, however, were not entirely ontological. He felt that talk of noumena bred social and political conservatism because it encouraged an uncritical attitude toward prevailing intuitions. To be fair, Mill was more concerned with the Anglicized Kantianism of Whewell and Hamilton than with Kant's own doctrine. Nonetheless, the point is that it was in part the perceived practical impact of this philosophical doctrine that set Mill off on his own theoretical project. As he said in the *Autobiography*,

> The notion that truths external to the mind may be known by intuition or consciousness, independently of observation and experience, is I am persuaded, in these times, the great intellectual support of false doctrines and bad institutions. By the aid of this theory, every inveterate belief and every intense feeling, of which the origin is not remembered, is enabled to dispense with the obligation of justifying itself by reason, and is erected into its own all-sufficient voucher and justification. There never was such an instrument devised for consecrating all deep-seated prejudices. And the chief strength of this false philosophy in morals, politics, and religion lies in the appeal which it is accustomed to make to the evidence of mathematics and of the cognate branches of physical sciences.[14]

[12] John Stuart Mill, *Dissertations and Discussions* (New York: Holt, 1882), 2:16–17.

[13] Quoted in F. Parvin Sharpless, *The Literary Criticism of John Stuart Mill* (The Hague: Mouton, 1967), p. 145 n. 43.

[14] Mill, *Autobiography*, p. 233.

Thus, although Mill's *Logic* begins with a consideration of mathematical truth and causation and ends with the "Art of Life," Mill initially made his way in just the opposite direction.[15] If Kant's practical philosophy rested on the synthetic a priori truths of mathematics, then the most powerful critique of that doctrine would be one that showed how even mathematical truths were inductively ascertained. This approach helps explain Mill's otherwise puzzling desire to publish an inexpensive copy of the *Logic* for workers because he believed it might have a social impact.[16]

Though Mill does not directly attack the idea of a transcendental deduction, his interpretation of deductive logic in general suggests that he would have had little patience with this mainstay of Kant's philosophy. What, Kant had asked, must speculative reason be like in order for the world to appear as it does? The parallel question for practical reason was, What must the structure of practical reason be like so that we can hold the principled views we do and act on them as we often do? The immediate problem with any transcendental argument of this type is the difficulty of showing why speculative and practical reason *must* be organized as Kant said in order for the world to be as he thought. Where does the necessity originate? If it originates in a grand teleological scheme, there is little compelling evidence to offer the skeptic. Mill was not simply skeptical: he believed that deductions, whether transcendental or not, really amount to complicated inductive arguments. Even could he have been persuaded of the natural teleology Kant found comfort in, he would have been no closer to accepting Kant's deductive arguments.

Briefly, this is how Mill interpreted deductive arguments in order to sweep away what he considered the foundations of rational intuitionism. Truths of consistency—what have been called logical truths—were of little consequence to Mill, for they were not a "means of coming to a knowledge of something which we did not know before."[17] Truths of reason, in contrast, bring us new knowledge, knowledge of the relation of particulars to other particulars. According to Mill, the major premise in a deductive syllogism (e.g., All men are mortal) is based on a prior set of determinations. As a general statement it contains no new knowledge. "No reasoning from generals to particulars can, as such, prove anything, since from a general principle we cannot infer any particular but those which the principle itself assumes as known."[18] These known particulars are the product

---

[15] Alan Ryan, *The Philosophy of John Stuart Mill* (New York: Pantheon, 1971), chap. 15. I am heavily indebted to Ryan's books on Mill for the following summary of the relation between Mill's political theory and his writings on logic.

[16] Alan Ryan, *J. S. Mill* (London: Routledge and Kegan Paul, 1974), p. 60.

[17] John Stuart Mill, *A System of Logic, Ratiocinative and Inductive*, in *CW*, 7:183.

[18] Ibid., p. 184.

of a prior inductive search, and they are what make deductive arguments truths of reason, not merely truths of consistency.

There are two logical problems with Mill's argument to mention in passing. First, one wonders if it is really possible to establish the premise "All men are mortal" simply by reasoning from "particular to particular without passing through generals." Mill's own universal law of causation might be considered a partial justification here, but it fails on its own terms. There is still to this day no noncontroversial account of the relation between particular and general terms. Mill has simply skimmed over a large philosophical problem. Any help he might have hoped to gain from his theory of causation, which focuses on a specific kind of general term, is unavailable because like any causal law, the Millian universal law of nature that allows Mill to talk about causation as more than a mere temporal sequence must itself be arrived at inductively, according to Mill.[19]

Second, in his zeal to prove that even geometry is an inductive science, Mill ignored the possibility of a more interesting form of deduction in which the major premise is a hypothetical (e.g., "If all men are mortal . . ."). This is the way we commonly think of deduction today. On this account it would be self-contradictory to deny the familiar conclusion "Socrates is mortal," given the minor premise "Socrates is a man." It would not be, as Mill argued, simply a denial of one of the particular observations the major premise had been based on. A hypothetical major premise is not inductively arrived at the way Mill felt major premises in a syllogism had to be.

Once we recognize the political purpose of the *Logic*, however, these errors become less important, and some of Mill's more explicit political disagreements with Kantianism become clearer. Mill felt that Kant had failed "grotesquely"[20] in his effort to deduce specific moral duties and political principles from the idea of universalizability, since a formal idea had no sound basis in particular observations. With no substantive major premise to work from, Kant had no chance of turning up new knowledge. Similarly, Mill was not much enamored of the Kantian idea of a hypothetical contract through which the rationality of practical principles could be tested.[21] Again, he believed that testable principles must be inferred from careful observations: otherwise they are merely intuitions. Although Mill did not believe one could logically prove practical principles in the rigorous way Kant hoped to,[22] he did think there were good and bad reasons for holding such principles based on the historical and political notion of a progressive being.

[19] Ryan, *Philosophy of John Stuart Mill*, pp. 83–84.
[20] John Stuart Mill, *Utilitarianism*, in *CW*, 10:207.
[21] Mill, *On Liberty*, p. 274.
[22] Mill, *Utilitarianism*, p. 208.

For historical reasons, according to Mill, the scope of liberal principles of right also had to be widened. Although both Kant and Mill felt that some kind of individual right to equal liberty was an essential part of what it means to be a person, there are important differences in application. Besides having different ways of deriving this right, they disagreed on who was entitled to it, against whom it was held, and how much it could be compromised in the name of other values. For Kant, equal liberty was a natural right from which more specific duties of justice were derived. Though he showed some sympathy for distributive justice, there does not seem to be much connection between his primary account of right and his views on distributive justice. Mill believed that the individual right to equal liberty was a prerequisite for the development of full human potential. As a right that carried with it correlative duties for others, it circumscribed an area of spontaneous individual choice whose social utility was as much the barrier it erected against majority tyranny as it was its guarantee of economic productivity.

Finally, on the issue of motivation, Mill broke decisively with the Kantian tradition. Mill believed that the "springs to action" were not limited to Hobbesian appetites and aversions, but he did not believe that the motivational basis for moral conduct and political action could be reduced to a choice between Hobbes and Kant. In his essay on Bentham, Mill wrote that "the first question in regard to any man of speculation is, what is his theory of human life?" For Mill Bentham's theory was only partially true. It ignored other qualities of life that, though not responsive to coercive pressure, were still indispensable if the "Art of Life" was to be carried on.

> The sense of honour, and personal dignity—the feeling of personal exaltation and degradation which acts independently of other people's opinion, or even in defiance of it; the love of beauty, the passion of the artist; the love of order, of congruity, of consistency in all things, and conformity to their end; the love of power, not in the limited form of power over other human beings, but abstract power, the power of making our volitions effectual; the love of action, the thirst for movement and activity, a principle scarcely of less influence in human life than its opposite, the love of ease . . . the love of loving, the need of a sympathizing support, or of objects of admiration and reverence.[23]

These "springs" constitute the moral and aesthetic side of human nature, and they play a central role in Mill's political doctrine. They provide the impetus for resisting social conformity.

The same argument occurs in the *Logic*, where Mill contrasted his "moral science" (what we would call an empirical social science) with the

[23] Mill, "Bentham," pp. 95–96.

"chemical" method of Macaulay and the "geometric" method of his father and Bentham. He faulted Macaulay for ignoring the fact that general principles about society still depend on the laws of individual human nature. Mill's objection to Macaulay is vague, but his critique of the "geometric" method is more powerful, for here he clearly states his view that a science of politics cannot be grounded in a partial theory of human nature.

> There is little chance of making due amends in the superstructure of a theory for the want of sufficient breadth in its foundations. It is unphilosophical to construct a science out of a few of the agencies by which the phenomena are determined and leave the rest to the routine of practice or the sagacity of conjecture. We either ought not to pretend to scientific forms, or we ought to study all the determining agencies equally and endeavor, so far as it can be done, to include all of them within the pale of the science, else we shall infallibly bestow a disproportionate attention upon these which our theory takes into account while we mis-estimate the rest and probably underrate their importance.[24]

The science of politics that Bentham and James Mill developed was flawed not simply because it did not generate testable hypotheses that could serve as guides for an impartial administrative apparatus insulated from the tyranny of the majority. It also was flawed because the conception of human nature it was based on and advanced was one-sided.

Now recall that I have argued that the real political goal of Kant's method of moral casuistry is to orient citizens toward each other as independent persons under the laws of a republican state. I have argued further that this method of moral casuistry is politically impotent. It does not prepare citizens for a shared public life; it seeks only to prepare them to resist encroachments on their private lives by external authorities. Mill's method of political emulation is designed to take individuals into the public domain, not just steel them against it. Mill does not so much refute Kant as extend his work into a new age in which individuals must be able to resist majority tyranny yet acquiesce to expert authority when appropriate. Mill did not have to bring quasi-religious, moral pressure to bear on recalcitrant citizens still clinging to feudalism and an antipolitical Lutheranism. He sought a new form of political character immune to "intellectual pacification."[25]

In an article in the *London Review* of April 1835, Mill made this observation: "The celebrity of England, in the present day, rests upon her docks,

---

24 Mill, *System of Logic*, p. 893.
25 Mill, *On Liberty*, p. 242.

her canals, her railroads. In intellect she is distinguished only for a kind of sober good sense, free from the extravagance, but also void of lofty aspirations; and for doing all those things which are best done where man most resembles a machine, with the precision of a machine."[26] This kind of useful knowledge was an integral part of England's accumulating wealth, and Mill had experienced it firsthand. Recalling his long years as a de facto public administrator at India House in the *Autobiography*, Mill again noted this somber methodical frame of mind, but this time with less disdain, since it was his own mind that was in question. "But the occupation accustomed me to see and hear difficulties of every course, and the means of obviating them, stated and discussed deliberately with a view to execution; it gave me opportunities of perceiving when public measures and other political facts, did not produce the effects which had been expected of them, and from what causes; above all it was valuable to me by making me, in this portion of my activity, merely one wheel in a machine, the whole of which had to work together."[27] Machinelike intelligence was not the only form of intellectual wealth Mill identified, however. The work of the intellectual poet, as Mill called him, was an important, albeit less visible, ingredient in constituting national character. And it is through this poetic mind that Mill gradually introduces the value of historical knowledge into his theory. According to Mill, anyone who claims to persuasively interpret power and citizenship must possess the skills of the intellectual poet as well as the expertise of the political economist and the breadth of learning of the historian.

In his essay "Two Kinds of Poetry," Mill suggests that in the work of some poets like Wordsworth we find a confluence of philosophic and poetic insight. The poet who is in command of his emotions, who gives them structure, can approach both philosophic and poetic truths. Mill ends this essay abruptly, but his concern with the content as well as the evocative form of poetic expression is clear. In addition to the sober good sense of methodical industry, the wealth of Mill's England was to be found in its ability to look beyond the world of docks and canals to more fundamental truths about human nature that were practical in their own right. Not only did the intellectual poet present a vision of nature that lay beyond the reach of the politician, the economist, and the lawyer, he could bring his audience closer to that vision, moving them in a progressive direction. This deep respect for the intellectual poet takes a more historical and less philosophical direction in Mill's political writings after 1840.

---

[26] Mill, *Dissertations and Discussions*, 1:122.
[27] Mill, *Autobiography*, p. 233.

## From Poetry to Autobiography

Our story begins with Mill's well-known disillusionment with Benthamite utilitarianism and his discomfort with party politics in the early 1840s.[28] Rather than understand Mill's early mental crisis as a humanistic break with Bentham and a reaction to the regimen his father imposed on him, it is possible to read it as the beginning of an extended period of transformation that includes his later disappointment with the political solidarity of antiaristocratic parliamentary forces and his belief that they needed more in the way of political education. By the 1840s political education was no longer just one of several youthful concerns: it was an all-encompassing project for Mill that propelled the *Logic*, the *Principles*, *On Liberty*, and finally the *Autobiography*.

It might be argued that Mill's response to the limited parliamentary success of Philosophic Radicalism was to take cover in scholarship, not to put his interest in poetry and history to work in an attempt to reorient citizens toward political power. I suggest that this is at best only partially true. The *Logic*, the *Principles*, and *Representative Government* constitute a new applied conception of political education designed to create a form of political character that goes beyond the competence and loyalty that may come with workplace and municipal participation, an egalitarian home life, and close attention to the newspapers. To give these texts the practical significance Mill wanted them to have, he first had to reconstitute the place of the philosopher in politics. He had to legitimate his own voice outside the London Debating Society and the circle of Philosophic Radicals.

The first hint of this innovative move is to be found in Mill's interpretation of Plato's *Gorgias*. Mill was deeply struck by Callicles' challenge to Socratic moral argument,[29] the same kind of moral argument he had been reared on and that still registered so powerfully in *On Liberty*. If most people were no better than Callicles and no readier to join in moral argument and political debate, then access to the political domain had to be restricted and the political domain itself had to be scaled down. Mill's views on plural voting are notorious: he would give an explicit advantage to educated citizens.[30] But more important, he hoped to contract the political domain by having the legislative assembly express the wants of the voters through a review of legislation proposed by administrative specialists.

---

[28] Joseph Hamburger, *Intellectuals in Politics* (New Haven: Yale University Press, 1965), p. 111.

[29] Mill, "Comment on Plato's *Gorgias*," p. 76.

[30] John Stuart Mill, *Considerations on Representative Government*, in *CW*, 19:476–77. In the *Autobiography*, p. 259, Mill abandons plural voting, and for that reason I do not want to make too much of it.

Mill's legislature has no direct lawmaking powers.[31] Representatives do not express the wishes of their constituents in this way. Rather, the legislature's expressive function is better understood as that of one body designed to instruct citizens in the art of interpreting their system of interdependent liberties responsibly when conflicting purposes exist for distribution and redistribution of the goods that give these liberties their effective worth.

A legislature designed to meet this task itself expresses the virtues Callicles denies. Furthermore, it also expresses the virtues described in the *Autobiography*, the virtues of a man who keeps his books in order and pays his financial and also his intellectual debts, tells the working class exactly what he thinks of their uncultured ways, and then reaps the admiration, political support, and personal peace of mind he deserves for his forthrightness.[32]

The power Mill sought in order to counter Callicles, a power he had earlier found in intellectual poetry and hoped he could adapt to reverse the failure of Philosophic Radicalism, was the power of a more historically informed method of self-reflection and debate. Mill believed that the skills and sensibilities he had acquired under the tutelage of his father and Ricardo and from the friendship of Roebuck, Sterling, and Maurice could be extrapolated into a theory of national character. This was so not because his skills and sensibilities had a classical pedigree, but because his account of them in the *Autobiography* was itself a political application of these skills. The *Autobiography* shows that it is possible to prepare people for representative government and the art of conceptualizing their liberties as an interdependent system by centering moral argument on the limits of "civic independence" and the need for representative but administratively competent political institutions. The *Autobiography* is a poetic companion volume to *On Liberty* and *Principles of Political Economy*.

The road that led Mill to the *Autobiography* can be traced in a number of ways. Though he began the first draft twenty years before he died in 1873, we should not discount the simple explanation that Mill wanted to record his life while he was still able. As the entries to his diary show, in the early part of 1854 he and Harriet Taylor were both pessimistic about their chances for continued good health.[33] Though this may partially explain why Mill wrote an autobiography, however, it does not explain why he wrote the one he did. I argue that the *Autobiography* is a poetic idealization of a Socratic debater come of age in a new world of mobile capital and administrative expertise. To make this argument, there is no need

---

[31] Mill, *Representative Government*, pp. 422–34.
[32] Mill, *Autobiography*, pp. 273, 275.
[33] Robson, *Improvement of Mankind*, p. 51.

to discredit all other possible motives Mill may have had for writing an autobiography. Whatever his personal reasons, whether conscious or unconscious, they remain compatible with the argument here, which turns on Mill's political understanding of poetry.

Mill settled on his political conception of poetry only after rejecting a number of positions. As I have said, in his early literary criticism he suggested that some poetry is dominated by emotion and some is a more intellectual, didactic observation of the emotions. Shelley exemplifies the first type, the poet of nature, and Wordsworth the second, the poet of culture. In these early essays Mill wrestled with the problem of poetic truth but never resolved it to his own satisfaction. Neither type of poet, though their skills and sensibilities are not philosophical, finds the pursuit of truth anathema. On the contrary, "The greater the individual's capability of happiness and of misery, the stronger interest has that individual in arriving at truth; and when once that interest is felt, an impassioned nature is sure to pursue this, as to pursue any other object, with greater ardour, for energy of character is always the offspring of strong feelings."[34] But here Mill is still saying only that a poetic mind is more disposed to pursue truth, not that it has any special purchase on some political truth denied to other equally energetic minds.

The next step was to bring poetry and literary criticism closer together. Two years after "What Is Poetry?" and "The Two Kinds of Poetry," he gave this advice to Tennyson: "The noblest end of poetry as an intellectual pursuit [is] that of acting upon the desires and characters of mankind through their emotions, to raise them towards the perfection of their nature. This, like every other adaptation of means to ends, is the work of cultivated reason; and the poet's success in it will be in proportion to the intrinsic value of his thoughts, and to the command which he has acquired over the materials of his imagination, for placing those thoughts in a strong light before the intellect and impressing them on the feelings."[35] Poetry, like criticism, is the work of cultivated reason whose end is the improvement of mankind, not the expression of deep emotions and not the observation of one's own emotions. Poetry and criticism differ less than the poetry of nature and the poetry of culture. The critic and the poet both aim at a truth that lies outside themselves: the achievement of desires and characters of mankind that are in conformity with the perfection of their nature.

In time an important element of historical awareness is added to this rational conception of poetry. Wordsworth, Shelley, and Tennyson give

[34] Sharpless, *Literary Criticism of John Stuart Mill*, p. 90.
[35] Ibid., p. 113.

way to Carlyle and Vigny. The poet's truth claim is no longer the quasi-scientific one that he is best able to observe his own associative psychology in the interest of human perfection. It is a claim based on his understanding of the place of the whole human being in the process of historical development. It was in coming to terms with St. Simonism that Mill arrived at this historical conception of a poetic truth. Mill rejected the Owenite view that individual initiative and creativity were shams. People do make choices, and the poet more than anyone else helps them make decisions that are profoundly in tune with the needs of their times. The critical poet can bring the historical process into focus and clear the way for responsible free choice. This difficult switch in Mill's position came with his reading of Tocqueville and Vigny and through his correspondence with Thomas Carlyle. In Mill's review of *The History of the French Revolution* we can see his cautious sympathy for poetic history in a Comtean key. Carlyle, Mill's epic historian, captured the disjunction between the aspirations of the Revolution and the limits it quickly encountered in the minds of people not ready for democratic participation. Mill agreed with Carlyle that people in situations like this need the help of a heroic individual who can inspire them to meet the demands of democratic life.[36]

Although Mill sympathized with Vigny and Carlyle, theirs was the poetry of an earlier time. His own views on the significant developments in his day could not be identical to theirs. Mill did attempt to reach his audience through a similar form, however. He fashioned a poetic self-idealization that accented the historical breadth and theoretical depth of his own schooling and did not try to rephrase the recent past in blank verse.

Like anyone else's self-image, Mill's goes through many changes in his own lifetime and again, in different ways, under the retrospective eye of the autobiographer. To gauge some of these changes, most commentators have focused on Mill's treatment of his contemporaries and on some of the more conspicuous silences in the final draft. This ground has been plowed many times over. What I think bears closer scrutiny is the Platonic framework Mill himself tacitly relied on to re-present "the life." It is the life of Plato, the life of the philosopher in politics, that guides Mill's hand as he constructs a progressive public character.

The importance of Plato for the *Autobiography* is not that he lends philosophical respectability to Mill's own educational training. Plato's central role can be understood as an outgrowth of Mill's reading of the political and economic conflicts of his own time and the needs he felt people's attention should be directed toward. By the time Mill wrote the *Autobiography* he had tempered his Socratic conception of theorizing with a more Pla-

---

[36] John Stuart Mill, "Carlyle's *French Revolution*," in *CW*, 20:131–66.

tonic one, a conception more firmly anchored in a commitment to a specific social division of labor, an analysis of the dangers that face a modern democracy, and a belief in the need for an exacting preparation for citizenship. Mill's growing interest in Plato makes itself felt in the very organization of the *Autobiography* as well, for there he chooses to portray himself as someone who is struggling against sophists and earlier poets for the right to direct the political education of the demos and who sees the need to supplement the Socratic method with a more constructive political theory.

It is traditional to divide Mill's life into three parts. The first part extends roughly up to his mental crisis in 1826. The second covers approximately the next fifteen years, and the third, the years after that. In the second period, when Mill's theory of poetry is still evolving and has not yet reached its Carlylean apogee, he is very active in politics, primarily as a journalist. In this heated period the Socratic Mill views the newspaper press as the bulwark of democracy. In 1836 he writes, "There are now in this country, we may say, but two modes left in which an individual mind can hope to produce much direct effect upon the minds and destinies of his countrymen generally,—as a member of Parliament, or as an editor of a London newspaper."[37] But by the mid-1840s Mill's involvement with the Philosophic Radicals had tapered off, and he was much less active as a journalist. The newspaper, what he termed the functional equivalent of the ancient agora,[38] had failed to move people toward an organic society. Plato then joined Socrates as his guide. The political philosopher, Mill came to believe, grasps the importance of the key figures of an age and places them in the most instructive light for the masses. These figures, when given the proper interpretation, are the Millian analogues to the Platonic forms, serving as political imperatives in a time of disorder and danger. Politics need not be a cynical business: there are points of reference, benchmarks against which we can measure our progress even in an age of transition. The most important benchmark in the mid–nineteenth century was "the life" of a responsible person capable of engaging his fellow citizens in open debate on the merits of an issue without rancor or resentment over the outcome and also capable of understanding and applying the new wisdom of political economy.

Thus, though Mill's life does seem to fall into three periods, I would like to divide it based on a more theoretical distinction. The Socratic Mill is largely found between Mill's earliest philosophical and literary articles and his exit from intense political involvement. The Socratic Mill resembles the intellectual poet more than the Carlylean critic in that he has

[37] Mill, *Dissertations and Discussions*, 4:215.
[38] Mill, *Representative Government*, p. 378.

made no claim to historical knowledge. His aim is to see his own associative self more clearly and to do this by challenging the insights of others. Some of Mill's later writings, especially parts of *On Liberty*, are Socratic in this sense. The Platonic Mill is primarily the Mill of the mid-1840s on, but again there are exceptions. His center is the *Autobiography*, in which he shows us how to add historical content to the exemplary pursuit of "individuality" put forward in *On Liberty*.

At times Mill suggests that the Socratic elenchus is the most valuable part of Plato's work and that Plato's more positive views are unpalatably dogmatic.[39] In contrast, the Platonic Mill calls our attention to the substantive rather than the dogmatic side of Plato's work. In an early article in the *Monthly Repository* in 1831 Mill wrote, "[A] book which gives evidence of any rare kind of moral qualities in its author is a treasure to which all the contents of all other books are as dross. What is there in the writings of Plato or Milton so eternally valuable to us as the reassurance they give that a Plato or a Milton might have been? Been in this very world of ours, where, therefore, we also according to the measure of our opportunities may, if we like, be the like."[40] According to Mill, an example of such an inspirational book is Plato's *Gorgias*. In his review of Grote's *Plato* published in 1866, Mill praises Plato's characterization of Socrates, not the Socratic method. "It is precisely this picture of the moral hero, still *tenax propositi* against the hostility and contempt of the world, which makes the splendor and power of the Gorgias. The Socrates of the dialogue makes us feel all other evils to be more tolerable than injustice in the soul, not by proving it, but by the sympathy he calls forth with his own intense feeling of it. He inspires heroism, because he shows himself a hero."[41] The final line should read, "because Plato shows him a hero as he takes up a progressive position within the 'rivers' of historical change."

## Socratic Engagement

Mill embraced the Socratic method as a model for agitating for parliamentary reform and as a way of criticizing mechanical solutions to the danger posed by public opinion. Whether in the London Debating Society, the House of Commons, or the pages of the *Westminster Review*, the Socratic Mill felt that any practical solution must begin with a rigorous logical analysis. The Socratic method was a "discipline for correcting errors, and clearing up the confusions incident to the *intellectus sibi permis-*

---

[39] Mill, *Dissertations and Discussions*, 4:290.
[40] Quoted in Sharpless, *Literary Criticism of John Stuart Mill*, p. 215.
[41] Mill, *Dissertations and Discussions*, 4:292.

*sus,* the understanding which has made up all its bundles of associations under the guidance of popular phraseology."[42] The "close searching *elenchus*" forces you to either define your terms unambiguously or admit that you do not know what you are talking about, no matter how widely held your opinions are.

Mill's early circle of friends was optimistic that the middle and working classes were on the verge of forming a strong parliamentary alliance based on just such an analysis. The Philosophic Radicals believed there were two opposed interests in society, the aristocratic and the democratic. These were the only two interests because they were the only two consistent doctrines. Whiggery was philosophical confusion and should not be taken seriously. As long as the Philosophic Radicals held this belief in "the People" (a potential parliamentary force united by consistent, albeit sub rosa, interests in more frequent elections, an open ballot, universal manhood suffrage, and repeal of the Corn Laws), the motivational problem was easily solved: a common sense of justice could be awakened in the working class and the middle class that would allow them to see their real foe, the aristocracy, and stop quarreling among themselves. The major organ for political education that was to awaken this sense of justice during this period of optimistic parliamentary activity was the press. Before we consider Mill's views on the Socratic value of the press, something more should be said about the context in which he gave it such importance.

In the first half of the nineteenth century, with technological development in agriculture and manufacture reaching new heights and religious authority in precipitous decline, the industrial entrepreneur and a little later the professional writer, lawyer, and bureaucrat made their primary demand for political recognition the reform of the franchise. They challenged the property qualification. Using selected ideas from Locke, Smith, and Bentham, Mill took an active part in giving the new industrial entrepreneur and his auxiliaries an articulate justification for their position. Mill believed that the freedom to make binding legal contracts and the legal ownership of capital, not just land, were the basis of political and economic progress and provided a setting for social cooperation on an unprecedented scale. For Mill or his audience, recognizing this sphere of human interaction as politically significant, as the place where human character could develop and the wealth of society was produced, did not rest on an act of faith or a transcendental deduction. The rapid growth of industrial capital, in contrast to the earlier transition from feudal estates to landed capital, was making an immediate impact.

Unlike landed capital, which developed slowly through the long period

---

[42] Mill, *Autobiography,* p. 25.

of European absolutism, industrial capital was reaching across national boundaries along an increasing number of rail connections, for the first time creating involuntary unemployment and generating cyclical economic trends.[43] Old forms of political recognition and authority that had been based on the ownership of land within a spatially fixed political domain began to lose their legitimacy. In this charged atmosphere, abolishing the property qualification brought government-sanctioned free trade when free trade was a threat to the power of landed capital and guaranteed very little to the new working class. Lower food prices through a repeal of the Corn Laws, for example, could easily be accompanied by lower wages as well as lower rents. Mill felt that high rents and food prices were deplorable: they interfered with the efficiency of the market. He also felt that low wages were avoidable: they resulted from overpopulation, which could be solved by teaching the masses to control their numbers. It was in the context of this highly political economic transformation that Mill turned to the press.

To Mill the press was not simply a medium for amplifying informed opinions for the benefit of the masses; it could, but did not always, play a more subtle Socratic role. To understand this role, we must keep in mind Mill's own statement of the conditions of political stability: cohesion and loyalty. Writing in 1840, Mill said that by cohesion he meant

> a principle of sympathy, not of hostility; of union not of separation. We mean a feeling of common interest among those who live under the same governments, and are contained within the same natural historical boundaries. We mean, that one part of the community do not consider themselves as foreigners with regard to another part; that they set a value on their connection; feel that they are one people, that their lot is cast together, that evil to any of their fellow-countrymen is evil to themselves; and do not desire selfishly to free themselves from their share of any common inconvenience by severing the connection.[44]

Mill also argued that there is a feeling of loyalty that is basically the same whether you are talking about loyalty to an absolutist state or an emerging parliamentary regime.

> This feeling may vary in its objects, and is not confined to any particular form of government; but whether in a democracy or a monarchy, its essence

---

[43] Asa Briggs, *The Making of Modern England* (New York: Harper and Row, 1959), p. 210. Also, see John A. Garraty, *Unemployment in History* (New York: Harper and Row, 1978), chaps. 5, 6.

[44] John Stuart Mill, "Coleridge," in *CW*, 10:135.

is always the same; viz. that there is in the constitution of the State something which is settled, something permanent, and not to be called in question;
something which, by general agreement, has a right to be where it is, and to
be secure against disturbance, whatever else may change.[45]

Cohesion within natural historical boundaries and loyalty to the regime
that maintains them were the two conditions for stable, progressive politics to which Mill believed the press could contribute. In *Considerations on
Representative Government* he suggests, through a classical parallel with the
agora, how the press might accomplish this.

In the ancient world, though there might be, and often was, great individual
or local independence, there could be nothing like a popular government
beyond the bounds of a single city-community; because there did not exist
propagation of a public opinion except among those who could be brought
together to discuss public matters in the same agora. This obstacle is in general thought to have ceased by the adoption of the representative system. But
to surmount it completely required the press, and even the newspaper press,
the real equivalent, though not in all respects an adequate one, of the Pnyx
and Forum.[46]

Socrates had galvanized the citizens of Athens, forced them to reexamine
the ideas of justice, piety, and education, and thus made the agora a more
political place. The press was to perform a similar function by clarifying
the political conflicts capitalist development was creating and by giving
people a visible and central institution through which individual loyalty
could be brought out into the open and telescoped in an effective political
way within its proper natural historical boundaries.

Can the press restrain the disintegrative impact of industrial capital on
these natural historical boundaries and shore up deepening class antago-
nisms without challenging the right of freedom of contract that nourishes
capitalist production? Clearly it depends on how much restraint is needed
and the availability of foreign markets. But it also depends on how receptive people are to the press as that "something permanent" they must feel
loyal to if capital accumulation is to proceed in a politically stable environment. The press itself, Mill hoped, would make them more receptive
without manipulating them. Mill knew that the *London and Westminster
Reviews, The Times, The Poor Man's Guardian*, and *The Gorgon* did not all
treat political conflicts in the same manner, nor did he think they should.
It was through editorial debate that they created a functional equivalent to

45 Ibid., pp. 133–34.
46 Mill, *Representative Government*, p. 378.

the agora, a public space that limited the bounds of political disagreement. The press was to be a permanent center in this spatially diffuse political domain because through it representatives could reach their constituencies, special interests could lobby for public support, and intellectuals could have their say. More than Parliament itself, the press represented that "something permanent" that everyone could feel loyal to. Championing a free press sounds fairly commonplace today, but this was not true in the early nineteenth century. Until 1836 there was a newspaper stamp tax (the "tax on knowledge") that effectively limited circulation of some newspapers by raising their prices and that the Philosophic Radicals, especially Francis Place, vehemently opposed.[47] Mill struggled for a free press because he felt it would be the nucleus of a new political order, a place where people could learn to understand both the promise and the danger of the revolutionary changes in social relations and economic wealth he was beginning to see.

What this means is that besides the many administrative and legislative reforms Mill supported through the press, the press was to be valued for its own sake. Mill hoped that the "dismal" future some political economists predicted could be avoided if population was held down and people learned to apply themselves as energetically to nonmarket projects as they did to business matters. In *The Principles of Political Economy* he writes, "The desirable medium is one which mankind have not often known how to hit: when they labor, to do it with all their might, and especially with all their mind: but to devote to labor, for more pecuniary gain, fewer hours in the day, fewer days in the year, and fewer years of life."[48] An active free press not only made for more informed public opinion and more efficient public administration, it symbolized the public-spirited nonremunerative work that Mill believed society could use more of. If more people took debate and argument seriously, there would be less shallow striving, less conformity, and a more competent political center from which to take the measure of the unprecedented changes wrought by capitalist development.

The press's role in administrative reform was to publicize administrative decisions and practices so the public could be informed of what their representatives had condoned or rejected. The press's role in deliberative politics involves another notion of validity that is potentially more powerful. Administrative policy can be judged by the validity of its underlying principles. But Mills idea of sound political deliberation entailed another notion of reliability that is peculiar to political beliefs and positions. Mill was a staunch advocate of well-researched public administration and legis-

---

47 Hamburger, *Intellectuals in Politics*, p. 128.
48 John Stuart Mill, *Principles of Political Economy*, in *CW*, 2:105–6.

lation, but he was careful to distinguish them from deliberation and discussion. He felt that government should streamline its administrative branch along lines similar to the structure of private business. The only thing that can be done better by a group in government than by an individual, he argued, is deliberation. Mill would have a small number of professional managers administer the government and a larger number of elected representatives "talk" out the needs that should inform public policies. And this talk would be an object of interpretation for the press.[49]

Sound administrative choices result in the efficient allocation of resources and the controlled expansion of participation. Deliberation also contributes to this expansion by filtering the demands of the people through the "expressive" mechanism of the representative assembly. But this is not all. In *On Liberty* Mill outlined what he considered the other side of true social and political beliefs. Logical consistency must be supplemented with something more, something an active free press is particularly suited for. "Complete liberty of contradicting and disproving our opinion is the very function which justifies us in assuming its truth for purposes of action; and on no other terms can a being with human faculties have any rational assurance of being right."[50] For something to be true for the purposes of action, it must be discussed and debated openly. The truth, not only the meaning of a practical proposition, depends on open discussion. Knowing the truth so that we can act on it requires that we be able to give reasons for believing that something is true for the purposes of action, that it belongs in the political domain for good reason. When we cannot give this kind of reason, we are not warranted in claiming that our beliefs are true in a practical sense, and presumably we would have trouble putting our knowledge to work in any particular situation.

Discussion, Mill believed, is also the best way to understand what we mean when we advance a particular belief. "The fact, however, is, that not only the grounds of the opinion are forgotten in the absence of discussion, but too often the meaning of the opinion itself, the Words which convey it cease to suggest ideas, or suggest only a small portion of those they were originally employed to communicate. Instead of a vivid conception and a living belief, there remain a few phrases retained by rote."[51] Thus the press keeps the truth and meaning of political discourse alive by staking out a place where the majority's voice and the market's hold are limited. Mill is calling attention to something more than the notion that only vigorously debated beliefs can improve or approach the truth, or the notion

---

[49] Mill, *Representative Government*, p. 428.
[50] Mill, *On Liberty*, p. 231.
[51] Ibid., p. 247.

that a practical truth has to make sense to someone who claims to follow its dictates. Creating a political domain through the press means providing a place where political truths can flourish; these are the truths that majorities fail to see because they do not conform to their prior expectations and that businesslike administrators working on their own individual projects may miss because they are too close to see how the market has swarmed over "natural historical boundaries."

In sum, there are two sides to the Socratic Mill. The first is the logical analyst concerned with the details of effective regulation, increased production, decreased population, and the gradual redistribution that can then follow. The second is the Mill who knows that detail work is not enough and that unless special arrangements are made to secure a place outside the market and beyond the reach of legislative majorities, no one will be able to see what shape things are taking in general, and then political loyalty and order will be in jeopardy. It is this second side, even more than the first, that leads Mill to put such a high value on the press. It represents a public space and not just an instrument for advancing capital accumulation. It is that something that people can feel loyal to at a time when political institutions have been lost to majority tyranny and the market monopolizes individuality. But it is the first side, the logical analyst, that is carried over into Mill's Platonic understanding of political education.

## Platonic Maturity

In addition to this Socratic idea of practical truth forged in public debate, *On Liberty* contains a forceful statement of the Platonic worth of individuality: "The initiation of all wise or noble things, comes and must come from individuals; generally at first from some one individual. The honour and glory of the average man is that he is capable of following that initiative; that he can respond internally to wise and noble things, and be led to them with his eyes open." [52] Even the average man is capable of being moved in a practical way by the example set by his betters. F. P. Sharpless has called attention to Mill's account of Plato's life and the parallel course of Mill's own development. Sharpless argues that "the disinterested love of virtue and heroic spirit of the *Gorgias* is the same inspiration that Mill's life and many of his works produced on his readers." [53] The flaw in this argument is that neither Plato nor Mill had a disinterested love of virtue. Mill's Platonic self-understanding is a political response to the histori-

[52] Ibid., p. 269.
[53] Sharpless, *Literary Criticism of John Stuart Mill*, p. 230.

cal limits that Kantian moral casuistry had reached, and it attains its full height in the *Autobiography*.

With parliamentary failure and economic crises in 1836 and then again in 1842, Mill grew pessimistic about reaching "the People" with a wide-barreled form of political education through a Socratic press. In response to the question whether he really wanted a "radical government," Mill replied in 1840: "I have long done what I could to prepare them for it, but in vain; so I have given them up, and in fact they have given me up." [54] Mill did not fully abandon the press in order to reach the people's sense of justice through an entirely new medium. What really changed was his understanding of the motivational issue itself. Political loyalty and cohesion became more problematic in his mind. They fell outside the range of a Socratic theory that aimed at consistent policymaking and the construction of a political space centered on the newspaper press. Mill, commenting on Plato, tells us we must do more than curb our acquisitiveness and join in open debate. He is interested in how we can improve our desires in a more political way. After comparing the *Republic* and the *Laws*, Mill makes an interesting comment. Rather than simply remarking on the obvious differences between these two dialogues and preferring, as we might expect, the latter for its more realistic and more detailed outlook, he has this to say:

> While Plato has thus two independent plans for the constitution of a political society, his notion of the end to be aimed at never varies. The business of rulers is to make the people whom they govern wise and virtuous. No political object but this is worth consideration. With respect to the other things usually desired by men and communities, he does not indeed always maintain the scornful tone assumed in the Gorgias, where all the statesmen of Athens . . . are reproached for having "filled the city with harbors, and docks, and fortifications, and tributes, and similar rubbish," instead of improving their desires, "the only business of a good citizen." In other places (as in the Second Alcibiades, Euthydemus, Menon, Leges) he contents himself with saying, that it is better not to have such things at all, than to have them, if devoid of the wisdom without which they cannot profit the professor; or, with Sokrates in the Apologia, that wealth does not produce virtue, but virtue wealth, and all other things that are desirable. But, either as the sole desirable thing, or as the means of obtaining all others, the wisdom and the virtue of the citizens (considered as identical) are the only proper end of government. [55]

This is a peculiar position for a Socratic philosopher to take. What could be further from the *Apology* than the *Laws*? Here Mill beckons us to see

---

[54] Hamburger, *Intellectuals in Politics*, p. 265.
[55] Mill, *Dissertations and Discussions*, 4:323–24.

that despite all their differences, the earlier Socratic dialogues and the later "dogmatic" ones have this in common: they bring to our attention the relation between material needs and the work of the political philosopher. Differences on this issue, Mill suggests, are only intramural disputes. The basic position is that wisdom and virtue, not material wealth, are the only proper end of government.

In one early comment on the *Gorgias* Mill set the stage for improving desires in a political way and not just giving people the power to resist social conformity and the logic of the market. This comment should be read as a prelude to the *Autobiography*.

> But no arguments which Plato urges have power to make those love or desire virtue who do not already; nor is this ever to be affected through the intellect, but through the imagination or the affections.
>
> The love of virtue, and every other noble feeling, is not communicated by reasoning but caught by inspiration or sympathy from those who already have it; and its nurse and foster-mother is admiration. We acquire it from those we love and reverence; from our ideal of those, whether in past or in present times, whose lives and characters have been the mirrors of all noble qualities; and lastly, from those who, as poets or artists, can clothe those feelings in the most beautiful forms, and breathe them into or through our imagination and our sensations.[56]

This inspirational figure is the missing element in the *Gorgias*. Mill was touched by Plato's genius in this dialogue, but in the dialogue itself, he thought, the Socratic method had failed. Mill believed that what stood between sound moral and political principles and a moral and political life in the *Gorgias* was the flawed character of the major figures. They did not understand that moral casuistry could have a desirable practical impact if it was in tune with the flow of history and the place of individual genius in that flow.

The three sources of the love of virtue that Mill mentions in this comment are incorporated into one heroic self-image in the *Autobiography*. Through this self-imaging he hoped to join political knowledge and energy with poetic sensitivity and a commitment to historical truth, to join Tocqueville and Vigny. What distinguished these two from most English writers in Mill's eyes was their passionate interest in politics and poetry and their ability to see the limits older doctrines were facing in Europe in 1830. In the work of Tocqueville and Vigny, even more than in that of Byron, Wordsworth, and Shelley, politics and poetry are each "colored by

56 Mill, "Comment on Plato's *Gorgias*," pp. 76–77.

the other."[57] Mill hoped to capture the "spirit of the age" as they had and put it to work in the service of progress, not the diffuse notion of "the People's" interest.

To support this interpretation we can turn to the opening paragraph of the *Autobiography* itself. Here Mill gives the reader ample warning that what is to be presented has a very peculiar political significance. Mill suggests it is a public, not a private, audience that will find something of interest in his story. Stillinger has shown that the early drafts of the *Autobiography* successively shift from a private to a more public voice.[58] For example, Mill becomes less critical of his father, less self-congratulatory, and generally unconcerned with the personal details we associate with autobiography. Mill does not think his autobiography should be preoccupied with anything so elusive as his particular self. As unusual as he thought his own education was, he did not believe much sense could be made of the notion of an extraordinary self. He refers to the *Autobiography* as "the life"; it is not a personal remembrance but the development of a life of social and intellectual associations.

The most personal moment in the book is Mill's account of his mental crisis. But even here an important political point is being made. Mill blames analysis itself for his collapse. "The habit of analysis has a tendency to wear away the feelings; as indeed it has, when no other mental habit is cultivated, and the analyzing spirit remains without its natural complements and correctives."[59] Following Locke and Hartley, Mill believed human psychology was a matter of accumulating associations. In this process, pleasurable and painful feelings become associated with events and experiences. It was based on this model of associational psychology that James Mill trusted that self-interested individuals could learn to value the happiness of the greatest number. His son abandoned this dream when he saw that the "analytic spirit" could so fully dominate our thoughts and our associations that the passions and virtues once in force atrophy and lose their direct association with events and actions in the world. Mill felt that he was virtually the victim of his own theory of human nature. The truth of the theory was no consolation to him at this time because, as he said, "to know that a feeling would make me happy if I had it, did not give me the feeling."[60]

The disintegrative effects of associational psychology are also alluded to in the third chapter of *Utilitarianism*. Mill notes that "moral associa-

[57] John Stuart Mill, "The Writings of Alfred de Vigny," in *CW*, 1:466.

[58] Jack Stillinger, ed., *The Early Draft of John Stuart Mill's Autobiography* (Urbana: University of Illinois Press, 1961), introduction.

[59] Mill, *Autobiography*, p. 141.

[60] Ibid., p. 143.

tions which are wholly of artificial creation, when intellectual culture goes on, yield by degrees to the dissolving force of analysis." [61] To remedy this he struggles with the idea of a natural sentiment of sorts. But the struggle ends on a negative note. The desire for social cooperation can be of use under the right educational and legal sanctions. Anyone who doubts that such loyalty can be generated without an appeal to God need only read Comte's *Traité de politique positive*. The problem, as Mill sees it, is that this kind of regimented social organization headed by an intellectual clerisy leaves no room for individual liberty. He is aware of the depth of the motivational problem in *Utilitarianism*, but he can find no answer to it there.

What raised the young Mill from this sorry state, according to the Mill of the 1850s? A number of things sustained him in later years, he tells us, beginning with Wordsworth and including his own treatment of the problem of freedom and necessity. But the initial step was more fortuitous. "I was reading, accidentally, Marmontel's *Memoirs*, and I came to the passage which relates his father's death, the distressed position of the family, and the sudden inspiration by which he, then a mere boy, felt and made them feel that he would be everything to them—would supply the place of all that they had lost. A vivid conception of the scene and its feelings came over me, and I was moved to tears. From this moment my burdens grew lighter." [62] Mill would have us believe that he was touched by the heroic act of a mere boy moved by sudden inspiration to step up and fill his deceased father's role in the family, and that the sight of his own emotional response brought him out of his depression. In retrospect, Mill felt that he was taken by the ability of the boy to be everything to them. He yearned, as he composed the *Autobiography*, for such a heroic figure—one that might inspire factions to put aside their differences, that might evoke a common heritage and a future of cooperation all might be loyal to and at the same time draw strength from. While this passage obviously gives us a glimpse into Mill's ambivalent feelings toward his own father, it also represents Mill's hope that individual efforts modeled on family solidarity can be unifying by being inspiring.

Returning to the opening paragraph, we find three explicit justifications for the *Autobiography* that support this public interpretation of Mill's account of his mental crisis. First, Mill suggests it is valuable to record an education that is "both unusual and remarkable" so that previous standards of learning can be seen in a better light. This is clearly a reference to the debilitating associational theory his father had so scrupulously applied to his education. Next, he suggests that "in an age of transition of opin-

---

[61] Mill, *Utilitarianism*, pp. 203–59.
[62] Mill, *Autobiography*, p. 145.

ions, there may be somewhat both of interest and of benefit in noting the successive phases of any mind which was always pressing forward, equally ready to learn and to unlearn either from its own thoughts or from those of others."[63] The phrase "age of transition" has a special meaning for Mill. It refers to his theory of human progress, which he derived in part from the Comtean distinction between critical and organic periods. Like critical periods, an age of transition is one in which there is great individual freedom of thought and action and at the same time a general lack of consensus about what is right and wrong.[64] Furthermore, during an age of transition such as Mill felt he was living through, the best-educated people do not hold political power. "In all other conditions of mankind, the uninstructed have faith in the instructed. In an age of transition, the divisions among the instructed nullify their authority, and the uninstructed lose their faith in them. The multitude are without a guide; and society is exposed to all the errors and dangers which are to be expected when persons who have never studied any branch of knowledge comprehensively and as a whole attempt to judge for themselves upon particular parts of it."[65] The successive phases of any mind in an age of transition are bound to be jolting, not simply because new lessons will have to be learned and old rules discarded. The real problem an age of transition poses for education is a political one. Divisions among the instructed make it difficult not simply to know what to believe in, but to lead the multitude. When the ruling elite is not aware of the dangers half-truths and tired doctrines pose for the masses, they may retard society's progress and even bring on political disorder. This second justification for the *Autobiography* is not a justification for the life of the mind. Mill is not suggesting that it is useful to see how one particular mind made the philosophic climb from error to scientific proof or from fact to feeling. He is advising us to attend to the political vicissitudes an age of transition holds for those in search of reliable political knowledge.

Finally, Mill states that he ought to acknowledge his intellectual and moral debts by writing this *Autobiography*. This is a difficult point. It raises a question about the nature of the knowledge Mill feels he has acquired such that it requires this type of fiduciary response. Discharging debts implies that one's relationship with the original source of an idea or argument has been brought to a proper close. Knowledge then can be passed along when proper credit is given: it becomes refutable, amendable, or even available for wholesale adoption. Once our debts are discharged, we can do

---

[63] Ibid., p. 5.

[64] For Mill's general appraisal of Comte, see his *Auguste Comte and Positivism*, in *CW*, 10: 263-68. He summarized his view several times in the *Autobiography*, including p. 175.

[65] John Stuart Mill, "The Spirit of the Age," part 2, in *CW*, 22:238.

what we please with the arguments and ideas we have acquired so long as we stay within the bounds of logical argument. By clearing the books we make our past manageable and our position marginal within the discourse we have inherited. In an age of transition nothing could be more valuable than to step out of the whirling stream of events and ideas, as Tocqueville and Vigny did, to compose a picture of the whole. Mill does this in his own way by creating a picture of fiduciary harmony. Though it begins among intellectuals, professionals, and entrepreneurs, there is no a priori reason others cannot eventually join in these transactions. Mill's desire to publish a number of his writings in inexpensive editions for workers and his support of the dictum "Make everyone a capitalist," put forward by the Society for the Diffusion of Useful Knowledge, strongly suggest that he meant it when he argued that there was a way, albeit a gradual one, out of an age of transition. For the Platonic Mill, no matter what associational ladders were available to reach greater political competence and acquire a sense of justice, and no matter how vigorous was public debate, loyalty and cohesion also depended on a fixed moral referent. The exemplary "life" was the product of a wide array of associations and the moral courage to speak one's mind. Without such a life to reflect on, most democratic citizens would not be able to resist the pressure to conform and the temptation to buy their way out of trouble. Mill presented his own recovery as an act of critical self-reflection on the origins of his own desires and an engagement with other minds, even if these other minds were "one-eyed."

## Missing Voices

The inspiring family scene that Mill claimed had triggered his emotional recovery raises a larger question for his political theory as a form of political education. How central is the family as a prepolitical association for the development of democratic political character? Can the sentiments and principles nurtured in an egalitarian family prepare citizens adequately for the challenges Mill is most concerned about? Mill's response to this question, of course, can be measured against contemporary standards. But it also offers us another opportunity to gauge the limits of his sight-based theory of political emulation. Voice, I argue, is especially powerful in the family, where masks are easy to see through and voices are complexly interwoven. However limited Mill's case for an egalitarian family may be—and I return to this issue in chapter 7—it also reveals the one-dimensional nature of his theory of political emulation. In Mill's own *Autobiography* as well as in the ideal egalitarian family he favors, too many voices are missing.

*The Subjection of Women*, written in 1861 and published in 1869, is primarily an argument for the legal equality of women, but several comments on the relation between national politics and the family as a secondary association are of interest. In this essay Mill considers the oppression of women the gravest injustice in the modern world. Not only is it wrong in principle to deny women equal legal status and bind them in domesticity, but the consequences are wholly unwanted. Women have not been able to lead happy, fulfilling lives, and men too have suffered in this situation. "All the selfish propensities, the self-worship, the unjust self-preference, which exist among mankind, have their source and root in, and derive their principal nourishment from, the present constitution of the relation between men and women." Furthermore, "The moral regeneration of mankind will only really commence when the most fundamental of the social relations is placed under the rule of equal justice, and when human beings learn to cultivate their strongest sympathy with an equal in rights and in cultivation." [66] Why, we might well ask, have men acted in such a reprehensible and self-defeating way? Mill admits that the limits men have imposed on women's efforts to advance politically and economically have in a sense benefited those men who, had they been forced to compete against women on an equal basis, would have found themselves in less comfortable positions. He suggests, however, that there is a more fundamental reason for this oppression that involves men's close everyday contact with women, their relationship with women in the family. "I believe that [women's] disabilities elsewhere are only clung to in order to maintain their subordination in domestic life; because the generality of the male sex cannot yet tolerate the idea of living with an equal." [67] The real resistance to equal rights can be located in men's attitudes toward equality in the family.

Although men do benefit from the competitive advantage these attitudes reinforce in other spheres, the reason they resist equality is that in the family more than in any other association they cannot face women on an equal footing, and so women are disproportionately burdened with household and family responsibilities. Mill does not shy away from the implications of this argument. An egalitarian family system would be the most devastating blow to male domination because it would bring men face-to-face on an intense daily basis with the fact that women are their equals. It is this intensity that makes the family more than one among many secondary associations. "Citizenship, in free countries, is partly a school

---

[66] John Stuart Mill, *The Subjection of Women*, in *CW*, 21:324, 326.
[67] Ibid., p. 299.

of society in equality; but citizenship fills in a small place in modern life, and does not come near the daily habits or inmost sentiments. The family, justly constituted, would be the real school of the virtues of freedom. It is sure to be a sufficient one of everything else." [68] If we combine Mill's special valuation of the family, his reservations about local participation, and his abbreviated treatment of workplace democracy, it is difficult to argue that his main contribution to liberal political education is his theory of participatory democracy.

My view is that the family plays another role in Mill's political theory that is not the role of a secondary association. What better place for future citizens to learn to be receptive to the virtues of freedom? In a family in which mother and father face each other on an equal footing, the child learns to identify with an adult who treats other adults in a reciprocal way regardless of sex. Seeing their parents respect each other as equals, Mill suggests, will give children a deep attachment to freedom and equality.

Now recall the passage in the *Autobiography* about Marmontel's *Mémoires*. The "mere boy" Mill was so moved by, the person who indirectly gave him the strength to come to terms with his own family philosophy, was someone who "would supply the place of [the family] they had lost." Egalitarian family heads like this precocious one are inspirational forces expressing reciprocity and bidding us to follow suit. Mill rejected his Benthamite identity, the product of a highly inegalitarian family life and, like the first family of the "mere boy," one that was fated to pass away. Mill then found his own way within a more egalitarian marriage that enabled him to bring Bentham and Coleridge together in one doctrine, more reliable and more motivating than Kantian intuitionism. Like the boy, Mill hoped that through the *Autobiography* he too could stand for the family that should have been: a family head who matures from Socratic enthusiasm and experimentation to Platonic wisdom and stability, who can recognize his spouse as an equal and inspire his children to do the same.

One would expect a theorist of participatory democracy to treat the family as an important secondary association. Mill was a staunch advocate of the egalitarian family, but not because he viewed participation in the family as preparation for primary political participation. The family was important for his view of political education because it could be a cohesive egalitarian group that could still be represented by one figure without eroding, in fact, while contributing to the loyalty of its other members.

This idealized view of the egalitarian family as a school for inspira-

---

[68] Ibid., p. 295.

tional leadership strikes me as a perfect example of Mill's fixation on looks. Mill's egalitarian family is a cameo of liberal equality. All the subtle tones, the nuanced and hushed voices, and the sighs and exasperations that bind families together have been scrubbed away. There is a deceptively soft luster to this marble cameo; there are no shadows, just as there is a sense in which the visual metaphors that dominate Mill's treatment of politics proper are insufficient to guide democratic deliberation.

This deafness is illustrated in one of Mill's most famous passages, the introductory paragraph of chapter 3 in *On Liberty*. In the previous chapter of *On Liberty* Mill had argued for the "liberty of thought and discussion" on the grounds he summarizes here and extends to freedom of action. Now these grounds (fallibility and the beneficent effects that "collision" has on competing half-truths and contestation has on those who may be formally right in their beliefs) are bolstered.[69] When thought and action are free, within the appropriate limits, they promote happiness and progress for the individual and for society as a whole. They do this primarily because they permit individual experimentation, which is the sign of a healthy character. The strength to experiment without harming others is one of the signs of "a man as a progressive being."[70]

In one stroke Mill has extended the argument for liberty of thought and discussion to action, and he has justified all three in terms of a very specific moral ideal of individual and social progress embodied in considerate but daring human character. He goes on to describe the value of individual experimentation, "genius," and "originality" in thought and action for society as well as for the individual experimenter. Most people, he asserts, see very little social utility in tolerating individuality taken to this extreme. Mill responds that the "first service which originality has to render them, is that of opening their eyes: which being once fully done, they would have a chance of being themselves original."[71] Originality is not merely to be valued because of the contributions unusual individuals may make to society in the form of discoveries. Originality is exemplary. Far from being restricted to science and literature, exemplary originality is especially important in political life. Democratic leaders need the wise counsel of individuals who can resist the "tyranny of majority opinion." This wise, original counsel is not directed simply at the leaders. "The honour and glory of the average man is that he is capable of following that initiative; that he can respond internally to wise and noble things, and be

69 Mill, *On Liberty*, pp. 260–61.
70 Ibid., p. 224.
71 Ibid., p. 268.

led to them with his eyes open."[72] Originality is a model of a surging intellectual vitality, not just spontaneous resistance to social conformity.

Liberty of thought, discussion, and action is valuable because of what it allows the masses to see. It creates an environment within which a visible, exemplary individuality can flourish, or at least survive. This emphasis on seeing individuality and its social value carries over to Mill's interpretation of the limits that can and should be placed on liberty. Thought, discussion, and action not only are justified on the same grounds, they are ultimately limited for the same reason: harm to others. This is the proviso Mill mentions in the opening paragraph of chapter 3. The boundaries on individual liberty have to be seen in terms of the harm or possible harm (the risk and peril) that might be caused to others. "Whenever, in short, there is a definite damage, or a definite risk of damage, either to an individual or to the public, the case is taken out of the province of liberty, and placed in that of morality or law."[73]

Mill realizes that he has to say more about this notion of a definite risk of damage. The offense some people take at the religious practices of others, the unintended inconveniences that some may suffer because of mere chance or the workings of the market, and the blows to their self-esteem when critics attack them or acquaintances spurn them are not, Mill believes, grounds for limiting liberty of thought, discussion, or action. Even when lack of concern and care for oneself is "injurious by . . . example,"[74] so long as "constructive" injuries like this do not violate any specific duty to the public, or lead to any "perceptible hurt" to others, they should not be limited by any external force.[75] In sum, we have to be able to see the harm done to others or the public duty violated before society can legitimately limit individual liberty in thought or action. The boundary between self- and other-regarding actions, including speech acts, may be jagged, but it is visible to the discerning eye.

Mill uses the example of the "excited mob assembled before the house of the corn-dealer" in the long introductory paragraph to chapter 3 to illustrate how opinions, like actions, are not entirely protected against state or social control. The key in this case is whether "the circumstances in which they are expressed are such as to constitute their expression a positive instigation to some mischievous act." Incitement of this sort is a function of the specific social meaning of the utterance. How is it likely to be understood and responded to by the excited mob? The harm here is hypotheti-

---

[72] Ibid., p. 269.
[73] Ibid., p. 282.
[74] Ibid., pp. 280–81.
[75] Ibid., p. 282.

cal, and the only thing the reader has to go on is Mill's tacit suggestion that an excited mob is likely to respond to the inflammatory words "starvers of the poor," whether they are spoken loudly or written boldly on placards.

If we restrict ourselves to Mill's visual metaphors, however, it may not be possible to see the risk of damage. In fact, there may be significant differences between a voice proclaiming that corn-dealers are starvers of the poor, picket signs displaying the same message, and—to take an actual parallel case—leaflets showering down on the avenue.[76] Even an excited mob may not pose a definite risk of damage without a galvanizing voice that can rivet its attention and drive it into action. A similar objection could be made to the famous example of falsely shouting fire in a crowded theater. Unless we can hear the intonation—that is, unless it is clearly a credible voice of panic—it may not create a definite risk of damage. The boundary line marking off potential harm to others may not be visible even to the most discerning eye. We may want to hear what things sounded like then and there before we condemn the utterance.

Despite Mill's efforts to describe the lines surrounding the domain of individual liberty, there seems to be a need for hearing as well as seeing how thought, discussion, and action affect others. Tone—whether it is humorous, ironic, or vicious—may well influence our political judgments in the cases Mill cites. That is not to say that what we see is unimportant; in the case of the excited mob there is certainly a need to see how the mob is moving. Is it surging forward, or is it undirected? But there is also a need to gauge the voices. Is the voice of the leader confident or resigned? Does the mob simply echo the leader's slogans or aggressively make them its own?

Like his accounts of the egalitarian family and of the excited mob, Mill's *Autobiography* is missing other important voices. We hear about the views of his father, Bentham, and the rest, but we do not hear their voices. Their views are blended together to create an inspirational picture of a mature life, but it is a life that is immaculate. There is no dissonance, and no place for democratic compromise and disagreement—only debate and decision. It is Mill's great strength that his theory of political emulation is able to make the invisible visible. The *Autobiography* is a stirring "experiment in living." We see women (with the conspicuous exception of his own mother) in a relatively clearer light, and we see the major influences on Mill and his age more sharply. This is no small matter. But it is one thing to be seen, another to be heard. Democratic politics depends on both. In the end, it was the image of great men that Mill sought to evoke, not the sounds and voices of democracy: "A great man had, in the unbounded publicity of

[76] *Abrams v. United States* 250 U.S. 616 (1919).

Athenian political life, extraordinary facilities for moulding his country after his own image." [77]

[77] Mill, *Dissertations and Discussions*, 3:232–33. No sooner does Mill recall this inspirational "image, however, then he goes on to another metaphor: "And seldom has any people, during a whole generation, enjoyed such a course of education as forty years of listening to the lofty spirit of the practical wisdom of Pericles must have been to the Athenian demos." Even in *On Liberty*, in *CW*, 18:245, Mill occasionally seems aware of the importance of hearing people out. Those who hold patently false beliefs ought to speak for themselves because they will "defend them in earnest, and do their very utmost for them." It is not just that all views should be represented but that those who hold false beliefs will do the best job representing them. In the case of our knowledge of women's psychology: it is "wretchedly imperfect and superficial, and always will be so, until women themselves have told all that they have to tell." *The Subjection of Women*, in *CW*, 1:279. At odds with this, however, is Mill's criticism of the "Communist" principle of collective decision making that requires that "every adult member of the body would have an equal voice in determining the collective system design for the benefit of all." Mill calls this the "most fruitful source of discord in every association." *Chapters on Socialism*, in *CW*, 5:745.

# CHAPTER SIX

# John Rawls Speaking
# for Stability

The "original position" is essential, Rawls argues, for gaining practical acceptance for political liberalism in general, not only for justifying his preferred conception of liberal theory, justice as fairness. It is through this philosophical method that principles of justice for society's basic institutions and practices can be agreed to, principles governing the legitimate exercise of state power can be identified for liberal democracy, and guidelines for reasoning on matters of public importance can be set that enable citizens to apply these general principles and act on their own political virtues.[1] The original position has become more, not less, important as Rawls's theory has evolved, and this assessment includes its significance for Rawls's theory as political education. It is, I argue, a Socratic method of "public reflection and self-clarification"[2] that orients citizens toward existing structures of expert authority in the spirit of moderate reform and accommodation.

To see Rawls's theory in this critical light, we have to approach it from an unlikely angle, the problem of stability, and listen to its "conversational style."[3] Rawls recently has said that the problem of stability motivated his

---

[1] John Rawls, *Political Liberalism* (New York: Columbia University Press, 1993), pp. 225–26.

[2] Rawls, *Political Liberalism*, p. 26.

[3] Rawls, *Political Liberalism*, p. xiii. Rawls introduces these "lectures" by saying that he hopes to preserve their original "conversational style," that is, the style in which they were delivered to philosophical audiences. They are not, certainly not as much as *A Theory of Justice* was, conversations with a broader audience in informal give-and-take. They are, just as *A Theory of Justice* was, conversational in the sense that they engage the reader in several voices at the same time that they encourage the reader to select from his or her repertoire of voices.

own revisions, and it is the problem of stability that gives his account of political liberalism in general its coherence.[4] Rawls has proposed two solutions to the problem, one psychological and one political. After connecting his analysis of stability to the traditional and modern problems of political education, I argue that the original position rests on orienting metaphors that reassure Rawls's readers that they can feel at home in a stable world of policymaking. The original position enables readers to hear themselves among the domesticated voices of professional experts and other clients and consumers. It introduces them to this conversational style. In contrast to Millian liberal theory, Rawlsian theory as political education relies primarily on voices rather than exemplary images to humanize neocorporatist politics.

## Psychological Stability and Political Education

Rawls formulates the problem of psychological stability as a question. Will individuals with the capacity for a sense of justice and their own individual conceptions of the good think that it is also a good thing to be moved by the particular principles of justice as fairness in a well-ordered society? Or will they find that living in such a society makes it hard for them to act on their sense of justice? If it is the latter, then even a well-ordered society is likely to be unstable; and when considering just reforms, individuals who do not know where they are going to be situated are not likely to want to be vulnerable to this kind of inner tension during the process of reform. The prospects of psychological stability will make the "strains of commitment" to justice as fairness too great.

Rawls's answer to this question has two parts. The primary response rests on an interpretation of normal moral development, and the second part rests on more speculative claims about how tendencies toward envy, intolerance, and excessive self-reproach (what Rawls calls "special psychologies") can be mitigated. This is where political education comes in. I begin with Rawls's primary concern, normal moral development, and turn to how noncooperative tendencies can be curbed.

---

[4] Rawls, *Political Liberalism*, p. xvii. Like *A Theory of Justice* (Cambridge: Harvard University Press, 1971), *Political Liberalism* is a product of painstaking revision. Both books grew out of earlier important articles and both books circulated widely in manuscript form before their final publications. In this chapter I refer to some of the articles and to the unpublished 1989 book-length manuscript, "Justice as Fairness: A Briefer Restatement," as well as the two books originally published in English. I do not make detailed cross-references to parallel passages, but I focus on those passages that elaborate the role of the original position as a mediating philosophical method, wherever they happen to occur in Rawls's work.

Rawls specifies two ways the psychological problem of stability can arise under normal conditions, free from complications like the "special psychologies." Here Rawls follows the now standard economic analysis of public goods. Because individuals are somewhat "isolated" from each other—that is, because they make their social decisions on their own and not through a process of collective deliberation—"there is the free-rider problem." Second, even if "all citizens were willing to pay their share, they would presumably do so only when they are assured that others will pay theirs as well." To remedy this, Rawls argues, a sense of justice must also support state enforcement of rules against defectors and free riders. Both the isolation and the assurance problems require that individual citizens have a sense of justice that will ensure the provision of public goods, from national defense to clean air.[5]

So while economic analysis can locate the problem of psychological stability, according to Rawls it does not provide an adequate solution. Rational choice cannot be manipulated or constrained to overcome isolation and suspicion. The key is to describe favorable circumstances within which individual moral development is likely to occur in such a way that the principles of justice as fairness, which are designed for the basic structure of society, will also prove "regulative" for most individuals. In other words, the question is not what rational actors will choose under certain constraints, but what individuals trying to assess the prospects of reform from the perspective of the original position should believe morally reasonable persons generally will be inclined to do in circumstances of near justice. Rawls believes he can show that they will be inclined to support justice as fairness.

The argument he presents leans heavily on the theories of moral development of Jean Piaget and Laurence Kohlberg. From these theories he distills three laws that govern the growth of moral sentiments, especially mutual trust and friendship, again in relatively favorable circumstances.[6] As children mature in these circumstances, certain natural attitudes form toward their parents that gradually give way to rudimentary moral feelings of love and trust in their protective authority. When children fail to win the approval of this parental authority they fear punishment, but gradually they also begin to feel guilty. This "morality of authority" is "primitive"; its virtues are "obedience, humility, and fidelity to authoritative persons." It is only a temporary station along the way to a more reflective sense of justice.[7] Later, as they become members of voluntary associations outside

---

[5] Rawls, *Theory of Justice*, pp. 267–68.
[6] Ibid., pp. 490–91.
[7] Ibid., p. 466.

the family, the potential for "authority guilt" gives way to a more complex "association guilt." In these voluntary associations individuals learn to value the friendship and trust of others with whom they stand on an equal footing. When they betray this trust or fail to carry through on the obligations of friendship, they will feel association guilt, a sign that the moral sentiments of trust and friendship have taken hold more firmly. There is a strong similarity between the moral development that occurs in the family and what happens in cooperative associations, however. In both cases, argues Rawls, "other persons act with evident intention to affirm our well-being and at the same time they exhibit qualities and ways of doing things that appeal to us and arouse the desire to model ourselves after them."[8] In both cases the moral sentiments that are formed are contingent on the particular persons who serve as models.

The passage from the morality of association to the morality of principles is somewhat different from the first passage out of the family morality of authority. In this case it is not that individuals expand the sphere of their activities or develop additional moral sentiments. The morality of associations is complete in this regard. What happens, Rawls argues, is that individuals realize that these associations and the family itself depend for their existence on the wider basic structure of society. And even though they do not have the kind of face-to-face association with fellow citizens that they have with family members, friends, and associates, they will feel guilty if they let their fellow citizens down by defecting or by exploiting cooperative social arrangements. A sense of justice now manifests itself in the desire to maintain the basic structure of society that makes social cooperation possible and the further desire "to work for (or at least not to oppose) the setting up of just institutions, and for the reform of existing ones when justice requires it."[9] Feelings of guilt now will be more intense, even though they will not be contingent on personal ties and loyalties, and moral sentiments will be more secure because they have a rational basis.

Authority, guilt, and trust are the foundations of a mature sense of justice. The authority of parents prepares the ground for the shared authority of voluntary associations and the more abstract authority of the principles governing the basic structure of a well-ordered society. Although parental authority is not a model for political authority, parents play an essential role in conveying to children the sense of self-worth and self-esteem that they need to enter voluntary associations on their own. Similarly, the particularistic friendships and ties private citizens develop within these voluntary associations teach them to value a more consensual form

---

[8] Ibid., p. 472.
[9] Ibid., p. 474.

of authority and other social practices such as promising, and this makes possible the final step to a more abstract morality of principles. In other words, citizens learn how to trust each other and cooperate on an impersonal societal level through the experiences they have within the family and small voluntary associations. Those who do not feel guilty when they defect or mislead other citizens most likely have not had these experiences and are incapable of the basic moral feelings that have their roots in them. They cannot experience justifiable resentment or moral indignation when others treat them unjustly, and conversely, they do not grasp the rational basis for treating others justly.

It should be obvious that psychological instability is very similar to the traditional problem of liberal political education. Recall that the traditional problem was one of balancing impersonal public duties that could be shirked against more personal private relationships that one felt more deeply about. The difficulty in sustaining this balance arose because defecting, free riding, and constantly trying to renegotiate previous agreements are supposed to be psychologically easier than disappointing family members or friends. To keep from neglecting impersonal public duties, either public life must become personalized, coercive measures and negative sanctions must make defecting and free riding too costly, or a gradual process of political education must instill in citizens some degree of political loyalty and public responsibility. In modern liberal societies the first two do occur, but they cannot be publicly affirmed too often. Citizens are not supposed to be infatuated with public figures or enthralled by pomp and circumstance as a regular part of their lives, even though they often are. And coercive measures are supposed to be minimized, not regularly utilized to discourage free riders. The process of political socialization and the experiences within voluntary associations in which mutual trust can grow are supposed to remedy the psychological deficiencies liberal theorists like Locke and Tocqueville were concerned about, and that Rawls also seems to be aware of. Without mutual trust and confidence that others will do their part, Rawls suggests, a well-ordered society is not likely to be any more stable than its major competitors. Where Rawls differs from Locke and Tocqueville is in his emphasis on the rational basis for mutual trust and confidence. The moral sentiments are grounded in natural attitudes, but they can be extended and strengthened only through reflection on the meaning of fair cooperation, not just the long-term implications of individual self-interest.

It is important to note that Rawls's account of psychological stability is not purely hypothetical; he is not simply speculating on the stability of some future ideal, well-ordered society. This is not always easy to remember. Rawls often talks about a well-ordered society as if it were wholly disconnected from the present state of affairs, and he distinguishes the deliberations of parties in the original position concerned about a well-ordered society from the perspectives of citizens in such a society and also from the conversations and disagreements we have as we weigh the relative merits of competing political theories.[10] Now, though it is important to keep these various perspectives separate, they all operate within the same temporal framework of reform; that is, they all serve the same practical purpose. By using them correctly, we should be in a better position to fashion the most reasonable doctrine for reforming our public life in light of our history and traditions.[11] The primary purpose of Rawls's ideal theory is to guide actual social and political reform: "An ideal conception of the social order is set up which is to regulate the direction of change and the efforts of reform."[12] Of course, there are obvious differences between Rawls's program of reform and detailed legislative and social reform programs. He emphasizes that political theory takes "the longest view," but it is still a view focused on reform.[13]

For example, in discussing the stability of a well-ordered society Rawls reminds the reader that the "crucial point is how the general facts of moral psychology affect the choice of principles in the original position."[14] One might think this means that Rawls is concerned only with how parties in the original position behind the "veil of ignorance" would assess the stability of the well-ordered society, not how—here and now—we should assess the attractiveness of this ideal in terms of its practical stability. Psychological stability is described in terms of "congruence" between the good and the right "in" a well-ordered society, and the decision about relative stability is supposed to be made "in the original position," but this is Rawlsian shorthand for talking about how we are to assess stability in the process of reform. When Rawls asks us to evaluate the stability of a well-ordered society from the perspective of the original position, he is reminding us that he means stability under the reforms of justice as fairness, not within a society in which citizens are crass psychological egoists with no commitment to fair cooperation.

The reason for this somewhat confusing shorthand is that Rawls is attempting to establish the relative stability of his own theory or public conception of justice as well as that of the ideal reforms enjoined by the theory.

---

[10] John Rawls, "Kantian Constructivism in Moral Theory: The Dewey Lectures, 1980," *Journal of Philosophy* 77 (September 1980): 533.

[11] Ibid., p. 519.

[12] Rawls, *Theory of Justice*, p. 565.

[13] John Rawls, "The Idea of an Overlapping Consensus," *Oxford Journal of Legal Studies* 7, no. 1 (1987): 24.

[14] Rawls, *Theory of Justice*, p. 462.

*A Theory of Justice* is addressed to several audiences, as we shall see later, and one of them is philosophers who understand the efficacy of their own methods in terms of the internal coherence or "stability" of the theory. For them stability is understood in terms like congruence between the right and the good, because without this kind of stability, their own theory cannot compete effectively against rival theories. Rawls's desire to show that justice as fairness is more stable than utilitarian theories is a practical desire to contest the hegemony of utilitarianism as the philosophical basis for public policy analysis and policymaking. For social scientists and professionals, however, stability means something else. They want to know about free riders and social coordination. The following passage suggests that Rawls thinks the two are related:

> It is evident that stability is a desirable feature of moral conceptions. Other things equal, the persons in the original position will adopt the more stable scheme of principles. However attractive a conception of justice might be on other grounds, it is seriously defective if the principles of moral psychology are such that it fails to engender in human beings the requisite desire to act upon it. Thus in arguing further for the principles of justice as fairness, I should like to show that this conception is more stable than other alternatives.[15]

A stable conception of justice will be adopted in the original position and also will engender in people the desire to act on it. The first way of putting it appeals to the philosophical notion of congruence: parties in the original position will adopt principles of right that will be congruent with their own conception of the good. Described this way, the theory is stable. The second way of formulating psychological stability appeals to the desire to identify a vision of a well-ordered society and reforms leading to it that will be practically stable given the normal course of moral development under favorable conditions. Acting on this public conception of justice is likely to be psychologically stable, and this way of putting it appeals to less philosophically minded reformers.

What about the so-called special psychologies? Rawls's treatment of these potential sources of instability is more ad hoc than his account of normal moral development. The possibility of racial, ethnic, and religious intolerance, he acknowledges, cannot be ruled out even in a well-ordered society, so the parties in the original position must consider these sources of instability when assessing reforms in line with justice as fairness. But, Rawls asserts without much argument, as long as intolerant minorities do

---

[15] Ibid., p. 455.

not directly threaten social and political order, tolerating them will "persuade them to a belief in freedom."[16]

Envy is a second source of "special" psychological instability, in particular the envy felt by the poor toward those economically better off. Rawls has three reasons for minimizing any concern about envy the parties in the original position might have. First, envy is not the same as resentment, and resentment is precisely what justice as fairness is designed to reduce. Envy is not based on rational argument, whereas resentment is, and since even those reforms (enjoined by the principles of fair equality of opportunity and the difference principle) that permitted economic inequalities would be justifiable to the "least advantaged" members of society, they would not be the cause of resentment for long. Then, once the problem is narrowed down by distinguishing envy from resentment, Rawls admits that the perception of unreasonable disparities in income and wealth may still give rise to destabilizing levels of envy. Two things work against this, however. The publicly affirmed conception of justice as fairness, in which equal political and civil liberties are given the highest priority, denies the identification of self-worth with one's particular share of the more "objective" primary goods. According to the publicly affirmed conception of justice as fairness, "no one supposes that those who have a larger share [of income and wealth] are more deserving from a moral point of view."[17] A second reason for believing destabilizing envy will be contained, Rawls asserts, is that people tend to live their lives in "noncomparing groups." Members of poorer groups will not be that visible to the rich, and so uncomfortable feelings of "grudgingness" will not afflict the rich. Similarly, the poor will not see much of the rich, and so their feelings of envy will not be constantly aggravated.

The third source of "special" psychological instability, according to Rawls, can be described as overwhelming feelings of self-reproach and self-doubt. If individuals are repeatedly reproaching themselves for having planned their lives poorly when they should have known better, they may succumb to paralyzing self-doubt. Although Rawls does not explore this syndrome in detail, the implication is that self-reproach leading to self-doubt may also make it difficult to form relationships of trust and confidence. The reason he offers for minimizing the importance of this special psychology is that it is reasonable for parties in the original position to assume that in the course of reform individuals will plan their lives according to a principle of responsibility to self.[18] They will not sacrifice their future well-being for short-term satisfactions because it is rational

[16] Ibid., p. 219.
[17] Ibid., p. 536.
[18] Ibid., pp. 421–22.

for them to think of themselves as "one person over time." Given this assumption about what it means to be "one enduring individual," rational life plans are not likely to be regrettable because present selves will make responsible plans for their future selves.

One way to evaluate Rawls's interpretation of normal and special psychological stability would be to examine the theories of moral development, the psychological laws, and the sociological generalizations he relies on. Since Rawls has raised doubts about the details of part 3, however, this would be superfluous. What are not are the problems of political education that Rawls's accounts of psychological and political stability presuppose and how the original position orients us toward these problems. Before moving on to political stability, therefore, I want to call attention to the role of the language of games in Rawls's account of psychological stability. I will return to this complex topic later, but I introduce it here because it reveals a dimension of Rawls's theory as a practical response to the problem of psychological stability that is carried over in the later analysis of political stability.

The simile "justice as fairness" rests on the assumption that the more the basic structure of a well-ordered society resembles fair voluntary games, the more likely it is to be just. Justice can never be the same as fairness because political societies, Rawls asserts, are usually not freely chosen, and they depend on a state monopoly over the use of force. Neither of these things is true of voluntary games like chess or baseball. But the basic structure of a political society can be organized to approximate fairness because justice and fairness are both forms of reciprocity. What fairness in games shares with justice in nonvoluntary social practices that people are born into is a higher-level commitment to reciprocity, where reciprocity refers to the absence of arbitrary distinctions and the proper adjudication of competing claims.[19] For example, a fair game of baseball would not vary the number of strikes a batter is allowed during one time at bat based on the batter's religious convictions and would not permit one team's batters to call their own balls and strikes while the other team had to accept the judgment of an umpire. Similarly, a just trial would be based on fixed rules of law that did not discriminate against a defendant based on religion.

In ruling out arbitrary distinctions and specifying what a proper or balanced adjudication of competing claims would be, justice as reciprocity bears some resemblance to fairness as reciprocity. The game simile does not seem to be exerting any undue influence or distorting the account of nonvoluntary institutions and practices. Rawls seems well aware of the dif-

[19] John Rawls, "Justice as Reciprocity," in *Mill: Utilitarianism*, ed. Samuel Gorovitz (Indianapolis: Bobbs-Merrill, 1971), p. 242.

ferences between games and other social practices in which rules specify rights and responsibilities, offices and powers. For example, he does not think the parties in the original position should compete with one another; their rationality is much more self-centered.[20] But there are other features of games that are more problematic and that seem to color Rawls's understanding of psychological stability and, later, political stability.

Before mentioning them, I have to take Rawls's account of psychological stability one step further. When, he argues, individuals recognize that circumstances are such that it is a good thing to be moved by a sense of justice and can act on these moral sentiments, then they will be both autonomous and able to enjoy the good of community. Rawls describes community as a pluralistic "social union of social unions." This social union, however, is not merely an open society in which opportunities to form new voluntary associations abound. It is a political community, he argues, because individuals who have acquired a morality of principles and who value the basic structure and the rich associational life it makes possible will take pleasure in the diverse activities that other members pursue as well as in their own life plans. They will recognize that without the willing cooperation of others permitted by the basic structure, their own associational life and individual plans would not be possible. Rawls goes so far as to say that it is through social union that "each person can participate in the total sum of the realized natural assets of the others."[21] Now, this image of a liberal community seems to go well beyond the tolerant association of associations that Rawls describes as a precondition for psychological stability. There are, as he notes, new elements of affection and friendship implicit in this social union of social unions. Such a social union is stable in a full psychological sense.

> Because such a society is a social union of social unions, it realizes to a preeminent degree the various forms of human activity; and given the social nature of humankind, the fact that our potentialities and inclinations far surpass what can be expressed in any one life, we depend upon the cooperative endeavors of others not only for the means of well-being but to bring to fruition our latent powers. And with a certain success all around, each enjoys the greater richness and diversity of the collective activity. . . . What binds a society's efforts into one social union is the mutual recognition and acceptance of the principles of justice; it is this general affirmation which extends the ties of identification over the whole community and permits the Aristotelian Principle to have its wider effect. Individual and group accomplishments

[20] Rawls, *Theory of Justice*, p. 144.
[21] Ibid., p. 523.

are no longer seen as just so many separate personal goods. Whereas not to confirm our sense of justice is to limit ourselves to a narrow view.[22]

To bring this community to life and explain how individuals will be able to sustain these ties of identification over the whole community, Rawls once again turns to voluntary games.

Like other social practices, he notes, games are organized by rules that specify the end of the game; games permit individual players to participate for a variety of personal reasons; and the social value of a game may be quite different from the value it has for individual participants. But the crucial thing about voluntary games is that regardless of the different motives and purposes individual players may have, they must all share one overriding end: "a good play of the game." This is not just an additional feature of some games. It is, in Weberian terms, an ideal interest of all the players: "The public desire to execute a good and fair play of the game must be regulative and effective if everyone's zest and pleasure is not to languish." What is a good play of the game? At the very least, it depends on the sides being evenly matched so that the best in both sides is brought out, in line with Rawls's Aristotelian principle. There is also an element of mutual respect between the players as they realize the efforts they have all made to prepare for the contest and the concentration they are maintaining in the play of the game. And there is a feeling of being suspended in time as the players are carried along in the flow of the game.[23]

If this is what it takes to build a fully stable "social union of social unions," what does a good play of the game mean in the context of nonvoluntary practices?

In much the same way that players have the shared end to execute a good and fair play of the game, so the members of a well-ordered society have the common aim of cooperating together to realize their own and another's nature in ways allowed by the principles of justice. This collective intention is the consequence of everyone's having an effective sense of justice. Each citizen wants everyone (including himself) to act from principles to which all would agree in an initial situation of equality. This desire is regulative, as the condition of finality on moral principles requires; and when everyone acts justly, all find satisfaction in the very same thing.[24]

---

[22] Ibid., pp. 571–72.

[23] See Mihaly Csikszentmihalyi, *Flow: The Psychology of Optimal Experience* (New York: Harper and Row, 1990). I thank Martin Benjamin for bringing this concept of flow to my attention.

[24] Rawls, *Theory of Justice*, p. 527.

The simile, now really a metaphor, seems to be stretched too far. What does it mean to be evenly matched in a nonvoluntary social practice? And can we realistically expect this to be the case? Metaphors like "leveling the playing field" and "bringing everyone up to the starting line" are misleading, I argue later, because of the way they allow market models of equilibrium to slip back into Rawls's analysis of stability. In these metaphors designed to capture some rough equality of skills and talents, the game is a euphemism for the depoliticized free market of neoclassical economic theory. Rawls explicitly rejects modeling political life on this abstraction,[25] but here it threatens to slip back into his account of psychological stability through the ideal of a good play of the game.

Second, what does it mean for the players to be in the flow of a nonvoluntary social practice? Many, possibly most, voluntary games are officially silent. Time should move along rapidly as the players find a rhythm, and each move or play of the game seems to complement or improve on the last. Long volleys in tennis in which each player pushes the other to the limit seem to capture this idea, but similar things occur in team sports as well—say, soccer. It is not clear, however, what this kind of flow would involve in a nonvoluntary political practice such as parliamentary debate, legislative caucusing, or courtroom arguments. If stability depends on political talk of these and other types, then the silent back-and-forth flow of a voluntary game may not capture what is good about these political contests.[26]

It could be argued that nonvoluntary social practices are more like language games than athletic contests, and in language games the concept of flow is not out of place or misleading. Something like the flow of a good conversation exists when parliamentary debate is lively and to the point, when caucus members speak their minds in the spirit of mutual respect, and when attorneys present forceful, precise arguments in an adversarial procedure. Some flow builds even in less structured political conversations and discussions, and many Socratic dialogues are good examples of this verbal flow. Games do not have to be euphemisms for coercive market exchanges. The dangers of likening political debate and discussion to a flowing Socratic dialogue will have to be postponed briefly until we discuss the particular Socratic method Rawls recommends to guide this kind of conversation. For the moment I only wish to call attention to the way the full psychological stability of a social union seems to depend on bol-

---

25 Ibid., pp. 360–61.

26 To be sure, there is plenty of talk in athletic contests, from "infield chatter" to attempts at outright verbal intimidation. But this kind of talk seems either peripheral to a good play of the game or contrary to it.

stering the individual sense of justice with a game metaphor that may prove to be loaded.[27]

## Political Stability and Political Education

Along with the problem of psychological stability which Rawls now believes too heavily rested on his failure to appreciate certain fundamental features of pluralism and the limitations of practical reason, Rawls has turned his attention to the problem of political stability—not to be confused, he says, with the security of a political regime.

> Let us say that a political conception of justice (in contrast to a political regime) is stable if it meets the following condition: those who grow up in a society well-ordered by it—a society whose institutions are publicly recognized to be just, as specified by that constitution itself—develop a sufficient allegiance to those institutions, that is, a sufficiently strong sense of justice guided by appropriate principles and ideals, so that they normally act as justice requires, provided they are assured that others will act likewise.[28]

As this passage suggests, political stability retains a degree of psychological complexity.[29] As Rawls goes on to elaborate how this sufficiently strong sense of justice will develop, however, it becomes clear that other things are involved besides moral psychology. Certain social preconditions are necessary, and a particular form of "public reason" has to be established.

Let us begin with the social preconditions. For Rawls, "the fact of pluralism" in general refers to the diversity of comprehensive and fundamentally opposed basic moral, religious, and philosophical views of the world that have proliferated in post-Reformation liberal societies. Only the oppressive use of state power has been able to eliminate this other-

---

[27] Of course there are other reasons for objecting to certain kinds of game metaphors, besides those that are market euphemisms, when describing nonvoluntary institutions and practices. This is especially true for sports metaphors. In some contexts these metaphors can reinforce exclusionary practices. This has been true for women in liberal democratic societies, where the use of sports metaphors has reinforced their exclusion from public life. Being unfamiliar with this language, women are tacitly excluded from political conversation. Rawls does not condone this arbitrary exclusion, even though he seems unaware of this aspect of sports language when he relies on baseball as an example of a practice structured according to constitutive rules. See John Rawls, "Two Concepts of Rules," in *Theories of Ethics*, ed. Philippa Foot (New York: Oxford University Press, 1967), p. 163.

[28] John Rawls, "The Domain of the Political and Overlapping Consensus," *New York University Law Review* 64 (May 1989): 239.

[29] Rawls expands on this in *Political Liberalism*, pp. 81–88.

wise "permanent feature of the public culture of democracy" since then.[30] Also, there is little reason to believe that substantive agreement among these opposing comprehensive views is likely to occur through rational inquiry and discussion. Human reason does not appear to be capable of sustaining this kind of "burden."[31] Yet the fact of pluralism is not something we should lament: it enhances the lives of liberal citizens in the same way that the social division of labor does by multiplying the opportunities for cooperative and complementary activities.[32] That there are Kantian liberals, Millian liberals, utilitarians, and religious believers of almost all sorts in modern liberal societies is a fact. Liberal theory should not strive to replace these competing comprehensive doctrines with a new comprehensive moral doctrine, but rather should seek out the common political ground on which the adherents to these conflicting comprehensive views can tolerate one another on fair terms. To do this, "it says on the surface, philosophically speaking."[33]

Mediating between competing comprehensive moral views, however, requires that most of these views already be reasonable. There must be "reasonable pluralism" before there can be a "reasonable overlapping consensus" on principles of justice. Reasonable pluralism refers to the diversity of comprehensive doctrines that "reasonable citizens will affirm" in a liberal democratic culture, and a reasonable overlapping consensus is what public reason can advance when the "fact of reasonable pluralism" exists.[34] Rawls summarizes this complex of ideas in the following way:

> To conclude: given the fact of reasonable pluralism, what the work of reconciliation by public reason does, thus enabling us to avoid reliance on general and comprehensive doctrines, is two things: first, it identifies the fundamental role of political values in expressing the terms of fair social cooperation consistent with mutual respect between citizens regarded as free and equal; and second, it uncovers a sufficiently inclusive concordant fit among political and other values seen in a reasonable overlapping consensus.[35]

To understand political stability, then, we have to understand what Rawls means by free public reason and how the original position establishes this restraining "guiding framework of deliberation and reflection"[36]

30 Rawls, "Domain of the Political and Overlapping Consensus," pp. 234–35.

31 Ibid., pp. 235–36.

32 Rawls, *Theory of Justice*, p. 529.

33 John Rawls, "Justice as Fairness: Political Not Metaphysical," *Philosophy and Public Affairs* 14 (summer 1985): 230–31.

34 Rawls, *Political Liberalism*, p. 36.

35 Ibid., pp. 157–58.

36 Rawls, "Idea of an Overlapping Consensus," p. 16.

within which citizens who disagree about moral, religious, and philosophical issues can sustain a commitment to free and equal citizenship as they continue to practice and believe in their conflicting moral, religious, and philosophical comprehensive doctrines.

Stability for Rawls is no longer a matter of squaring individual moral development in a well-ordered society with the demands of justice as fairness so as to avoid too much free riding, to ensure citizens of mutual compliance, and to foster a "good play of the game." This concept of full psychological stability is too rigid for ensuring stability, given the general fact of pluralism and the limitations or "burdens of judgment."[37] Because psychological stability neglects the facts of pluralism and reasonable pluralism, either it is unrealistically utopian as a criterion for legitimate political reforms or it becomes an invitation to the oppressive use of state power. If liberal theory is to help ensure stability from one generation to the next, it must find more ecumenical methods of teaching citizens with conflicting comprehensive moral views how to separate their political views from their comprehensive moral views when they are deliberating and reflecting on the basic structure of society and its reform. Only then, Rawls argues, is there likely to be a stable overlapping reasonable consensus on the fair terms of social cooperation.

Rawls describes three main elements in such a political consensus among reasonable persons.[38] The first is that certain fundamental individual rights and liberties must not be on the political agenda. A constitutional democracy in which basic rights and liberties can be bargained away or extorted through the political process will make citizens too suspicious of one another. They will be tempted to engage in defensive preemptive strikes. The content and priority of basic rights and liberties must be "fixed, once and for all" so that social cooperation can be established on a "footing of mutual respect" without hostility and suspicion. This seems to be solidly rooted in the public culture of some, though certainly not all, liberal societies.[39] Second, political conflicts and disagreements must be worked out according to a "conception of free public reason." This means that methods of inquiry and standards of evidence used to debate matters of justice must be accessible to common sense and must rely on noncontroversial

[37] "Burdens of reason" in the manuscript, "Justice as Fairness: A Briefer Restatement," becomes "burdens of judgment" in *Political Liberalism*, pp. 54–58, but without substantial change in meaning.

[38] Rawls, "Idea of an Overlapping Consensus," pp. 19–21.

[39] Rawls describes the complex way one such liberty, freedom of speech, has been fixed within American constitutional law in "The Basic Liberties and Their Priority," in *The Tanner Lectures on Human Values*, vol. 3, ed. Sterling M. McMurrin (Salt Lake City: University of Utah Press, 1982), pp. 55–79.

scientific procedures and findings. This is especially true for the state's reasons, which must be simple enough to allay any fears that complexity is masking a comprehensive moral doctrine or mere arbitrariness, whether or not it actually is. Finally, for a stable, overlapping reasonable consensus to exist, the publicly affirmed conception of justice and the idea of "free public reason" that guides its political implementation have to encourage "the cooperative virtues of political life: the virtue of reasonableness and a sense of fairness, a spirit of compromise and a readiness to meet others halfway, all of which are connected with the willingness if not the desire to cooperate with others on political terms that everyone can publicly accept consistent with mutual respect." When these three further conditions are met, then strategic, self-serving, and temporary commitments to justice as fairness and the constitutional regime it enjoins will gradually give way to sincere and stable support. Mutual trust and confidence, Rawls suggests, gradually increase as citizens enjoy "the success of shared cooperative arrangements."[40] The basic structure of society that initially had been accepted as a mere modus vivendi then becomes the object of a stable overlapping consensus.

Although this anticipated growth in trust and confidence depends in part on the development of a normal moral psychology and on what people will tend to feel and do in their everyday lives, the real linchpin in this process, as Rawls says, is the concept of free public reason. Without it the constitutional guarantee of basic rights and liberties will remain a mere modus vivendi. Without these accepted guidelines governing reasoning on public matters, citizens will be uninformed and suspicious of others and the state. Without them citizens will not be able to balance their desire to realize their individual conceptions of the good with their commitment to fair social cooperation. The traditional problem of liberal political education will remain unsolved even if their individual moral psychology is in order.

How does this process work, and what role does the original position play in it? At a minimum, free public reason means that the principles guiding public policies in the name of the public should be publicly known. They cannot depend on the ignorance of citizens for their efficacy as some forms of utilitarianism might. This is the publicity condition Rawls has favored for some time for evaluating any proposed conception of justice. But free public reason also means that these publicly known principles should respect citizens as free persons. They are principles that free and equal citizens would choose. Finally, free public reason implies that the reasons supporting the choice of a public conception of justice and the policies that follow from it must be accessible to common sense and based

---

40 Rawls, "Idea of an Overlapping Consensus," p. 22.

on noncontroversial standards of evidence and procedures. The reasons governing reform, not just the principles chosen by reasonable parties in a hypothetical situation, must be publicly known and acceptable to reasonable persons if citizens are to develop political virtues of compromise and respect the fixed constitutional "essentials" of their society. This is what generates the right kind of support for a well-ordered society.

> The problem of stability is not the problem of bringing others who reject a conception to share it, or to act in accordance with it, by workable sanctions if necessary—as if the task were to find ways to impose that conception on others once we are ourselves convinced it is sound. Rather, as a liberal political conception, justice as fairness relies for its reasonableness in the first place upon generating its own support in a suitable way by addressing each citizen's reason, as explained within its own framework.[41]

As Rawls explains in a footnote, this means the reasons that must be accessible to common sense and based on noncontroversial standards of evidence and scientific procedures are subject to the constraints imposed in the original position.[42] This is what "within its own framework" means.

That it is "the original position as a device of representation"[43] that enables us to know what free public reason requires should come as no surprise. All along Rawls has referred to "reasonable persons" in order to explain what reasonable pluralism presupposes and what a reasonable overlapping consensus involves: agreement among reasonable persons. What does it mean to be a reasonable person? A reasonable person is willing to accept fair rules of cooperation among equals and acknowledge the "burdens of judgment."[44] If you sincerely want to establish such rules and avoid illegitimate state coercion, and if you admit that human reason has certain limitations, then it would be unreasonable for you to insist on anything other than some form of political liberalism to regulate the basic structure of society. How does a reasonable person follow this imperative? By reasoning from the original position. For example, it would be unreasonable to argue for slavery because "it violates principles that would be agreed to in the original position by representatives of persons as free and equal." A reasonable person, then, is someone who knows what will wash in the original position or who knows, Rawls says, this time paraphrasing Thomas Scanlon, what "violates principles that cannot be reasonably rejected by persons who are motivated to find a free and informed basis of

41 Rawls, "Domain of the Political and Overlapping Consensus," p. 247.
42 The slightly revised wording and footnote in *Political Liberalism* occur on p. 143.
43 Rawls, "Domain of the Political and Overlapping Consensus," p. 247 n. 32.
44 Rawls, *Political Liberalism*, p. 94.

willing agreement in political life."[45] Why step behind the veil of ignorance, where you will likely be convinced to accept liberal principles of
justice and legitimacy? Because that is what enables you to be reasonable
on such matters.

In an early review of *A Theory of Justice* Ronald Dworkin argued that the
original position was essential for Rawls's theory because it was a procedural expression of a certain moral conception of the person. "The original position is therefore a schematic representation of a particular mental
process of at least some, and perhaps most, human beings," that is, those
governed by a sense of justice and a capacity to formulate their own conception of a good life. Therefore, to accept reasoning from the original
position is to respect the rights of individuals "to equal concern and respect in the design and administration of the political institutions that
govern them."[46] Dworkin's answer to the question, Why step behind the
veil of ignorance? was that in doing so one affirmed a certain moral conception of the person.

Others, like Thomas Nagel, initially thought the original position might
be shelved for better arguments in favor of Rawls's principles of justice.
The principles themselves, not the method of selecting them, carried the
most moral value for Nagel. The original position only models, but does
not justify, Rawls's "egalitarian liberalism."[47] My interpretation of the
original position is closer to Dworkin's. The original position is not so
easily shed by modern liberal theory—not because it expresses in procedural form a truth about our moral psychology, but rather because it cap-
sulizes a form of abstract reasoning that has entered the public culture:
The original position is a formal humanistic restatement of the Socratic
method of reasoning that experts, clients, and professionals can rely on to
settle their differences.

## Revising the Socratic Method

Thus far I have shown the centrality of the original position for the
Rawlsian problems of psychological and political stability while indicating
their similarity to the traditional problem of liberal political education. I
also have suggested that psychological stability involves a suspicious game
metaphor that is carried over in the later account of political stability. In

45 Ibid., p. 124. For Rawls's view of the similarity between his conception of reasoning
from the original position and Thomas Scanlon's contractualism, see p. 49 n. 2.

46 Ronald Dworkin, "The Original Position," in *Reading Rawls*, ed. Norman Daniels
(New York: Basic Books, n.d.), pp. 25, 50.

47 Thomas Nagel, "Rawls on Justice," in *Reading Rawls*, p. 15.

this section I say more about the original position before returning to the importance of the game metaphor. I explain why it makes sense to think of the original position as a Socratic form of political education, and I suggest how it points beyond the traditional problem of political education that Rawls's concepts of psychological and political stability presuppose to something more akin to what I have called the modern problem of liberal political education.

In his 1957 article "Outline for a Decision Procedure for Ethics," Rawls argues that there is a need for a "heuristic device which is likely to yield reasonable and justifiable principles" that are "embodied in the many dictates of common-sense morality."[48] Rawls then sketches a test for the reasonableness of any particular principle arrived at in this way. If the principle arrived at convinces a large number of competent judges, if it handles anomalous cases better than other adjudicative principles, and if it tends to lead competent judges to give up their considered judgments when they conflict with the principle, then it is reasonable.

Who is to use the heuristic device of explication and the reasonable test? Obviously it would have to be someone familiar with actual disputes like the ones Rawls's article describes in the area of freedom of speech; someone who is familiar with the rulings of competent judges in these cases and also familiar with the inconsistencies and changes in judicial doctrine that new and better principles would correct. Rawls makes it clear that his competent judges are not like Ronald Dworkin's ideal judge, Hercules. They have a judicial character but ordinary intelligence. They make considered judgments, but they do not derive them from a set of preestablished principles. His audience, it seems, are those scholars, legal commentators, and other professionals concerned about the principled consistency of actual judicial decision making. He is offering them a "discipline" for entering legal conversations that is sufficiently modest that it does not irritate practitioners and sufficiently oriented toward practical problems to be useful to them. Although this brief article is terse and its methods are sketchy, it signals Rawls's practical ambition as a mediator of expert social practices.[49]

This political purpose still guides Rawls's philosophical method. At certain times Rawls has described the original position as a device that gives procedural expression to a Kantian moral view of the self that, it appears, needs no further defense.[50] This description is consistent with Dworkin's

---

[48] John Rawls, "Outline for a Decision Procedure in Ethics," *Philosophical Review* 66 (1957): 181.

[49] Rawls reviews the competing doctrines and tests in the area of free speech in his Tanner Lectures, "The Basic Liberties and Their Priority." In the 1950s this was a vehemently contested area of the law.

[50] Rawls, *Theory of Justice*, p. 256.

reading of the original position. But Rawls seems to have abandoned this view for the more situated political conception of reasonableness.[51] The questions are, How does this method advance this political end? and What exactly is the nature of this social cooperation it seeks to advance? Is it simply coordinated activity adequate to overcome the traditional problem of political education, or is the trust and confidence sought *among* citizens *in* the expert authority of others?

We can begin with Rawls's assertion that the original position is an abstract and nonhistorical method. It is nonhistorical in the sense that it does not refer to some previous time or "state of nature" before the establishment of political institutions or civil society in general. It is a method of reasoning we can enter at any time for the purpose of constructing fair principles of social cooperation that would govern the basic structure of our (closed, self-sufficient) society. We need not pretend we are apolitical or prepolitical persons to do this. In fact, the alternative principles of justice we will consider are those given to us by our actual liberal tradition and that make sense to us because they are part of it.

The original position is abstract in the sense that it is an attempt to abstract from the particular situations of those who employ it in order to generalize the familiar idea of cooperation between individuals. That is, although individuals with disagreements over the scope of their political rights or conflicting claims to social resources, say, are interested in achieving some cooperative arrangement for themselves, they may not be able to see beyond this familiar problem. The original position enables them to envision an ideal of social cooperation among all free and equal citizens, not just a cooperative agreement for themselves. "The way in which we think about fairness in everyday life ill-prepares us for the great shift in perspective required for considering the justice of the basic structure itself."[52] The original position has to be abstract if it is to identify a conception of social cooperation that is general enough to respect citizens as free and equal persons, not, for example, as neighbors arguing over who is responsible for the damage from a fallen tree.

It is this abstractness that enables the original position to serve as a political "device of representation." The "parties" in the original position do not represent their own interests: each represents the interests of a free and equal citizen. The conditions Rawls describes as part of the

51 Here I note a parallel with Rawls's method of "reflective equilibrium" in "Justice as Fairness: A Briefer Restatement," pp. 24–25, where he characterizes that method as having the "practical aim" of advancing "civic concord and social cooperation." I have discussed this in "John Rawls and the Political Education of Applied Ethics," *Social Theory and Practice* 11 (fall 1985): 307–54.

52 Rawls, "Kantian Constructivism in Moral Theory," p. 551.

original position, like moderate scarcity, and the constraints placed on reasoning, which include the "veil of ignorance" and the "burdens of judgment," shape how these representative parties will deliberate and reflect. Rawls believes that the conditions and constraints he favors best honor the status of citizens as free and equal persons. For example, because the parties do not know the socioeconomic status of those they represent, the value of political equality will be reflected in the arguments and claims they put forward, and eventually in the principles chosen. For individuals who step behind the veil of ignorance, entrusted with the authority to devise principles of justice, the conditions and constraints that guide their deliberation and reflection enable them to consider how cooperation might be embodied in the basic structure of society for all free and equal citizens. In other words, the abstract and nonhistorical original position serves a Socratic function. It is an ad hominem device in the sense that it takes persons as they are, with only a particularistic understanding of social cooperation, and guides their deliberations and reflections so that they can understand cooperation on a social scale. It makes them trustworthy enough to deliberate over and reflect on the basic structure of society, which will have profound effects on the life chances and desires of all citizens, including themselves.

This means that the parties in the original position and those they represent are actually the same people—you and me, as Rawls likes to say. We view our cooperative arrangements from behind the veil of ignorance and learn to distinguish this view from particular agreements and cooperative arrangements we may make on a more personal level. Rawls sometimes refers to the parties in the original position as trustees, but this should not be taken in a Burkean sense. He also says they "are to reach an agreement on certain principles of justice, and doing this they follow the instructions of those they represent."[53] This statement could also be misleading if we think of the parties as separate from those they are representing. The original position enables you and me to trust ourselves to make choices about the basic structure and in that way still follow our own instructions. Combining the two models of representation, Rawls says, "whether they are citizens acting as deputies for themselves or whether they are trustees, they are free to act in the best interests of whomever they represent within the framework of reasonable constraints embedded in the original position."[54] This otherwise puzzling indifference toward the role of the representative

[53] John Rawls, "Social Unity and Primary Goods," in *Utilitarianism and Beyond*, ed. Amartya Sen and Bernard Williams (Cambridge: Cambridge University Press, 1982), p. 165.
[54] Rawls, "Kantian Constructivism in Moral Theory," p. 548.

makes sense when we realize that the parties in the original position and the citizens they represent are the same persons with different voices.

It is the influence of a cooperative basic structure on the desires of citizens that necessitates this important role for the original position. Rawls regularly emphasizes that justice as fairness does not simply take individual preferences as given. A just basic structure will reshape people's desires and interests. The conditions and constraints of the original position enable the representative parties to distinguish for their constituent selves the difference between their ordinary desires and those desires or "highest-order interests" they have as free and equal citizens.[55] The original position is an attempt to give individuals some distance on their existing desires and preferences so that they can decide which interests the basic structure should favor or discourage. By imagining themselves as parties with the responsibility of representing the highest-order interests of persons through the principles they choose to govern the basic structure of society, they are able to mediate between their social and economic desires and their political needs as free and equal citizens. The original position is the medium or bridge that takes people beyond their immediate nonpublic desires into a situation in which they can look back on those desires from a critical perspective. This perspective is not, Rawls emphasizes, anything like the "impersonal perspective" Thomas Nagel has described. It is, to repeat, the point of view of reasonable persons who are willing to accept fair rules of cooperation among equals and to acknowledge the limitations or "burdens of judgment."[56] The view from behind the veil of ignorance, unlike the "view from nowhere" is always the view "from somewhere" of "persons, individual or corporate."[57]

This interpretation of the original position as a bridging or enabling device of representation that gives persons some critical distance on their existing desires is confirmed by two additional features of it that Rawls has revised since *A Theory of Justice*. The first is the notion of primary goods. In *A Theory of Justice* Rawls described primary goods as simply those things that rational persons want more rather than less of and that are necessary for carrying out one's life plan and realizing one's conception of the good. Without this assumption, Rawls argued, it was not clear that there would be agreement on principles of justice in the original position.[58] In response to several critics, including Nagel, Rawls recognized that the primary goods he in fact favored (income, wealth, power, opportunities,

---

[55] "Highest" is also distinguished from "higher" in *Political Liberalism*, p. 74.
[56] Rawls, *Political Liberalism*, p. 94.
[57] Ibid., p. 116.
[58] Rawls, *Theory of Justice*, p. 62.

rights, liberties, and the bases of self-respect), though not biased toward an individualistic conception of the good, were indeed interpretations of the needs of free and equal democratic citizens. "Primary goods are things needed and required by persons seen in the light of the *political* conception of persons, as citizens who are fully cooperating members of society, and not merely as human beings apart from any normative conception. These goods are things citizens *need* as free and equal persons living a complete life; they are not things it is simply rational to want or desire, or to prefer or even to crave." [59] Furthermore, Rawls claims, "Citizens' needs are objective in a way that desires are not; that is, they express requirements of persons with certain highest-order interests who have a certain social role and status." [60] That social role and status is free and equal citizenship. The primary goods satisfy the objective needs that free and equal citizens have when they are members of a fair system of social cooperation. This revision of the theory of primary goods represents an interpretation of the needs of persons struggling to agree on fair terms of cooperation. It reinforces the function of the original position as a method for distancing oneself from personal desires and particularistic views.

The second additional feature of the original position that confirms its special enabling function is what Rawls describes as full publicity. In *A Theory of Justice* Rawls argued that one of the formal constraints on the choice of principles in the original position was, as I have noted, that they had to be publicly affirmed. [61] Since then he has emphasized the educational importance of a public conception of justice. One dimension of this larger conception of publicity is free public reason, which I have already discussed. In addition, the full justification of justice as fairness must be "publicly known or, better, at least publicly available." [62] Rawls admits that not all citizens will have the time, inclination, or ability to follow the reasoning for justice as fairness all the way through. Even if this is true, however, that the theory is fully available will create a "social milieu" in which "citizens are made aware of and educated to" justice as fairness. [63] Rawls has pushed this idea of an educating social milieu further in *Political Liberalism*. There he argues that citizens, not politicians or government officials, are the primary audience of justice as fairness.

---

[59] Rawls, "Justice as Fairness: A Brieter Restatement," p. 38. More fully, *Political Liberalism*, pp. 187–90.

[60] Rawls, "Social Unity and Primary Goods," p. 172.

[61] Rawls, *Theory of Justice*, p. 133.

[62] Rawls, "Kantian Constructivism in Moral Theory," p. 545.

[63] Ibid., p. 553.

Justice as fairness provides a publicly recognized point of view from which all citizens can examine before one another whether their political and social institutions are just. It enables them to do this by citing what are publicly recognized among them as valid and sufficient reasons singled out by that conception itself. Society's main institutions and how they fit together into one system of social cooperation can be assessed in the same way by each citizen, whatever that citizen's social position or more particular interests.[64]

Later he characterizes this feature of a "political conception of justice" as a "wide role" that gives citizens "a way of regarding themselves that otherwise they would most likely never be able to entertain."[65] "Full publicity" means that the framework for deliberation and reflection embodied in the original position should be available so that citizens can learn how "to justify their institutions to one another." In Socratic terms, the original position is not merely addressed to citizens in a language they can understand but is designed to impress on them the objective character of their political needs and enable them to carry on the process of justification with one another. In other words, the original position is not just a method for arriving at guidelines for public reason; by virtue of its modeling of reasonableness and full autonomy, it is a central part of what it means to reason about things that free and equal citizens hold in common.

To eliminate some of the vagueness in this wide role, Rawls suggests in *Political Liberalism* that "to check whether we are following public reason we might ask: how would our argument strike us presented in the form of a supreme court opinion? Reasonable? Outrageous?"[66] Judges, Rawls maintains, are exemplars of public reason when they bracket their "own personal morality" and "the ideals and virtues of morality" in general. Their judgments "must appeal to the political values they think belong to the most reasonable understanding of the public conception and its political values of justice and public reason." When they judge this way, they participate in the "wide, or educative, role of public reason."[67] As unusual as this approach may be in current practice, it nonetheless reveals Rawls's sympathy for judicial reasoning, something that we noticed in his early work and that is reminiscent of Mill's politics of emulation. What makes free public reason reasonable, then, in addition to its commitment to political equality and its recognition of the "burdens of reason," is a judicial frame of mind.

[64] Rawls, *Political Liberalism*, p. 9.
[65] Ibid., p. 71.
[66] Ibid., p. 254.
[67] Ibid., p. 236.

This sympathy for the educative importance of professional styles of reasoning manifests itself in another aspect of the original position that Rawls in *A Theory of Justice* calls the "four-stage sequence," and by revisiting this argument we can gain a fuller understanding of this seemingly atavistic praise of exemplary judicial reasoning.

The four-stage sequence is a way of formulating issues and conflicts so that they are understood at a particular level in the policymaking process. The sequence is not chronological: it is designed to help us identify the appropriate place to voice our needs and introduce reforms. In mastering the original position citizens learn what information is relevant and what kinds of arguments they can make given the kind of claim or grievance they have. Economic claims that would be the basis of proposed reforms, Rawls argues, belong at the legislative stage, where citizens assume the perspective of a representative legislator who must be apprised of society's demographic contours and socioeconomic trends. These claims would include things like workers' demands for occupational safety, consumers' demands for stricter product liability laws, and capitalists' demands for subsidies, bailouts, and tax abatements. When justifying reforms of this sort to each other in terms of objective needs behind the veil of ignorance, citizens might adopt the perspective of a reform-minded legislator, but the arguments themselves would have to be convincing to economists, labor lawyers, and other planners.

Other disputes and concerns, like those over the scope of civil liberties and civil rights, require intervention in policymaking at the level of constitutional reform, and here the appropriate perspective is that of the delegate whose horizon extends further than the legislator's and excludes even the aggregate data legislators consider. But again, even though the arguments are made by citizens to other citizens from the hypothetical perspective of a delegate to a constitutional convention, the content of the arguments must be acceptable to constitutional lawyers, legal philosophers, and political theorists. They set the standards these citizens will want to meet in making their arguments to one another. Finally, at the other end of the spectrum, claims against criminal behavior or for welfare entitlements should be made before the proper judicial or administrative authorities, and the standards of sound argument will once again be determined professionally even though they are to be made among citizens.[68]

The four-stage sequence is not just a road map for reformers and those with grievances or claims. It enables citizens to identify the level at which they must make their case and the language appropriate to that level.

[68] Rawls, *Theory of Justice*, pp. 195–201.

Should they take their case to an administrative law judge or a local magistrate? Should they lobby, campaign, or circulate petitions? Should they document their research or cite the relevant constitutional provisions? The answers to these questions depend on where in the policymaking process they can get the best hearing. Sometimes it is in court under procedures of due process that protect individual rights relatively well and follow "black letter" law where it exists. At other times the setting is more administrative, and there due process guarantees are less well established and appeals to discretionary policy judgments more effective. Sometimes new legislation is the most likely remedy, and in other cases a constitutional amendment is necessary. Of course, none of this is permanently fixed. Which process or forum is appropriate will depend on a variety of factors. The point is that the original position, when understood as a four-stage sequence, has the power to orient citizens toward one policy arena or another. This is a very serious matter given the different obstacles facing citizens at these four levels of policymaking, the very different guarantees and protections they have within them, and the professional standards of sound argument that vary from one level to another. The original position as a framework for deliberation and reflection does not teach citizens to make arguments to one another but teaches them to make arguments against one another in the appropriate terms before the appropriate officials. The original position is not the exclusive "forum of principle,"[69] it is a method for orienting citizens toward alternative policy arenas and policymaking levels with their respective professional languages.

Another way to understand this feature of the original position is to interpret the four-stage sequence as a method for specifying political membership. Rawls's ideal citizens are not free and equal political members *simpliciter*. Sometimes they must make their arguments to an administrative official who enjoys wide discretion. In that case their membership is much more restricted than if they were litigants in a civil suit. Sometimes they must marshal their strength to reform the constitution, and the obstacles they face are much more severe than those facing legislative reformers at the local level. Leaving aside justifiable inequalities in the primary goods, the sense in which they are free to campaign for constitutional change as equal members of political society is not the same as the sense in which they are free to lobby for legislative change. Even within Rawls's scheme, it is clear that membership varies dramatically from one level to the next. It may be that all citizens in a well-ordered liberal democratic society are

---

[69] Ronald Dworkin, "The Forum of Principle," *New York University Law Review* 56 (May–June 1981): 469–518.

free and equal, but the kind of freedom and equality they have will vary depending on where they "stand" in the policymaking process and what language they have acquired.

We tend to think of political membership in terms of geographical districts. Although this division remains important, membership is also divided along institutional lines. Citizens are members of institutional clientele groups, lobbying groups, and other constituencies. One of the first questions the parties in the original position must ask one another is where their dispute belongs. What membership group is the relevant one for deliberating and reflecting on this kind of issue or conflict? Although the methods of reasoning in the original position should be publicly available to all citizens so that they can justify their principles of reform to one another, the four-stage sequence suggests that the language they use should be appropriate to a particular stage. When we think about our differences as trustees and citizens, we must also think about the kinds of arguments that constitutional delegates, legislators, judges, or administrators will want to hear given the particular stage in which our differences fall and the standards of professional argument the appropriate officials will accept.

If this is a plausible reading of the four-stage sequence, then the problem of political education that the original position addresses is not just a matter of getting citizens to appreciate the difference between nonpublic forms of cooperation and cooperation at the level of the basic structure of society. The four-stage sequence points beyond the need for a secure sense of justice that will stabilize this abstract form of social cooperation. It addresses the need for a more differentiated form of political education that will enable citizens to recognize how policymaking works and how to engage in appropriate discussion. The four-stage sequence does not contain any answers to how citizens will learn to trust the judgments of the delegates, legislators, judges, and administrators they are arguing before, but it does suggest the need for some kind of trust in their standards of judgment. This is reinforced, as we will see, by the functional account of government Rawls gives and the relatively scant attention he pays to common modes of political deliberation, in contrast to extraordinary acts of civil disobedience.

To conclude this part of my interpretation of the original position, I will call attention to Rawls's own characterization of this method as an example of pure procedural justice. This will bring us back to the problem of metaphor and how it contributes to the enabling and educating force of the original position.

In *A Theory of Justice* Rawls argues that the original position is one example of pure procedural justice. "The idea of the original position is to set up a fair procedure so that any principles agreed to will be just. The aim is to use the option of pure procedural justice as a basis of theory."[70] The original position, like an honest betting game, leads to a just outcome (the choice of just principles), even though what counts as a just outcome is not specified prior to and independent of the procedures themselves. Unlike a utilitarian procedure, which begins by defining justice in terms of a particular conception of the good, then chooses principles that will maximize the good, the reason Rawls's principles of justice are indeed just is that they are chosen under certain conditions and constraints that ensure the justness of the procedure of deliberation and reflection. This does not mean that what the parties choose in the original position is just, whatever the consequences. The consequences matter enormously to Rawls, and that is why the background conditions, the constraints, and the alternatives to be chosen from have to be so carefully spelled out. But none of this negates the importance of pure proceduralism as an explanation for the value of the original position. A procedure that respects citizens as free and equal persons capable of acting on a sense of justice is one, Rawls argues, that we would prefer over other forms of justice (for example, a criminal trial) that begin with some preestablished or dominant end (the determination of guilt or innocence) that procedures (for example, the rules of evidence) are constructed to realize.

The most familiar pure procedure, and the one that seems to guide Rawls's thinking in this area, is the economic model of a free market. Buyers and sellers, left to themselves, will usually settle on mutually acceptable terms of trade so long as competition exists, barriers to entry are relatively low, and other sources of imperfect competition are controlled by government. The assumption of this market model is that economic life can reach a stable equilibrium according to its own laws and that politics is a necessary, coercive intrusion that must be relied on to rid this procedure of any impurities. Rawls uncritically accepts this model of economics and politics. The principles he considers political principles (fair equality of opportunity, the difference principle, and the just savings principle) are to be chosen at the legislative stage behind a partial veil of ignorance after constitutional principles fixing civil rights and liberties are in place and a system of very wide property ownership is guaranteed. In this free marketplace of ideas and property, Rawls believes, legislative political principles will not have to be relied on very much. This is especially true for the difference principle. It will not often come into play, because

[70] Rawls, *Theory of Justice*, p. 136.

in a property-owning democracy with smoothly functioning markets and open political assemblies, departures from equality will not be great.[71]

The hard question is, Do these assumptions about politics and economics implicit in the market model also affect the meaning of the original position itself (not just the content of the principles chosen there) as a pure procedure? One could argue that the model implies that parties in the original position will deliberate and reflect on the terms of fair cooperation in a manner that is supposedly independent of or prior to the operations of political power. Their deliberation and reflection are free and uncoerced. This sounds like what Rawls wants; the veil of ignorance protects them from such unwanted influence. If we follow this metaphor (deliberation and reflection in the original position are a free exchange among equal citizens) and the arguments and discussions in the original position begin to tilt too far in favor of one group or another, to the point where some voices are prematurely silenced, then political constraints may be needed. Gag rules and special nonharassment rules may have to be added to the customary rules of order so that the process of reform can proceed. Like the difference principle, these political adjustments should not often be necessary. Open debate in the original position and fair equality of opportunity so that all citizens' views are represented should be enough to ensure a pure procedure. Only occasionally will corrective measures have to be taken. As I discuss later Rawls uses the example of a professional sports draft in which the team with the worst record gets to pick first to illustrate the place of the difference principle alongside fair equality of opportunity,[72] and the same kind of adjustment might be made in maintaining the original position itself as a pure procedure. Some parties would be invited or encouraged to speak first during deliberation and reflection so that their softer voices are guaranteed a hearing.

What is the primary weakness of the original position as a form of free-market proceduralism? Just as politics plays a misleading secondary role in the market model of classical and neoclassical economic theory, so too is politics understated in Rawls's characterization of the original position as a form of pure (adjusted) procedural justice. Pure procedure behind the veil of ignorance is misleading because it strongly implies that power is exercised only as an extraordinary measure to make sure all voices are heard under generally very favorable conditions for deliberation and reflection. Ideas, arguments, deliberation, and discussion should be insulated

71 Ibid., pp. 265–84, and "Justice as Fairness: A Briefer Restatement," pt. 4. Also, Richard Krouse and Michael McPherson, "Capitalism, 'Property-Owning Democracy,' and the Welfare State," in *Democracy and the Welfare State*, ed. Amy Gutmann (Princeton: Princeton University Press, 1988).

72 Rawls, "Justice as Fairness: A Briefer Restatement," p. 37.

from politics as much as possible, and only when necessary should political corrections be made in the deliberative process framed by the original position. In fact, just as the so-called free market depends on a complex political system to establish particular property relations, liabilities, and rights, so too does the framework of deliberation and reflection called the original position presuppose an existing set of power relations. It is not an accident of nature that some voices are less audible than others and some parties more inclined to speak. To make this criticism stick will require that we listen very carefully to the dialogues organized by the original position between justice as fairness and its major rivals.

## Hearing Voices

Finding your own voice and speaking for yourself, especially in democratic politics, is hard to do. This may sound counterintuitive, and in one sense it is. Democratic politics, including what Rawls calls constitutional or liberal democracy, prides itself on letting its citizens speak for themselves.

Finding your own voice is indeed difficult, however, and one reason is the way we have neglected the subtleties and nuances of voice.

> Moreover, in real life as well we very keenly and subtly hear all these nuances in the speech of people surrounding us, and we ourselves work very skillfully with all these colors on the verbal palette. We very sensitively catch the smallest shift in intonation, the slightest interruption of voices in anything of importance to us in another person's practical everyday discourse. All those verbal sideward glances, reservations, loopholes, hints, thrusts do not slip past our ear, are not foreign to our own lips. All the more astonishing, then, that up to now all this has found no precise theoretical cognizance, nor the assessment it deserves![73]

Furthermore, finding your own voice always will be hard, if not impossible, if you assume that you have or should have only one voice. To take an obvious case, surely the voice that suits you in the marketplace is not the voice you feel at home with when speaking with your family on any number of sensitive subjects. You must always find your own voice in a particular context, whether the classroom, the courtroom, the selling floor, or the parlor. Therefore one thing that makes it hard is the need to distinguish between these contexts and use the right tone and accent within

[73] Mikhail Bakhtin, *Problems of Dostoevsky's Poetics*, trans. Caryl Emerson (Minneapolis: University of Minnesota Press, 1984), p. 201.

your own repertoire of voices. I take as strong evidence of this choice the regret and even shame we feel when we use the wrong tone of voice, even though we know it is one of our own.

In democratic politics this problem of sorting through our repertoire of voices is further complicated by built-in tensions. Ideally, democratic citizens are supposed to be strong advocates for their own interests but be willing to compromise with the opposition. Ideally, they are to accept norms of procedural fairness while striving for outcomes that are also substantively just.[74] Because democratic politics is built around these conflicting expectations and values, our democratic political voice must be capable of sounding impartial, judicious, and fair-minded at the same time as it is committed and adversarial. For example, when we give voice to our own interests at the expense of our adversaries, we do not want to be deaf to the value of procedural due process. A sound democratic character, again ideally, enables us to take stock of the demands of self-interest and still be moved by a sense of fairness.

Because it is hard to monitor ourselves in this way, democratic politics relies on a complicated division of labor. For example, political party officials, litigants, and lobbyists usually speak in adversarial tones; labor mediators, hearing officers, and other professionals are responsible for keeping alive compromise and procedural due process. But this is only a partial solution. If democratic politics is to avoid divisiveness on one side and a tyranny of professionals on the other, democratic citizens individually have to master these built-in tensions. This is not just a matter of finding the most efficient or most comfortable mix of procedural fairness and strong advocacy. Resolving the tension in one of these ways would only strike others as a mark of confusion or duplicity. Rather, finding your own democratic political voice seems to entail finding a voice that respects the opposing values and expectations built into democratic politics without trying to resolve or dissolve these tensions once and for all.

These tensions are heightened by yet another unavoidable feature of democratic politics. At the same time that democratic citizens cannot speak in a single voice, they must exercise power over themselves, and this requires considerable confidence. This is a problem not just for democracy as a whole, but for individual democratic citizens who feel the contrary pulls of procedural fairness and substantive justice. Caught between the competing expectations and values of democratic politics, they find it difficult to speak with confidence; yet to make themselves heard this is precisely what they must do. Understood in this sense, the challenge of demo-

[74] The persistent doctrine of substantive due process in jurisprudence testifies to this built-in tension.

cratic politics is not a matter of forcing yourself to sit through endless evening meetings. Democracy does not require heroic efforts at participation at any price. The particular challenge of democracy I am emphasizing is learning to come to terms with the competing demands of democracy so that neither substantive justice nor procedural fairness gains a permanent advantage over the other, *and* to do this in a sometimes violent, often unpredictable atmosphere where self-assurance is a discomforting necessity. These pressures on individual democratic citizens are enormous, and they make finding one's own voice a continuing challenge. They require what I call in part 3 political poise.

Rawls tells us that the original position is an enabling framework of deliberation and reflection. It enables citizens to agree as free and equal persons on reasonable patterns of social cooperation within nonvoluntary social practices that are similar to the cooperative rules of voluntary social practices, but more general and abstract than the voluntary forms of cooperation they are familiar with in their personal lives.[75]

How do the arguments leading up to this agreement sound? Are there forced confessions and stonewalling silences? Do participants ignore certain voices and precipitously trust others? Are some emotions more palatable and others filtered out? To address these questions, it is first necessary to distinguish in Rawls between what I will call simple and complex dialogues.

Simple dialogue is, figuratively speaking, spatially organized. The participants take up different positions vis-à-vis each other, and the tension between them manifests itself along lines of argument. As the lines are sketched, the views and counterviews of the opposing figures produce a shift in their horizons, and in some cases a fusing of horizons. In simple dialogue the opposing figures testify to what they have seen. When they challenge or cross-examine, they look for inconsistencies and gaps in the story that has been told. The motive force in simple dialogue is the question. It is by asking questions, not by giving answers, that simple dialogues move ahead. Gadamer has developed this interpretation of dialogue the most fully.

> It is of the essence of the question to have sense. Now sense involves direction. Hence the sense of the question is the direction in which alone the answer can be given if it is to be meaningful. A question places that which is questioned within a particular perspective. The emergence of the question opens up, as it were, the being of the object. Hence the logos that sets out this opened-up being is already an answer. Its sense lies in the sense of the question.

75 Rawls, "Justice as Reciprocity," pp. 242–68.

Among the greatest insights given us by Plato's account of Socrates is that, contrary to the general opinion, it is more difficult to ask questions than to answer them.[76]

Notice how much spatial imagery is packed into this small passage ("direction," "places," "perspective," "opens up," and "lies"). In part it is the result of Gadamer's belief that the reader's visual encounter with the text is a model for other forms of interpersonal dialogue. The questions the reader poses to the text are what determine the shared meaning that emerges, just as the questions Socrates poses determine the direction of the responses he receives. But one does not have to accept Gadamer's ontological assumptions about the act of reading to agree that this kind of simple dialogue, at least as an ideal, captures a variety of cooperative human encounters. Simple dialogue is not simple in the sense of being uncomplicated. It is simple in the sense that the figures' views meet within a single manifold, fuse or glance off one another, with consequences that can be tracked for a time, if not predicted. The pathways of simple dialogues can be very convoluted.

Competitive games are a natural metaphor for illustrating how simple dialogues work. They can be intricate, and usually they are vividly spatial. They pit characters against one another in a contest designed to identify winners and losers. Each move is based on seeing what the other side has done or is about to do. And like a game in which we can say there has been a good play of the game, in a good simple dialogue the conversation is uncoerced but each side's position has been vigorously put to the test. No one has been forced to confess or boxed into a corner and obliged to dissemble. The dialogues in Sophocles' *Oedipus the King* and Shakespeare's *King Lear* are examples of coerced simple dialogues. There is very little alternation of speaking and listening, there is little mutual respect, and the results that follow from bullying and threatening are tragic for both speaker and listener.[77] The same is true in games when a player uses slander and humiliation to gain an advantage. Courtroom questioning, perhaps the paradigm of simple dialogue, can go bad in this sense, but it does not have to. Witnesses do not have to be badgered or reputations slandered, and honesty need not be questioned, although this usually does happen.

In contrast to simple dialogue, complex dialogue is voice based. The speakers are—or at least try to be—aware of the changing tones, the inflec-

[76] Hans-Georg Gadamer, especially his *Truth and Method* (New York: Seabury Press, 1975), p. 326.
[77] Aaron Fogel, "Coerced Speech and the Oedipus Dialogue Complex," in *Rethinking Bakhtin: Extensions and Challenges*, ed. Gary Saul Morson and Caryl Emerson (Evanston, Ill.: Northwestern University Press, 1989), pp. 173–96.

tions, the phrasing, the accents, and the silences that inform the conflict. In addition, the interplay between the speakers' voices is more complex than that between the opposing positions in a simple dialogue because often each character has more than one voice. This complexity is not a liability or a matter of inconsistency or ambivalence: the richness of a complex dialogue is a product of the interplay of the multiple voices each character has. Whereas we (readers and interlocutors) strive for a single view or the most consistent set of views in a simple dialogue, in a complex dialogue the participants explore their different voices, cultivate new sounds, and in this way develop themselves. The most important feature of complex dialogue is the way it constitutes the character of those who learn to participate in it. By engendering new voices and exploring differences through impersonation and improvisation, complex dialogue can be a creative method.[78] Whereas simple dialogue attempts to eliminate inconsistencies and fuse horizons into a unified view of the whole, complex dialogue ideally is unfinished and remains open to new voices. The *Crito* is an example of a complex dialogue that works. By giving new, somewhat disappointed parental voice to some of his political views through the "Laws," Socrates enables Crito to hear what he otherwise would miss, and in the process Socrates' own resolve in this particular situation is strengthened. The alternative, to repress dissonant voices, only threatens to deepen conflicts and weaken political character on all sides.

In a good complex dialogue, or what Bakhtin calls active, internally persuasive, and double-voiced dialogue, the speakers use several voices, and the way these external and internal voices set each other off constitutes their characters. Sometimes one person will be reminded by another of what he or she has said even though the person has forgotten or repressed those words. The dialogue then depends on the interplay between the speaker's temporarily lost or interior voice, the present voice, and the tentative suggestions of the interlocutor.

> Everywhere there is an intersection, consonance, or interruption of rejoinders in the open dialogue by rejoinders in the heroes' internal dialogue. Everywhere a specific sum total of ideas, thoughts, and words is passed through several unmerged voices, sounding differently in each. The object of authorial aspirations is certainly not this sum total of ideas in itself, as something neutral and identical with itself. No, the object is precisely the passing

---

[78] See Martha Minow, *Making All the Difference: Inclusion, Exclusion, and American Law* (Ithaca: Cornell University Press, 1990), for an account of how justice can be "engendered" in the context of official violence through dialogical judicial decision making. I discuss Minow's work in the next chapter.

of a theme through many and various voices, its rigorous and, so to speak, ir-revocable multi-voicedness and vari-voicedness.[79]

The aim of the author is to bring this polyphonic dialogue into being by ac-tively parodying or accenting the second voices that characters draw on as constitutive sources of their own selves. This leads Bakhtin to suggest that Dostoevsky enables his characters to speak their own minds; he does not put words in their mouths but rather allows them to find their own voices: "In dialogue a person not only shows himself outwardly, but he becomes for the first time that which he is—and, we repeat, not only for others but for himself as well." [80] It is not easy to imagine writing a dialogue in which your characters literally take on a life of their own. It is too redolent of the sorcerer's apprentice. But if we concentrate on social dialogues instead of the novel, what Bakhtin may mean here is that complex dialogue is a process of character formation in which self-disclosure through complex social interactions can never be prescripted. Complex dialogue enables those who participate in it to learn to speak for themselves using words that can be neither entirely of their own making nor preordained for them.

The most important dialogue in Rawls's theory is between the social contract tradition and utilitarianism.[81] This dialogue is conducted on two levels. On one level Rawls raises objections to classical and average utili-tarianism as rivals to the theory of justice as a whole, not just the two principles of justice as fairness and their accompanying priority rules. This encounter is more like a one-sided debate than a dialogue. On a sec-ond level, he asks whether utilitarian principles of distribution would be chosen in the original position over some or all of the specific principles of justice as fairness that he favors.[82] The debate between contractualism and utilitarianism on what I have called the first level is indeed too one-sided to convince anyone who does not already share Rawls's most basic assumptions; on the second level it is more dialogical in both the simple and complex senses I have just described.

First the debate. As a "public political conception" of justice, to use Rawls's phrase, utilitarianism does not have a coherent and humane view

[79] Bakhtin, *Problems of Dostoevsky's Poetics*, p. 265.

[80] Ibid., p. 252.

[81] The characters in a dialogue can be identified in abstract generic terms (e.g., utilitari-anism), and the "contexture" in which they speak can be traced using deictic words, as in Rawls's recurrent use of "then" and "now" and his references to arguments made behind the veil of ignorance. See Jochen Mecke, "Dialogue in Narration (the Narrative Principle)," in *The Interpretation of Dialogue*, ed. Tullio Maranhão (Chicago: University of Chicago Press, 1990), pp. 195–215.

[82] This approach to utilitarianism is implicit in *A Theory of Justice*, and Rawls makes it explicit in "Justice as Fairness: A Briefer Restatement," pp. 67–69.

of what it means to be a cooperating member of a political society. It is not merely that utilitarianism does not take seriously the differences between persons or mistakes impersonality for impartiality.[83] Average utilitarianism is not, according to Rawls, a teleological theory, and therefore it is not vulnerable to the objection that in some circumstances a minority may be required to sacrifice its basic liberties (or other "primary goods") for the sake of greater overall utility.[84] What unites the two otherwise very different forms of utilitarianism is their common failure to value fellow citizens' need to settle on fair terms of cooperation.

Classical utilitarianism, according to Rawls, is a crude administrative theory that treats individuals as if they were merely separate lines along which pleasure or happiness can be achieved. This is not the perspective of a fellow participant in a social practice, but that of an administrator designing social practices for others.[85] The principle of average utility, he argues, is less crude but perhaps even more deeply flawed. Instead of artificially separating persons for the sake of more effective administration, the principle requires that we construct a fictitious average person with no coherent life plan against which to judge the meaningfulness of the primary goods that would give "it" pleasure or happiness.[86] Once again, the ideal of fair social cooperation plays no role in the theory.

These debates with utilitarianism are never fully joined in Rawls's work. The more powerful opposing utilitarian theories such as Derek Parfit's, which reject Rawls's conception of a person but not all ideals of social cooperation, are not given much of a hearing; because they rest on controversial metaphysical claims about personhood, Rawls argues, they can and should be avoided in political theory.[87]

The real dialogue with utilitarianism begins on Rawls's home court, the original position. If we accept the original position, including the theory of "primary goods," as a procedural expression of what it means to be a person engaged in a set of ongoing social practices, Rawls suggests, we can then engage utilitarian principles of justice on moral rather than merely administrative ground.

Rawls's most persuasive arguments against utilitarianism in the original position are less technical and depend on our viewing the principles of justice as fairness as a set that works together. The parties in the original position, he argues, look into the future and consider, first, Will it be

---

[83] Rawls, *Theory of Justice*, pp. 183–92.

[84] Ibid., pp. 563–66.

[85] Rawls, "Justice as Reciprocity," pp. 260–63.

[86] Rawls, *Theory of Justice*, pp. 173–74.

[87] Rawls, "Justice as Fairness: Political Not Metaphysical," p. 242 n. 24, and *Political Liberalism*, p. 31 n. 34.

hard for them to remain active and loyal members of a utilitarian society if somewhere down the road their basic rights and liberties are restricted for the sake of the material well-being of others? Rawls calls this the problem of "the strains of commitment." Second, and closely related, they ask, Will the future institutions and practices enjoined by utilitarianism be adequately stable in a political and psychological sense? That is, will utilitarianism as a public conception of justice encourage political virtues, make public decision making accessible to ordinary citizens, and fix the "constitutional essentials" of society in an acceptable way "once and for all"? Rawls argues that the parties in the original position will favor the two principles of justice on both these scores. They will feel more confident as trustees for free and equal citizens if they choose justice as fairness, for two reasons. (1) The lexical priority of the first principle of equal liberty and the principle of fair equality of opportunity over the difference principle will avoid the severe strain on the commitments of members of society that utilitarian trade-offs between liberty and economic goods might produce. And (2) justice as fairness will constitute an environment within which there is a greater chance for stable reform because utilitarianism cannot be endorsed as a public conception of justice without undermining the motivational basis of its own support.[88]

This exchange with utilitarianism, from behind the veil of ignorance, is what I have called a simple dialogue, and Rawls appears to win hands down. But things are not nearly as clear-cut when it comes to weighing utilitarianism against Rawls's most controversial and, many would argue, most important principle, the difference principle. The choice between the difference principle and some qualified utilitarian principle, possibly that of average utility joined with some guaranteed social minimum, is also conducted from behind the veil of ignorance. But this is a more complex dialogue in which voice plays a vital role.

To be sure, there are rational arguments for the difference principle that rely on assumptions about adequate social minima, unnecessarily high social maxima, and the irrelevance of risk aversion, but they are inconclusive.[89] The case for the difference principle depends on the notion that in the distribution of social and economic "primary goods" the long-term expectations of the least advantaged members of society should be taken into account in a special way. We should begin from the benchmark of equal citizenship, and the only permissible inequalities in social and economic primary goods are those that enhance the long-term expectations

[88] The problems of the strains of commitment and stability are treated in tandem early in *A Theory of Justice*, in section 29. Stability is then given a fuller psychological analysis in section 76.

[89] Rawls, *Theory of Justice*, pp. 150–58.

of the least advantaged to be equal citizens. Because their voices are not likely to be heard as clearly in the political process as the voices of those with greater resources—through no fault of their own—special attention should be paid to their long-term expectations behind the veil of ignorance. In *A Theory of Justice* Rawls tends to talk about the primary goods in apolitical terms as necessary means to whatever a rational person conceives to be the good.[90] This aspect of the theory of primary goods has been corrected, and the primary goods are redescribed as the goods "citizens" need to realize their rational life plans.[91] But the more general point remains. The instructions that representatives of the least advantaged receive are intentionally open-ended. The representative, Rawls says, must ask "which combination of primary goods it would be rational for [the representative individual from the least advantaged class] to prefer." This depends on the representative's "intuitive capacities" and "rational prudence," not on paternalistic "moral judgments."[92] The least advantaged must have their own representatives who can articulate the long-term expectations of people who typically do not have the resources that make it worth their while to conceptualize and value their long-term political interests over short-term material gains.[93] As we deliberate and reflect on the way social and economic primary goods will be distributed, we must make a special effort to hear the political voices of the least advantaged.

This does not mean trying to imagine how much representative members of the least advantaged class would want, given what other people have. Rawls makes it clear that decisions in the original position are not based on relative comparisons of well-being.[94] Rather, the original position encourages us to ask what the objective needs of equal citizens would be and then to voice these needs at the appropriate time in the "four-stage sequence" of public policymaking.[95]

Rawls restates this plea for special consideration based on the worth of political liberty in several ways.[96] He describes the difference principle as a

[90] Ibid., pp. 90–95.

[91] Rawls, "Social Unity and Primary Goods," p. 161, and generally, "The Priority of Right and Ideas of the Good," *Philosophy and Public Affairs* 17 (fall 1988): 251–76, and *Political Liberalism*, lecture 5.

[92] Rawls, *Theory of Justice*, p. 94.

[93] See Joshua Cohen and Joel Rogers, *On Democracy: Toward a Transformation of American Society* (New York: Penguin Books, 1983), chap. 3, for a clear summary of this structural problem in what they call a capitalist democracy. The same problem, although perhaps not to the same degree, would still arise in Rawls's "property-owning democracy."

[94] Rawls, *Theory of Justice*, p. 144.

[95] Ibid., pp. 195–201.

[96] For criticism of Rawls's initial distinction between liberty and the worth of liberty in *A Theory of Justice*, see Norman Daniels, "Equal Liberty and Unequal Worth of Liberty," in *Reading Rawls*, pp. 253–82. For Rawls's response, see *Political Liberalism*, p. 325.

principle of fraternity and says it symbolizes the sense in which individual talents and skills can be thought of as social assets rather than private property.[97] Rawls has taken heavy criticism for such claims, and he has responded by emphasizing the priority of equal liberty in the theory.[98] Yet the dialogue is not neutral with respect to the long-term interests of the least advantaged.

The most important voice, to be sure, is the voice of representative members of the least advantaged class. This is not merely a sympathetic, farsighted facsimile of the typical member of that class. It is also one of the inner voices Rawls believes belong to all liberal democratic citizens who think of themselves as continuous persons over time in search of political self-respect and meaningful work understood in terms of a personal career. It is not the only inner voice that plays a role in the dialogue between contractualism and restricted average utilitarianism at this point in the theory, however. Not only is the voice of the least advantaged accented and rephrased in a more convincing way by their representatives, but the already powerful voices of the more advantaged are modulated without being repressed. These are the familiar voices that have arisen against policies like equal funding for public education, national health insurance, and state-subsidized child care. Contesting the voice of the representative member of the least advantaged class from another quarter are the voices of future generations, reminding democratic citizens that just as their parents saved for them, so they should save for their children and their children's children. Applying the difference principle to distribution between generations would result in a rate of savings that tended to zero, and so an alternative perspective representing "family lines, say, with ties of sentiment between successive generations" is called up.[99] The original position can be interpreted as a method designed for citizens who individually are struggling to come to terms with these three conflicting inner voices.

Let me summarize this interpretation of the original position as a medium of inner dialogue up to this point. You and I, before entering the original position, are confronted with a debate between justice as fairness and utilitarianism. The debate seems to clearly favor the former so long as we accept certain assumptions about cooperation and the primacy of the basic structure as the subject of a theory of justice. Then the focus shifts to the original position, which preserves these assumptions about social cooperation and moral personhood but introduces others designed to blend

---

[97] Rawls, *Theory of Justice*, pp. 101–5.

[98] Rawls, "Basic Liberties and Their Priority."

[99] Rawls, *Theory of Justice*, p. 292. Rawls has altered this argument in *Political Liberalism*, p. 274.

reasonableness and rationality,[100] and a dialogue begins. Initially a simple dialogue with classical and average utilitarianism on one side and the principles of justice as fairness on the other favors the latter, but gradually the dialogue becomes more complex as the difference principle takes on greater importance for the theory. Rawls tries to downplay this importance by emphasizing the need to evaluate the theory as a whole—all the principles of justice as fairness taken together and their priority rules— but there is no getting around the fact that the difference principle gives social cooperation its distinct identity in the theory. It is at this point that the nuances of voice become much more important. Rawls argues that the view from behind the veil of ignorance has to be coupled with sensitivity to the voicelessness of the least advantaged in political debates and discussions where social and economic resources are distributed unequally. But by introducing this new voice, he also activates both the voices of those who would object in the name of their freedom to develop their own talents and skills with the property they control and the voices of those who would be disadvantaged in the future by reductions in current savings and investment. The former would argue that even though they inherited or acquired their fortune through no effort of their own, they have made good use of it and now have organized their lives around the expectation that things will stay roughly the same. Don't we, they say, have legitimate expectations too? The latter would argue that previous generations have been provided for, why not they?

These are not voices from the "sidelines," to use Bakhtin's language, which Rawls tries to minimize or dismiss so that the simple dialogue can continue. They are inner voices that persons behind the veil of ignorance hear as the rival theories vying for their support are constructed. Rawls's arguments for ameliorating general envy and correcting conditions leading to resentment, but not for responding to cases of particular envy or grudgingness, are complicated and not wholly convincing. They rely on controversial psychological and sociological assumptions like the claim that people live in "noncomparing groups."[101] But one effect of introducing these attitudes and emotions is to accent the voices of representative members of the least advantaged class and their opponents. Rawls suggests that when we speak to ourselves with envy in our voices, we will be ashamed and feel compelled to suppress this feeling because it cannot be justified on the grounds of political equality. The same is ostensibly true when we speak grudgingly, even if we try to hide behind claims of desert and natural entitlement. In our hearts we will know better, because there is no justification for this attitude that free and equal citizens would accept. In contrast, he suggests, when we speak resentfully and can show how our feelings of resentment flow from being treated as second-class citizens, this moral feeling will elicit respect and bolster self-respect.[102]

Rawls's complex dialogue does not merely present us with opposing arguments; it strives to engage us in a process of critical self-reflection. Ideally, it enables us to listen to how we would sound if we gave in to our competing inner voices. By accenting these inner voices in the emotional language of justifiable resentment, familial love, grudgingness, envy, and regret, Rawlsian inner dialogue encourages us to choose among them with a sympathetic ear for the social and economic sources of political inequality, now and into the future, which is precisely what the representative members of the least advantaged class—with some help from their representative counterparts in future generations—know best. This is how the otherwise elusive notion of reasonableness is pinned down in the original position.

## To Be Seen but Not Heard

Now we are able to take up the more difficult issue: the democratic limits of Rawlsian inner dialogue. At one point Rawls likens the humane adjustments to the principle of equal political liberty (the difference principle, the principle of fair equality of opportunity, and the just savings principle) to a professional sports draft in which the teams with the worst records choose first in the selection of new players.[103] The principle of equal political liberty, like rules of competitive professional sports, is supposed to be fundamentally sound. All that is needed, it seems, is to give last year's biggest losers first pick of the new recruits, and so on up the line. But like a professional sports draft that seems simple enough and designed to even things out over time, the difference principle, the principle of fair equality of opportunity, and also the just savings principle make sense only against the background of a very specific kind of game.

To understand just how complex the "game" is that Rawls thinks needs only minimal cyclical adjustments, consider his summary of the implications of the principle of fair equality of opportunity.

> Fair (as opposed to formal) equality of opportunity . . . means that in addition to maintaining the usual kinds of social overhead capital, the government tries to insure equal chances of education and culture for persons similarly

102 Rawls, *Theory of Justice*, pp. 530–41.
103 Rawls, "Justice as Fairness: A Briefer Restatement," p. 37.

endowed and motivated either by subsidizing private schools or by establishing a public school system. It also enforces and underwrites equality of opportunity in economic activities and in the free choice of occupation. This is achieved by policing the conduct of firms and private associations and by preventing the establishment of monopolistic restrictions and barriers to the more desirable positions. Finally, the government guarantees a social minimum either by family allowances and special payments for sickness and employment, or systematically by such devices as a graded income supplement (a so-called negative income tax).[104]

To establish these fair background conditions, the government must be equipped to monitor and regulate wages and prices, and in some cases even to change the definition of private property. It must be ready to subsidize new fledgling industries and retrain workers. It must be able to identify the poverty level, measure changes in the standard of living, and the like. It must tax inheritance and gifts without driving wealth or "human capital" out of the country. It must regulate and adjust the rate of savings to balance present consumption and the well-being of future generations. All this and many more complicated tasks must be carried out by the functional branches of government if the fair value of political liberty is to be maintained and fair equality of opportunity is to be available now and in the future. There are no markets independent of these institutions. This may not be a welfare state, and it may minimize the need for a heavy-handed use of the difference principle, but it is certainly a highly complex politicized economy. It has clear implications for the voices we would want to hear in the original position.

When the parties in the original position listen to their inner voices, what they hear must encourage them to trust in the expertise of government officials and professionals who can administer this complex political economy. This encouragement is partially overt. Even Madisonian representatives of the least advantaged class may not be sensitive to the Hamiltonian needs of future generations, so another voice must be heard if an adequate rate of savings and investment is to curb the excesses of the difference principle and the principle of fair equality of opportunity. But it is also conveyed through the psychological distinction Rawls makes between envy and resentment, and the subordinate status he gives to the claims of desert and need as mere maxims of justice.[105] It is not typical

---

[104] Rawls, *Theory of Justice*, p. 275.

[105] Rawls's discussion of desert also falls in this category, although it remains somewhat unfinished. See *Theory of Justice*, pp. 310–15, and "Justice as Fairness: A Briefer Restatement," pp. 53–55, where Rawls relies on a game metaphor to introduce a new distinction between moral desert and deservingness.

members of these groups who have a voice in the original position; rather, their voices must express the long-term political needs that all free and equal citizens have for the "primary goods" without envy or rancor. In fact, I am suggesting, the emotional content of their voices is as important as the arguments they make on behalf of the difference principle and the principle of fair equality of opportunity. Members of the least advantaged class are not going to be able to judge how well their representatives understand their long-term interests. They will have to trust them based on how they sound. Will they be able to make their case without envy or hostility in their voices? The answer, I think, is yes. But whether this is a good thing is another matter. It depends on the value we place on speaking in one's own voice in democratic politics and on the degree to which this is possible when democratic politics becomes fragmented into a politics of policymaking.

Democratic citizens draw on a wide variety of resources in order to participate in political life. Rawls explicitly emphasizes the material resources of income and wealth, but he also acknowledges that the social bases of self-respect are important. Among these, political freedoms and civil liberties are crucial. These resources may be necessary, but I do not think they are sufficient for giving voice to the experiences of frustration, pain, and despair that are barely audible behind the veil of ignorance. Possessing a fair share of Rawls's primary goods may enable the least advantaged members of a liberal democratic society to be seen, but to be heard they have to speak in their own voices, from their own experiences, with the sharp emotions that will convey to others the power of these experiences. Furthermore, it is not their inner dialogue but the inner dialogues of those who have not shared in their experiences that must be enriched. The original position filters out too much of the emotional content of this experience.

Rawls's impulse to keep our inner dialogues free of these emotions is reflected in his belief that "a more or less self-sufficient" nation-state [106] should define the boundaries of the basic structure that is the subject of a political theory of justice. There may be natural duties of benevolence that govern our relations with the poor of other countries, but these are not matters to be governed by principles of justice. This is not, he argues, a nativist prejudice. Despite the economic interdependence that may exist

[106] Rawls, *Theory of Justice*, p. 4. That a Rawlsian inner dialogue should be open to voices across national boundaries is one implication Thomas W. Pogge tries to draw from the principles of justice Rawls favors. See his *Realizing Rawls* (Ithaca: Cornell University Press, 1989). Rawls appears sympathetic to this position in *Political Liberalism* in that he prefers to speak speculatively about a "law of peoples" rather than of nations. He remains convinced, however, that the starting point must be some "closed background system," and this is "illustrated by nations" (*Political Liberalism*, p. 272 n. 9).

between rich and poor nations, alternative international forms of political organization needed to bring justice as fairness to bear in these relationships would be either oppressive or too fragile.[107]

On its face this seems like an uncharacteristically harsh view for Rawls, and one that is inconsistent with his basic assumption that we owe a duty of fair play to those with whom we are engaged in cooperative social practices. In fact, recently he has moved in a more conciliatory, cosmopolitan direction.[108] These revised views on human rights and international interdependence, however, are not directly to the point. The voices he wants us to listen to in the original position must still be at least capable of being domesticated. They are voices whose anguish makes sense because they have been cleansed of any fearsome superstitions or strange beliefs. Unless the voices democratic citizens hear in the original position are capable of this kind of domestication, they will threaten the "reasonable overlapping consensus" that Rawls believes coherent policymaking depends on in a pluralistic society. The voices of zealots, true believers, and rabidly intolerant sects simply cannot be permitted given the delicacy of constitutional arrangements. The sounds of frustration, pain, and despair that color these voices, Rawls implies, have no place behind the veil of ignorance, even when they can be tolerated within society at large. They are the most dangerous symptoms of the "special psychologies" besides envy that Rawls only mentions in passing: "attitudes toward risk and uncertainty, domination and submission, and the like."[109] There is nothing in the psychodynamics of the original position as an enabling framework of reflection and deliberation that is designed to lessen these special psychologies. They have to be peremptorily excluded.

In the case of some national minorities this exclusion of unregenerate foreign voices is rendered unnecessary by the filtering power of the policymaking process. The pain of Native Americans whose traditional lands have been parceled out for economic development and whose voices are muted in the policymaking process[110] is no less real than the pain of someone whose freedom of speech has been denied for political reasons.

---

[107] Rawls, "Justice as Fairness: A Briefer Restatement," p. 10. In *Political Liberalism*, pp. 244–45, Rawls expresses a greater optimism that justice to other peoples and the permanently disabled may be only a matter of extending justice as fairness to these cases once the simpler cases have been understood and other relevant values introduced. This is similar to Rawls's revised view of justice between generations mentioned earlier; all are now what he calls "problems of extension."

[108] John Rawls, "The Law of Peoples," in *On Human Rights: The Oxford Amnesty Lectures 1993*, ed. Stephen Shute and Susan Hurley (New York: Basic Books, 1993), pp. 42–82.

[109] Rawls, *Theory of Justice*, p. 541.

[110] Minow, *Making All the Difference*, pp. 102–6, 351–56.

The emotions in their voices are no less characteristic of the politics of policymaking than, say, resentment over limitations on political speech and other moral feelings that Rawls does acknowledge as politically relevant. But they have learned to speak two languages: one for themselves and one composed so that their views can be heard within the policymaking process.

The boundaries of the nation-state are not just geographic. They are also the emotional boundaries of inner dialogues. We know this during times of war when the suffering of the enemy can be seen but not heard and when the denial of violence is the unspoken common theme in official pronouncements and personal life.[111] The same denial, I fear, is true at other times in domestic policymaking arenas. What Mill said of the family can be said of domestic policymaking in general: "In the present day, power holds a smoother language, and whomsoever it oppresses, always pretends to do so for their own good."[112] Domesticated violence begins with the voices of official authorities, passes through a network of expertise, trust, and distrust, emerges in the form of assessments, findings, judgments, and policies, and then finally settles in the voices of the dispossessed, the expelled, and the other parties who do not often prevail within the policymaking process.[113] By widening the emotional boundaries of inner dialogues, we recognize the exercise of violence and the experience of pain within the politics of policymaking. Unless citizens learn to hear the sounds of domesticated violence behind this smoother language, they will not be able to hear the pain beyond their borders.

Rawlsian inner dialogue is attuned to only one segment of this broad register, the nexus of trust and distrust in expert authority. Because of this the original position, and the inner dialogue it organizes, reinforces the illusion that democratic policymaking is a predominantly nonviolent form of political rule. Representatives of these members of the least advantaged class speak in the "prudential" tones of resentment and justifiable envy, without rancor and outrage, in order to be heard. The least advantaged themselves cannot be heard in the original position; their allegedly strident voices are filtered out. The sharp pain of the welfare mother whose child has been placed in foster care against the mother's will, for example, cannot be adequately expressed in the preferred language of the original position. As an organized consumer of public services she is sometimes

111 See Susan Griffin, *A Chorus of Stones: The Private Pain of War* (New York: Doubleday, 1991).

112 John Stuart Mill, *The Subjection of Women*, in *The Collected Works of John Stuart Mill*, ed. John M. Robson (Toronto: University of Toronto Press, 1963-91), 21:299.

113 See Robert M. Cover, "Violence and the Word," *Yale Law Journal* 95 (1986): 1601-29.

visible in the policymaking process, but the original position domesticates her own account of her experience as it recognizes her need to be fairly represented. If her emotional language is to be a political resource for her, it can be realized only if others can begin to hear it as part of their own internal dialogues. In the next chapter I describe this missing voice, which falls outside the domestic boundaries of Rawlsian politics, and also illustrate how Mill's visualization of political education complements the inner dialogues mediated by the original position.

To conclude my reconstruction of liberal theory as political education, let me briefly summarize the main argument of Part 2. Hobbes sought to replace the power of "masterless men" with a more transparent Leviathan state that egocentric citizens could trust. One way this might happen is by adopting his method of geometric reasoning, but Hobbes did not work this through. For Kant, the problem of political education was to teach "independent" men to think for themselves in more juridical terms. Mill shifted the focus of liberal theory as political education from state power to the power of the majority: how could citizens be trusted to participate in the constitution of state power when they were so vulnerable themselves to the power of public opinion? They needed a model of "a man as a progressive being" to follow, not an abstract method of philosophical reasoning, if they were to reclaim their individuality and resist the temptations of wealth and power. With Rawls we find a return to abstract method as a medium for political education: "reasonable" citizens can reconcile themselves to the prospects of a life in a "well-ordered society" if they can domesticate their own voices. The original position as a "device of representation" gives them this kind of political skill. Rawls's own reluctance to recognize the practical role the original position plays as a mediating method of political education among policy analysts and professional ethicists notwithstanding,[114] it remains "central to the whole theory, and other basic notions are defined in terms of it."[115]

[114] Rawls, *Political Liberalism*, p. 242 n. 31.
[115] Rawls, *Theory of Justice*, p. 516.

# PART III

# CRITIQUE

# CHAPTER SEVEN

# Envisioning
# Democratic Theory

Liberal theorists such as Mill elevated political judgment to an elite task at the same time as they reduced political education to a balancing act. To understand how to balance their private desires and their public duties, most citizens provisionally should trust in the judgments of exemplary leaders. Mill's arguments for this division of labor were based on the assumption, encased in metaphor, that sound political judgments require unusually penetrating insight.

Contemporary liberal theorists, uncomfortable with this overtly hierarchical conception of citizenship, have turned to dialogue and conversation to describe political judgment and make it available to a wider range of citizens. In Rawls's case the dialogue is not presented in explicit terms but is implicit in the method of reasoning he develops. Other liberal theorists such as Bruce Ackerman and Michael Walzer have made the need for a dialogical politics more explicit. In either case the goal has been to constrain political debate and discussion so that regulative principles can be agreed on and sound judgments made that are appropriate to the politics of expert policymaking.

I have argued that Mill's sight-based theory and Rawls's more complex dialogical theory uncritically orient citizens toward a shallow, imagistic politics of consumption and an emotionally narrow clientism. The kind of political judgment these liberal theories have fostered is inadequate if one believes that democratic social practices can and should be more than clientism and consumerism and that democratic citizens are capable of making more self-critical judgments about the dynamics of power.

This chapter is divided into three sections. The first presents an account of the dominant consumerist sights in liberal society. I have already used the college classroom to illustrate the Weberian context within which the sounds of expert policymaking take shape; here I use the modern shopping mall as an allegory for describing the complementary formation of visual images in neocorporatist political life. The college classroom is not an idiosyncratic or peculiar political space in neocorporatist liberal societies. Many professional-client relationships in which liberal citizens learn how to hear the voices of power resemble this classroom experience. Similarly, the mall is a model for understanding how the visual experiences of consumers of all stripes, not just shoppers, are organized. In the second section I discuss the ways Emersonian liberal theories have relied on visual metaphors to separate the political judgments of experts from the political education of citizens. Finally, I revisit Mill's theory and distinguish my argument from some feminist critiques of liberalism.

## The Allegory of the Mall

Liberal society is a society of spectacles in two senses. The spectacles through which liberal citizens have learned to see their political world are, as Hobbes knew, "multiplying glasses."[1] These spectacles do not simply exaggerate the erosion of or improvements in their future standard of living, however. They also conflate the goods and services promised by Millian expert policymakers with the notion of a public good, and they enlarge the skills of the policymakers so that they can be trusted to rule over the production of these goods and services. Second, the spectacles of liberal society are themselves the objects that are multiplied. These spectacular monuments to consumption are not just mounds of consumer goods and endless lists of available services. They are the institutions through which consumer goods and services reach liberal citizens: the ever-expanding superhighways, computer networks, and retail systems that bring goods and services to market—the infrastructure that holds liberal society together, what liberal citizens hold in common.

The most familiar form this double spectacle now takes is the shopping mall.[2] It is in the mall that liberal citizens learn how to see themselves, and the mall epitomizes the spectacle of consumption.

The mall has been an easy target for liberal critics of mass society. In Michael Walzer's words, the mall is a "single-minded public space" where

---

[1] Thomas Hobbes, *Leviathan*, in *The English Works of Thomas Hobbes*, ed. Sir William Molesworth, 11 vols. (London: J. Bohn, 1839–45), 3:170.

[2] See William Severini Kowinski, *The Malling of America: An Inside Look at the Great Consumer Paradise* (New York: William Morrow, 1985), and Sharon Zukin, *Landscapes of Power: From Detroit to Disney World* (Berkeley and Los Angeles: University of California Press, 1991).

people move in and out with the least possible bother and with little openness to chance encounters and unanticipated public meetings. Unlike the traditional university, Walzer argues, single-minded public spaces discourage people from listening for new ideas and arguments. They may browse or graze, but their minds are on only one thing: consumption.[3] The courts have recognized this social transformation—it would be incredible if they had not—but they have been reluctant to protect political rights such as the right to petition and the right of assembly within the confines of the mall.[4] Entertainment and exercise, because of their clear business dividends, seem to have secured their place there, but rallying political support is generally unwelcome.

Beyond this, however, the spectacular shopping mall has a larger allegorical meaning. We can begin with Jean Baudrillard's description. "The mall," he argues, "offers the previously unexperienced luxury of strolling between stores which freely . . . offer their temptations without so much interference as glare from a display window." The mall is free of seasonal changes, of day and night, of even the most basic contrasts between work and leisure. The conflicts of the city, the family arguments, the losses, the anguish are gone; everything has been "mixed, massaged, climate controlled, and domesticated into the simple activity of shopping . . . in a perpetual Springtime." The chains that bind in the mall are not the false beliefs of Plato's shadow world. What holds us there is the ease with which we drift and slide, almost effortlessly, from one purchase to another. Consumption becomes a frictionless intercourse of credit cards passing back and forth.[5] This characterization is not a postmodernist's prejudice. The designers of the mall themselves single out its power to transform "destination buyers" into "impulse shoppers." The moment is called "the Gruen transfer (named after architect Victor Gruen)"—that point at which "a determined stride" becomes an "erratic and meandering gait."[6] The mall is the perfection of the early twentieth-century department store, the first

[3] Michael Walzer, "Urban Spaces: Pleasures and Costs of Urbanity," *Dissent*, fall 1986, pp. 47-75. "We educate," Amy Gutmann observes, "rational shoppers but not good people or virtuous citizens." In the context of her argument, this observation is not intended as a criticism. See her "Undemocratic Education," in *Liberalism and the Moral Life*, ed. Nancy L. Rosenblum (Cambridge: Harvard University Press, 1991), pp. 74-75.

[4] For example, *Amalgamated Food Employees v. Logan Valley Plaza*, 391 U.S. 408 (1968); *Lloyd Corp. v. Tanner*, 407 U.S. 551 (1972); *Hudgens v. NLRB*, 424 U.S. 507 (1976); and *Pruneyard Shopping Center v. Robbins*, 447 U.S. 74 (1980).

[5] Jean Baudrillard, "Consumer Society," in *Selected Writings*, ed. Mark Poster (Stanford: Stanford University Press, 1988), pp. 34-35.

[6] Margaret Crawford, "The World in a Shopping Mall," in *Variations on a Theme Park: The New American City and the End of Public Space*, ed. Michael Sorkin (New York: Hill and Wang, 1992), p. 14.

cathedral of consumption. In the new secular temple shoppers browse, almost like zombies, in a directionless search for unforeseen purchases. No longer do they have to be lured into the "Emerald City" by lavish display windows. New forms of advertising keep consumers informed; a new milieu of consumption keeps them shopping.[7]

The modern allegory of the mall, like the Platonic allegory of the cave, traces the path political education must travel. The difference between the two allegories is that Plato believed the vision of former prisoners gradually improves as they leave the cave, whereas the fate of those who leave the mall is to find themselves in what Baudrillard calls simulacra of the same model of visual self-absorption.

The mall manufactures an illusion of conflict-free intercourse. In it we do not just consume food, clothes, and entertainment; we consume ourselves in a seemingly endless line of mirrors. The mall makes the rituals of everyday encounters clean, predictable, and nonthreatening. There is no need for what Erving Goffman called the cautious "civil inattention" of two strangers catching each other's eye as they pass on a city street.[8] In the mall we obliquely notice one another with impunity. We can see ourselves as consumers with no stigma and no clash of narcissistic egos. In the mall we can all play the dandy.

What makes this self-reflection so beguiling is the way the mall drapes us in the most flattering light, powders and perfumes us. It makes us larger than life, and we see ourselves reflected not just in the eyes of other consumers but in the larger-than-life images of today's windblown, high-jumping heroes whose signatures reach out to us from all directions. It is this self-image, first seen in the fleeting glances of the other and then artificially reproduced and reinforced in silver and neon, that holds us. The same self-image is reflected in the electronic media, the mall we take home with us. In video games, videotapes, and constantly scrolling network shows, we see polished and nonthreatening reflections of ourselves as ideal consumers.

The mall's simulacra are not limited to the images broadcast over electronic media. The mall has become a model for other institutions:[9] shopping mall high schools, shopping mall churches, even city halls aspire to

---

[7] On the history of the department store and the role L. Frank Baum, the author of the *Oz* books, played in the development of show windows, see William Leach, *Land of Desire: Merchants, Power, and the Rise of a New American Culture* (New York: Pantheon, 1993), pp. 55–61, 246–61.

[8] Erving Goffman, *Behavior in Public Places* (New York: Free Press, 1963).

[9] For example, see Anthony G. Powell et al., *The Shopping Mall High School: Winners and Losers in the Education Marketplace* (Boston: Houghton Mifflin, 1985).

this new model of efficiency. The recombinant floor plan of the mall even extends beyond these institutions to counties and regions—new Disney-lands, neither suburbs nor cities, where new modules can replace old ones as quickly as a Disney store can replace a shoestore inside the mall.[10] It is over these new topographies that citizens shop for the land-use policies, education reforms, and other public policies that reflect their ideal self-images as consumers. Politics within this artificial atmosphere, Christo-pher Lasch has suggested, has a facade of civility, even congeniality. "We live in a swirl of images and echoes that arrest experience and play it back in slow motion. . . . We need no reminder to smile. A smile is perma-nently grave on our features, and we already know from which of several angles it photographs to best advantage."[11] But it is a narcissistic political civility. We see the same self-images in the look of the other in the offices and halls of the bureaucratically organized workplace, whether it is a pri-vate firm or a public agency.[12]

The allegory of the mall, like the allegory of the cave, contains an un-spoken story. In the allegory of the cave Plato never tells us who lights the fire, who creates the shadows, or who has to force the would-be philosopher-king back down into the cave after he has seen the light. The omissions in the allegory of the mall are equally important. Who cleans the mall? Who produces the goods and services consumers choose from? Where do these people shop, and how do they view the politics of policy-making?

Let's begin with a mall that bears some resemblance to the Emerald City. Within easy reach of the Washington, D.C., Metro lie two strikingly different malls, Pentagon City and the Crystal City Underground. Pen-tagon City is an example of the soaring gothic mall Baudrillard describes. Anchored by upscale department stores, Pentagon City provides a four-story atrium where shoppers can eat and rest between purchases. Much more than its namesake—notorious for its bungles and overruns—Penta-gon City shelters and refreshes the forces of consumption. Some Penta-gon City shoppers find its atmosphere too artificial, the perfume too sweet to take regularly. They prefer discount malls with oversized supermarket shopping carts and towering columns of partially unpacked merchandise. These "power malls" are to Pentagon City what the old Sears and Spiegel

[10] Edward W. Soja, "Inside Exopolis: Scenes from Orange County," in *Variations on a Theme Park*, pp. 94–122.

[11] Christopher Lasch, *The Culture of Narcissism: American Life in an Age of Diminishing Expectations* (New York: Warner Books, 1979), pp. 96–97.

[12] See, for example, Arlie Russell Hochschild, *The Managed Heart: Commercialization of Human Feeling* (Berkeley and Los Angeles: University of California Press, 1983).

catalogs were to the department store in its prime. They are more convenient, and they serve as supplements for Pentagon City shoppers who want the security of a full pantry as well as the pleasure of Pentagon City.

In contrast to Pentagon City (and its discount supplements), stands the Crystal City Underground, horizontally inserted between high-rise apartments and a labyrinthine parking garage. The Underground is anything but crystalline in structure or appearance. With its winding tunnels of small shops and arcades, crowded with commuters wearing plastic name tags with picture IDs, Crystal City is hurried, almost frantic. There are no perfumes, no food courts, and no discounts. The customers in the Underground are commuters who shop on the run.

Farther beyond the geopolitics of these malls lies another mall whose atmosphere is more threatening and whose patrons are more desperate. This is the panopticon mall of the inner city. Designed on the model of a prison with high-tech security devices and high-turnover, low-quality goods, malls like the King Shopping Center in the Watts district of Los Angeles are as far removed from the Crystal City Underground as Crystal City is from Pentagon City and the discount mall.[13] These inner city machines of forced consumption are suffocating. For shoppers accustomed to browse or bargain hunt, the urge to flee from them is overwhelming.

The Crystal City Underground is inhabited by those who participate in the consumer economy but must take what they are given. To those who glide effortlessly through Pentagon City or wheel fearlessly through the overstocked aisles of discount malls like the Price Club, a chain of "power malls," the inhabitants of the Underground are only vaguely visible shadows. Their work is invisible, where they live is invisible, only what they consume and carry with them can be seen—and that just barely. They enter the public domain through different portals and travel at different times. In sharper contrast yet, the King Shopping Center's customers do not commute, they do not stock the shelves at Pentagon City. They are visible only in sensational media events. Pentagon City may well depend on Crystal City for its labor; but its only relationship with the King Center is that of dread.

What kind of judgment does it take to navigate these malls, to see what is on the shelves and not see what is missing? In fact, judgment is barely involved. The mall teaches its customers how to choose, not how to judge. If the mall provides shoppers with a "grammar" for constructing a distinctive identity and "community of taste," this language of styles and designer

---

[13] Mike Davis, "Fortress Los Angeles: The Militarization of Urban Space," in *Variations on a Theme Park*, pp. 169–71.

labels is so decontextualized and confined that it can hardly be called sub-versive.[14] If we think of the mall allegorically, the spectacular politics of policymaking makes only one demand on its citizens: choose the images that reflect you best and that shield you from the unflattering or threatening images of others. These may be complicated choices involving alternative, subtly nuanced gestures, but they are not political judgments about how power operates on the consumer as a member of this self-absorbed, compartmentalized polity.

The sights of liberal society simultaneously are luminously clear and hidden. They make political judgment irrelevant to citizens who are asked only to choose among the most flattering images of themselves in the policymaker's gallery. Mill, of course, did not conciously condone this kind of aestheticized politics. But without the tradition of public discourse he initiated, a tradition that vests public trust in the visual powers of exemplary masculine leaders, today's spectacles and life in Pentagon City and its satellites would seem much less natural to "us."

The sounds of liberal society are very different. They operate as a counterweight to these public spectacles, but not as a corrective. They are not the voices of great orators or of the people united in song. They are, I have suggested, the muffled and sometimes dissonant sounds of professionals and clients wrestling with the meaning of the latest policy problems. That is to say, the sounds of liberal society are made up of voices of individual clients and professionals working over and through the maze of images that policymakers have manufactured for them. These sounds can be heard as lawyers, social workers, and divorcing parents try to work out a compromise child custody arrangement.[15] They can be heard as doctors, lawyers, hospital administrators, and relatives of patients in a permanent vegetative condition try to make their way through public policies providing for living wills.[16] They can be heard as teachers, school administrators, and parents try to agree on an individual program of instruction for a handicapped student.[17] They can be heard as land developers, neighborhood activists, small businessmen, and city managers try to decide in

[14] For a defense of shopping along these lines that ignores the malls of the other, see Anne Norton, *Republic of Signs: Liberal Theory and American Popular Culture* (Chicago: University of Chicago Press, 1993), pp. 70–71.

[15] Martha Fineman, "Dominant Discourse: Professional Language and Legal Change in Child Custody Decisionmaking," *Harvard Law Review* 101 (February 1988): 727–74.

[16] Allen E. Buchanan and Dan W. Brock, *Deciding for Others: The Ethics of Surrogate Decision Making* (Cambridge: Cambridge University Press, 1989).

[17] Joel F. Handler, *The Conditions of Discretion: Autonomy, Community, Bureaucracy* (New York: Russell Sage Foundation, 1986).

whose backyard the next highway, toxic dump site, or commercial strip will go.[18] And depending on how organized the parties are, they can reverberate back through policymaking arenas, triggering a new round of image making. This interplay between sights and sounds, between performers and audience, has been especially true in medical policymaking. The imagery of policymakers has elicited voices that have given rise to yet new waves of policymaking.[19]

The most distinctive feature of these voices is their professionalism. The voices of the professionals (and of clients presumptuous enough to imitate them) are marked by what Bakhtin calls subtle sideward glances, loopholes, and intonations.[20] These mannerisms are crucial to the trust that humanistic corporatism rests on. Balanced against the infantile imagery of consumerism are the comforting voices of trustworthy professionals — school principals, medical specialists, legal counsels, social workers, local planning consultants, and the like. To these voices liberal citizens turn when they are baffled by the myriad policies and services facing them.

Of course, these voices do not comfort all citizens in liberal societies today. Just as the mall, the site of imagistic politics, has its negation, the voices of clientism depend on absent voices as well. Those who speak another language, sometimes literally, draw little from these professional voices. They are left to fend for themselves in silence within the shadows of the Crystal City Underground and the King Shopping Center, without much professional help to lobby for better schools, low-income housing, public transportation, and the many other public services they depend on. As unwilling consumers of public services, they can only look on in disbelief at the imaginary world of politics screened for them daily and hope to overhear the conversations between those clients and professionals who have lessened their dependence on public goods through privatization.

As long as relatively informed clients and relatively organized consumers are content to let policymakers make political judgments for them — which means treating their own political education as a trivial matter and remaining deaf to the voices of the others and blind to the subterranean worlds they inhabit — there is little reason to believe this situation will change. Now I want to examine how liberal theory's Emersonian ego

[18] Sidney Plotkin, *Keep Out: The Struggle for Land Use Control* (Berkeley and Los Angeles: University of California Press, 1987).

[19] For example, President's Commission for the Study of Ethical Problems in Medicine and Biomedical and Behavioral Research, *Deciding to Forego Life-Sustaining Treatment* (Washington, D.C.: U.S. Government Printing Office, 1983).

[20] Mikhail Bakhtin, *Problems of Dostoevsky's Poetics*, trans. Caryl Emerson (Minneapolis: University of Minnesota Press, 1984), p. 201.

ideal has contributed to this complacency toward the sights and sounds of expert policymaking.

## Seeing and Judging

One might think that learning to make good political judgments should be an integral part of political education in a liberal society. "Common citizens," not just "academics" and "political observers," Ronald Beiner has argued, make political judgments as they read the morning newspaper and discuss current events, as well as in carrying out their conventional political responsibilities. A liberal political education presumably would make them more conscious of this faculty and more adept at using it.[21]

In fact, liberal theorists, whether republican or Madisonian, have stressed the importance of separating political education and political judgment. As we have seen, liberal theories of political education claim to reduce political education in large measure to socialization, whereas political judgment becomes the province of those trustworthy liberal citizens who have learned to domesticate their feelings. "Trust in the relation between ruled and ruler is not a supine psychic compulsion on the part of the former," John Dunn has argued. "Rather," in liberal societies "it is an eminently realistic assessment of the irreversibility of a political division of labour and a sharp reminder, from the former to the latter, of the sole conditions that can make that division humanly benign."[22] To solidify this political division of labor between citizen and policymaker, liberal theorists model their conception of political judgment on what Hans Jonas has called "the nobility of sight":[23] not all citizens are in a position to see how the boundaries that crisscross public and private life can be drawn, even if they know, roughly, a good boundary when they see one. Citizens should trust those with the keenest political vision.

Thomas Jefferson's famous letter to John Adams, praising the natural aristocracy and minimizing the blindness of the demos, captures this view of the dynamic between trusted but still corruptible leaders and ordinary citizens, who can be shortsighted through no fault of their own. "I think the best remedy is exactly that provided by all our constitutions, to leave to the citizens the free election and separation of the aristoi from the

---

[21] Ronald Beiner, *Political Judgment* (Chicago: University of Chicago Press, 1983), p. 8.

[22] John Dunn, "Trust and Political Agency," in *Trust: Making and Breaking Cooperative Relations*, ed. Diego Gambetta (Cambridge: Basil Blackwell, 1988), p. 87.

[23] Hans Jonas, "The Nobility of Sight," in his *The Phenomenon of Life: Toward a Philosophical Biology* (New York: Harper and Row, 1966).

pseudo-aristoi, of the wheat from the chaff. In general they will elect the really good and wise. In some instances, wealth may corrupt, and birth blind them; but not in sufficient degree to endanger the society."[24] Citizens usually can see well enough to trust the judgments of the natural aristocracy, and the natural aristocracy in most cases can be trusted to see more deeply—not because they stand above the demos, but because of their appreciation of structure. Jefferson conveys the social content of this natural faculty with his own representation of the Natural Bridge. First he describes the bridge's dimensions and internal structure. Then he compares the vertigo he experiences at the top with the delight gained from below through knowledge of its static forces: "You involuntarily fall on your hands and feet, creep to the parapet and peep over it. Looking down from this height about a minute, gave me a violent head ache. If the view from the top be painful and intolerable, that from below is delightful in an equal extreme. It is impossible for the emotions arising from the sublime, to be felt beyond what they are here; so beautiful an arch, so elevated, so light: and springing as it were up to heaven, the rapture of the spectator is really indescribable!"[25] To appreciate scenes like this, Jefferson argued, even a natural aristocracy must have a rigorous education in math and science before studying the fine arts. Like good architects, members must know what holds the arch up before they can see its heavenly direction. Only then will they have "the habits of reflection and correct action, rendering them examples of virtue to others, and of happiness within themselves."[26]

In general, according to liberal theorists, political judgment is knowing how, not just knowing that. Citizens can imitate the exemplary moral virtues of the natural aristocracy, but they will not have the time or inclination to put these virtues to work in politics—nor should they try. They can learn about what is at stake in politics and in retrospect what should have been done, but they will not possess the vision and concentration to do it themselves. They are, as Plato said, mere "lovers of sights and sounds."[27]

In a similar vein, Tocqueville believed Americans feverishly "clutch everything but hold nothing fast, and so lose grip as they hurry after some new delight." It is not that their grip is weak, but that they are driven by their "taste for physical pleasures" to constantly search for more. "A man who has set his heart on nothing but the good things of this world is always

[24] Thomas Jefferson, letter to John Adams, October 28, 1813, in *The Portable Jefferson*, ed. Merrill D. Peterson (New York: Penguin Books, 1977), p. 535.

[25] Thomas Jefferson, *Notes on the State of Virginia*, in *Portable Jefferson*, p. 54.

[26] Thomas Jefferson, *Report of the Commissioners for the University of Virginia*, August 4, 1818, in *Portable Jefferson*, p. 335.

[27] Plato, *The Republic of Plato*, trans. F. M. Cornford (New York: Oxford University Press, 1945), 476B, p. 183.

in a hurry, for he has only a limited time in which to find them, get them, and enjoy them."[28]

This compulsive restlessness is reinforced by certain habits of mind. Americans, Tocqueville observed, are a hands-on people, interested in theory only to the extent that it bears on the immediate demands of practice.[29] Although this might serve them well in business, it does not incline them to take pleasure in the delights and blessings they have or to look back over the road they have traveled. In the language of the visual arts, Tocqueville suggested that most Americans are inclined to see the world through the eyes of the Renaissance painter David, emphasizing anatomical detail at the expense of higher ideals. They rarely possess a Raphaelite sensitivity to feelings and thoughts that have no direct material payoff.[30]

This materialism (symbolized by the images of gripping and anatomical inspection), argued Tocqueville, is especially disabling in politics, which depends on a far-seeing, synoptic view of the whole: "I have tried to see not differently but further than any party; while they are busy with tomorrow, I have wished to consider the whole future."[31] Seeing in politics is no simple matter, and democratic citizens are peculiarly disabled in this regard because of their aversion to *theoria*, their taste for the anatomically correct, and third, their Cartesian style of thought. It is the way they reason about politics, not the passionate or spirited element of their souls, that keeps them from making sound political judgments. "Being accustomed to rely on the witness of their own eyes, they like to see the object before them very clearly. They therefore free it, as far as they can, from its wrappings and move anything in the way and anything that hides their view of it, so as to get the closest view they can in broad daylight. This turn of mind soon leads them to a scorn of forms, which they take as useless, hampering veils put between them and truth."[32] This untutored Cartesian urge to get the closest view, Tocqueville claimed, is peculiarly unsuited to politics, as Descartes himself recognized. It strips the world of its ancient tradition and gives individuals a false confidence in their own perceptions at the same time that they reject out of hand the judgments of others. In a country like the United States, where "the precepts of Descartes are least

---

[28] Alexis de Tocqueville, *Democracy in America*, trans. George Lawrence, ed. J. P. Mayer (Garden City, N.Y.: Anchor Books, 1969), p. 536.

[29] Ibid., p. 463.

[30] Ibid., p. 468. Other passages in *Democracy* seem to contradict this. For example: "No men are less dreamers than the citizens of democracy; one hardly finds any who care to let themselves indulge in such leisurely and solitary moods of contemplation as generally precede and produce the great agitations of the heart" (p. 598).

[31] Ibid., p. 20.

[32] Ibid., p. 430.

studied and best followed," citizens make decisions based on what they consider to be their personal unobstructed views and dismiss their "ancestors' conceptions." They have very little interest in constructing or revising shared understandings, especially ones wrapped in traditional terms.

Ironically, this Cartesianism, argued Tocqueville, ends up generating its own dogma. Democracies do need shared understandings: "For without ideas in common, no common action would be possible, and without common action, men might exist, but there could be no body social." What has filled this void in America is "public opinion." Unwilling to trust in the authority of the ancients, democratic citizens turn to "the mass, and public opinion becomes more and more mistress of the world." Public opinion, Tocqueville continued, "uses no persuasion to forward its beliefs, but by some mighty pressure of the mind of all upon the intelligence of each it imposes its ideas and makes them penetrate men's very souls." Eventually, he concluded, "trust in common opinion will become a sort of religion, with the majority as its prophet."[33]

It is at this point that political education becomes mandatory. Democracy can and should be educated, Tocqueville announced in the first volume of *Democracy in America*, and the French, whom Tocqueville had almost given up on, might still learn something from the experiment in the New World. In this famous passage, Tocqueville identified his audience as well as what he wanted them to see: "The first duty imposed on those who now direct society is to educate democracy; to put, if possible, new life into its beliefs; to purify its mores; to control its actions; gradually to substitute understanding of statecraft for present inexperience and knowledge of its true interests for blind instincts; to adapt government to the needs of time and place; and to modify it as men and circumstances require."[34] Those who direct society have a duty to improve democratic politics. They are the ones Tocqueville was trying to reach. It is their vision he wanted to sharpen so that they could educate the beliefs, mores, interests, and political practices governing the people. They are the ones who must follow him up out of the "city" so they can see the future danger posed by egalitarianism. On their return, they will have to use sound judgment if they are to gradually teach the people to assent to true statecraft. This is all that the "feverish agitation" of the American mind can absorb.[35] Their style of thought and their faith in public opinion do not allow them to learn to make sound political judgments themselves. The difficult decisions regarding the limits of freedom of speech, the extent of property

[33] Ibid., pp. 433–36.
[34] Ibid., p. 12.
[35] Ibid., pp. 408, 404.

rights, the separation of religion and politics should be made by those who now direct society. The people can and should be educated so that they will support these judgments and those empowered to carry them out.

Unlike those of other liberal theorists, even Jefferson, Tocqueville's treatment of political judgment is not based on an aristocratic disdain for the demos. Political judgment, according to him, depends on a special kind of insight into the past and foresight into the future that the demos do not have but that they can be taught to appreciate in others. In particular, according to Tocqueville, political judgment is the kind of judgment that lawyers, judges, and other intellectuals have and that democratic citizens, saddled with an aversion to abstract *theoria*, an instinctual Cartesian skepticism, a bare-bones aesthetic, and a faith in public opinion, can learn to trust.

Take the legal profession. Lawyers and judges have an aristocratic "distaste for the behavior of the multitude and secretly scorn the government of the people." They form the "strongest barriers against the faults of democracy." Their adherence to historical precedent, their reluctance to embrace change, their love of order all run contrary to the "instincts of democracy." The effects of the political authority of the legal profession, however, are not visible to all. "In the United States the lawyers constitute a power which is little dreaded and hardly noticed; it has no banner of its own; it adapts itself flexibly to the exigencies of the moment and lets itself be carried along unresistingly by every movement of the body social; but it enwraps the whole of society, penetrating each component class and constantly working in secret upon its unconscious patient, till in the end it has molded it to its desire."[36] No banners or professional lobbyists are needed to symbolize and protect the influence of lawyers and judges. Legal authority shapes itself to the contours of the body social until gradually "the language of everyday party-political controversy has to be borrowed from legal phraseology and conceptions." How, we might well ask, could this possibly occur? Some people pick up the language in school or on jury duty. Mostly it is the influence of "public men" who "are or have been lawyers" who infuse their ways of thinking into public affairs until almost every "political question," Tocqueville claims, "sooner or later turns into a judicial one." Words like "carried along," "penetrating," and "molded" refer to the "secret" way the political authority of the legal profession operates. There is no overt direct causation here, only a gradual, unobtrusive influence. Those who "direct society" must be able to see this secret influence and preserve it for the sake of "the whole of society."

At the same time, popular reliance on legal terms like *due process* ex-

[36] Ibid., p. 270.

acerbates democracy's unhappy tendency toward abstraction. Laypersons should not imitate lawyers. Like other general ideas, abstract legal terms permit citizens to range swiftly over a multitude of phenomena. But they obscure important differences and sacrifice rigor for speed:

> The abundance of abstract terms in the langauge of democracy, used the whole time without reference to any particular facts, both widens the scope of thought and clouds it. They make expression quicker but conceptions less clear. However, in matters of language democracies prefer obscurity to hard work. . . .
>
> Democratic citizens, then, will often have vacillating thoughts, and so language must be loose enough to leave them play. As they never know whether what they say today will fit the facts of tomorrow, they have a natural taste for abstract terms. An abstract word is like a box with a false bottom; you may put in it what ideas you please and take them out again unobserved.[37]

The abstract language of popular culture not only unwittingly obscures complex ideas and concrete reality, it is an invitation to duplicity. Those who must direct democratic society not only should avoid abstractions, they should be on their guard against those who rely on them in the name of the people. If they are to make sound political judgments, then they must watch for false bottoms.

Tocqueville thought that only those with insight into the past and a keen view of the future could discern the quasi-religious influence of public opinion and its delirious attachment to equality. But why is judging a matter of seeing? Could he just as easily have talked about a sensitive ear or being in touch with potential dangers?

Sight, Hans Jonas has argued, has a kind of "nobility" that hearing and touching lack. It promises much more to those willing to use it properly. First, sight presents us all at once with a manifold of objects at our beck and call. We need only open our eyes and survey those parts of our domain we choose. Not only does sight promise us this freedom from the objects we see (hearing must wait for sounds to reach us, and we have much less control over what can be heard), it gives us those objects in a manifold that exists, at least in part, outside time. Objects of sight do not roll in the way sounds and objects of touch do, chained to temporality. Sight offers us a look at how things are, here and now, not how they are coming into being. "Indeed only the simultaneity of sight, with its extended 'present' of enduring objects, allows the distinction between change and the unchanging and therefore between becoming and being. All the other senses operate

---

[37] Ibid., p. 482.

by registering change and cannot make that distinction. Only sight therefore provides the sensual basis on which the mind may conceive the idea of the eternal, that which never changes and is always present." [38] From a Tocquevillean perspective, this interpretation of sight is surely attractive: sight preserves freedom of choice; it ranges freely over its domain, capable of taking in much more than hearing or touching, at the same time that it can abandon one object for another. Sight makes freedom possible; hearing and touching are temptations to sacrifice freedom for greater pleasures. To resist the temptations of sight, we need only turn away. To resist the Sirens, Odysseus had to have himself bound to the mast, which proved in one sense that he had already succumbed.

Second, sight distills the image of the perceived object in a way that abstracts from the causal genesis of the object. We can read that genesis or history back into the objects we see, but sight alone does not take that in. In Jonas's words, sight "neutralizes" the dynamics between subjects and objects, separating the form of the object from its matter. The promise here is one of almost immaculate conceptual objectivity. "Seeing requires no perceptible activity either on the part of the object or on that of the subject. Neither invades the sphere of the other: they let each other be what they are and as they are, and thus emerge the self-contained object and the self-contained subject." [39]

Finally, in addition to the greater freedom and objectivity sight promises, there is an even grander promise: the promise of what is to come. Sight follows the converging lines of the present into the future. This increases the freedom that the simultaneity of the visual manifold creates. Distance, in perspective, is an invitation to move from the actual to the potential, to move forward and take a closer look. Beyond this, Jonas suggests, sight's ability to traverse distance along the lines of perspective, in a way that neither hearing nor touching makes possible, creates a rudimentary conception of infinity "to which no other sense could supply the experiential basis." [40]

This account of sight's relation to distance, then, is consistent with Tocqueville's oculocentrism. Tocqueville wants those who will direct society to be able to step back and see where democracy is going, to render its feelings and thoughts, outline its potential strengths and weaknesses. For example, he wants them to see the nonobvious stabilizing lines of convergence between religion and politics in a democratic society committed to the separation of church and state. By his own choice of metaphors

[38] Jonas, "Nobility of Sight," pp. 144–45.
[39] Ibid., p. 148.
[40] Ibid., p. 150.

for describing the problems of democracy and the remedies he favors, Tocqueville clearly endorsed vision as the nobler political sense. Those who cannot see the whole "city" before them, who cannot separate political forms from particular political matters, and who cannot see beyond their immediate circumstances into the political future are the ones who need a political education. They are the ones Tocqueville worried about most, and it is their habits of heart (materialism) and mind (Cartesianism) that have to be improved so they will know whose political judgments they should trust. Political judgment based on the ability to see the boundaries that separate church and state, self-regarding and other-regarding actions, town and country, nation and tribe, majority and minority, or citizen and alien in democratic societies claims to penetrate the veil of tradition. Envisioning how these boundaries should be set requires that someone see farther and more objectively than those within these contested boundaries.

There is an eerie silence surrounding this act of political judgment. There are no protests as old boundaries are erased and new group identities created. There are no ragged edges that continue to tear, and no aching bruises or empty spaces left behind. No postpartum depression. Sight-based political judgments make razor-thin incisions, and the suturing leaves only the shadow of a scar. Sight-based political judgments penetrate with laser swiftness and exit almost without a trace. To the extent that there is any sound at all, it is the imperious voice of the judge making his ruling known.

## Feminism and Voice

Feminsts have objected to this theory of practical reason, calling it phallogocentrism. The reasoning involved in sight-based political judgment allegedly centers on the assumed power of theoretical ideas to penetrate reality and give it new life. It is a myth of creation in which the only animating force is reason's penetrating power to pierce the veil of tradition. Women, lacking the embodiment of this power, are unfit to make political judgments. When women gaze into this man-made mirror, they see only what they would lack if they were men, and they hate themselves. Men, Hélène Cixous claims, "have made for women an antinarcissism! A narcissism which loves itself only to be loved for what women haven't got."[41]

Luce Irigaray has found a detailed version of Cixous's concept of "antinarcissism" in Plato's allegory of the cave, which she calls "a silent pre-

[41] Hélène Cixous, "The Laugh of the Medusa," *Signs: Journal of Women in Culture and Society* 1, no. 4 (1976): 878.

scription for Western metaphysics."[42] She suggests that Plato, in formulating his theory of political knowledge, has severed the connection between
men and women, either reducing women to surrogate males or relegating
them to being caretakers of men's unwanted functions. The cave, instead
of symbolizing the origin of life, is portrayed as a dark prison. The prisoners and the other actors are male, and the cave or womb represents the
denial of truth and freedom. For Irigaray this means that the setting inside
the cave, the characters, and their actions are all dictated by a patriarchal
theory of knowledge constructed on the outside, where an "immaculate
conception" is supposed to occur.

> Specula(riza)tion, at last, without images, without determinate representa-
> tions, without the shadow of a reflection that might still suggest a role played
> by some body. Irradiation freed, also, from point of view, form defensive
> delimitation, restriction on principle demanded by organs that are still too
> natural. The whole field of vision, including depth, will be equally flooded by
> a light dispensed, equally, in its omnipotence. Without deformation, trans-
> formation, or loss, and equally without blindness or blurring of any kind.[43]

Any return to the empty eye socket of a cave from this phallocratic kingdom, no matter how enlightened, still must face the threat of violence and
corruption. Within this "economy of desire" the womb represents the distortion of the images visible up on top and a continuing threat to swallow
the returning prisoner whole.

> Real "nature" is unveiled on the path up to the heavens, not on the track back
> into the earth. The mother. That place connected still with artful conception,
> haunted by magicians who would have you believe that (re)production can be
> executed by skillful imitators, working from the divine plans. The cave gives
> birth only to phantoms, fakes or, at best, images. One must leave its circle in
> order to realize the factitious character of such a birth. Engendering the real
> is the father's task, engendering the fictive is the task of the mother—that
> "receptacle" for turning out more or less good copies of reality.[44]

Where men produce insight, women are encased within their own being,
mere objects of speculation, unable to answer when direct questions are
put to them.
   The Greek word for womb is *hystera*, and Irigaray wants us to under-

---

[42] Luce Irigaray, *Speculum of the Other Woman*, trans. Gillian C. Gill (Ithaca: Cornell
University Press, 1985), p. 243.

[43] Ibid., p. 316.

[44] Ibid., p. 300.

stand the difference between speaking as a hysteric and "speaking (as) woman."[45] The language of hysteria is a caricature of the dominant male discourse. Like mime, it is distorted and partially paralyzed. It is the language of women as other, defined from a male point of view. "Speaking (as) woman" involves a radically different understanding of language and logic. Irigaray suggests that her own style in *Speculum of the Other Woman* is an attempt to realize this alternative discourse. Speaking (as) woman

> would reject all closure or circularity in discourse—any constitution of *arche* or of *telos*; . . . it would privilege the "near" rather than the "proper," but a "near" not (re)captured in the spatio-temporal economy of philosophical tradition; that it would entail a different relation to unity, to identity with self, to truth, to the same and thus to alterity, to repetition and thus to temporality; that it would retraverse "differently" the matter/form dyad, the power/act dyad, and so on.[46]

Irigaray summarizes the contrast between these two ways of speaking by comparing the "flat mirror" of male discourse with "a curved mirror . . . that is folded back on itself." Phallogocentric language is a product of men reading themselves into the world around them and writing others out, just as they would see only themselves reflected on the surface of a perfectly flat mirror. This discourse is modeled on "frozen nature," that is, the ice in which man, once out of the cave, first notices his own image. Alternatively, reflection in a "curved mirror" subverts any hard-and-fast distinction between subject and object; thus there would be no possibility of ownership and the appropriation of the other. Such a "syntax" would break the spell of the phallocratic economy of desire.[47]

Irigaray's injunction to speak (as) woman rests on the claim that just as our lines of vision should not simply reproduce our own individual selves as they do when we gaze at the mirror image of a mirror image, ad infinitum, one's own voice should not be unitary. Voice, unlike visual imagery, cannot be mirrored back infinitely along Euclidean lines without losing its vitality. If we listen, we will hear how our voices encircle us at the same time that they project us in different directions. Speaking (as) woman is a generative *and* self-reflective activity that would be impossible within the confines of the impotent narcissism of icy male discourse.

This is only one of many attempts by feminists to use voice critically to

[45] Luce Irigaray, *This Sex Which Is Not One*, trans. Catherine Porter with Carolyn Burke (Ithaca: Cornell University Press, 1985), p. 136.
[46] Ibid., p. 154.
[47] Here I am following Margaret Whitford, *Luce Irigaray: Philosophy in the Feminine* (London: Routledge, 1991), pp. 38–52.

evaluate moral and political philosophy in modern democratic societies.[48] Its primary virtue is the way Irigaray recognizes how visual metaphors of rationality and power have affected the voices of democratic citizens. Voice has been indentured to the nobler faculty of seeing, and in politics this has created an androcentric distortion. As political judges, men speak with a certainty that the power of their words can reflect reality; women are only mimes. These noblemen do not simply claim to see farther and more clearly because they have escaped from Plato's *hystera*; they depreciate the voices of those who are in no position to see as they do. The alternative is not to bring women out of the cave so that they too can gaze into "frozen nature," but to revalue the voices of men as well as women within the spaces where "concrete" identities are formed.[49]

Does this feminist argument apply to liberal theory? Tocqueville's remarks on women are brief and predictable. The passion for democratic equality has not destroyed the American family. It remains a stable patriarchy, for "the American woman . . . knows beforehand what will be expected of her, and she herself has freely accepted the yoke."[50] What distinguishes the American case, Tocqueville claims, is the respect men give their wives. The division of labor within the household is clear, and women are not forced to take on work they are unfit for. Attacks on them are punished severely. As for their ability to reason, American women are accorded all the respect that men doing their work would be given. "Americans constantly display complete confidence in their spouses' judgment and deep respect for their freedom. They hold that woman's mind is just as capable as man's of discovering the naked truth, and her heart as firm to face it. They have never sought to place her virtue, any more than his, under the protection of prejudice, ignorance, or fear." Like men, wives can face the naked truth without blinking. Americans "do not think that a man and his wife should always use their intelligence and understanding in the same way, but they do at least consider that the one has as firm an understanding as the other and a mind as clear."[51] A firm heart and a firm understanding equip American wives to handle the naked truth just like a man.

But more revealing than Tocqueville's faint praise of women is the essay

---

[48] Compare Mary E. Hawkesworth, "Feminist Rhetoric: Discourses on the Male Monopoly of Thought," *Political Theory* 16 (August 1988): 444–67, with Nancy Fraser and Sandra Lee Bartky, eds., *Revaluing French Feminism* (Bloomington: Indiana University Press, 1992).

[49] See Seyla Benhabib, "The Generalized and the Concrete Other," in *Feminism as Critique*, ed. Seyla Benhabib and Drucilla Cornell (Minneapolis: University of Minnesota Press, 1987), pp. 77–95.

[50] Tocqueville, *Democracy*, p. 593.

[51] Ibid., pp. 602, 603.

I have already discussed, *The Subjection of Women*, by his contemporary and admirer John Stuart Mill. I return to it to evaluate the merits of the feminist case against the liberal conception of judgment. Tocqueville never fully overcame his nostalgia for the ancien régime. In Mill we find a less reluctant theory of liberal democracy in which individual liberty remains the primary moral value because of its instrumental connection to progress. As I have said, Mill designed political institutions, especially representative legislatures and expert administrative offices, to complement one another and create the environment within which free individuals will improve themselves. To the extent that individuals need help, they can be assisted by exemplary figures like Mill as they vigorously debate one another. These are the sights and sounds Mill wanted representative democracy to offer. Within this universe, he argued, political judgment can take several forms (legislative, administrative, intellectual, and journalistic), but it remains an activity for these elites, whereas political education for the majority occurs through modest forms of local participation inspired by exemplary role models and debates within the press. Mill's vigorous case against the legal subjection of women in a liberal society reveals more vividly than Tocqueville's brief treatment of women how a visual conception of political judgment can rest on an androcentric conception of political education.

Mill repeatedly emphasized that the prejudices against women and the disabilities they suffer are assuredly the product of their unequal station and harsh treatment in modern societies. Their subjection is unjust to them and harms society as a whole. Therefore women should be freed from their subordinate place in the family, the workplace, and public affairs. But despite this dominant theme in the essay, Mill still made several invidious comparisons between men and women that should not be minimized as historical artifacts. As Jean Elshtain says, "Mill seeks equality *within* the family yet wishes to retain much of the traditional ambience of family life tied to women's domestication and men's assumptions of public responsibilities."[52]

For example, he argued that "in an otherwise just state of things" married women should not work outside the home when it is inconsistent with the requirements of "the management of the household."[53] Why this special solicitude for women homemakers? More to the point, why shouldn't the same limitation be placed on men or shared equally between men and

[52] Jean Bethke Elshtain, *Public Man, Private Woman* (Princeton: Princeton University Press, 1981), p. 144. Also, see Susan Moller Okin, *Women in Western Political Thought* (Princeton: Princeton University Press, 1979), pp. 226–30, and Carole Pateman, *The Disorder of Women* (Stanford: Stanford University Press, 1989), pp. 210–25.

[53] John Stuart Mill, *The Subjection of Women*, in *CW*, 21:298.

women? One plausible answer is that "Mill wanted to assure his Victorian readers that even without formal obligation, women would choose to raise a family."[54] Without denying this possible strategic motivation, we can still ask what assumptions Mill harbored about the tendencies of men and women to judge political issues from different perspectives.

The first assumption has to do with the value of an egalitarian home as the primary locus of moral and political education. It is within this new family that Mill believed an attachment to and understanding of freedom and equality can be cultivated. "The moral training of mankind will never be adapted to the conditions of the life for which all other human progress is a preparation, until they practise in the family the same moral rule which is adapted to the normal constitution of human society."[55] But if equality within the home is so important for all other associations and "human progress" generally, then surely the inequality Mill was prepared to admit between men and women in terms of their responsibilities for the household has to be justified. It is here that Mill slips back into the language of natural differences he otherwise took great pains to reject.

"Women as they are," Mill repeatedly emphasized, have a cast of mind that is different from men's. They attend to the present in a way that men do not: "With equality of experience and of general faculties, a woman usually sees much more than a man of what is immediately before her."[56] Men, on the other hand, have a more developed speculative faculty that enables them to see into the future. The two abilities are complementary, Mill argued, but the latter is clearly a more powerful tool for the improvement of mankind: "To see the futurity of the species has always been the privilege of the intellectual elite, or of those who have learnt from them; to have the feelings of that futurity has been the distinction, and usually the martyrdom, of a still rarer elite."[57] It is a tool that only a male "elite" is capable of mastering.

Mill emphasized the way a woman's practical, present-tense orientation complements the man's speculative mind. "Hardly anything can be of greater value to a man of theory and speculation who employs himself not in collecting materials of knowledge by observation, but in working them up by processes of thought into comprehensive truths of science and laws of conduct, than to carry on his speculation in the companionship, and under the criticism, of a really superior woman... A woman seldom runs wild after an abstraction." Without the help of women, men's work

---

[54] Nadia Urbanati, "John Stuart Mill on Androgyny and Ideal Marriage," *Political Theory* 19 (November 1991): 640.
[55] Mill, *Subjection of Women*, p. 295.
[56] Ibid., p. 305.
[57] Ibid., p. 294.

would not reach any practical conclusions. It would remain idle speculation. Women, Mill explicitly suggested, can lead men out of the world of
"transcendent philosophy" that is not "peopled with real beings, animate
or inanimate, even idealized, but with personified shadows created by the
illusions of metaphysics or by the mere entanglement of words."[58] Mill's
ambivalence toward Plato forces him to reject the notion that the Forms
can inseminate nature, but he clung to the deeper prejudice that the vision
of a male elite can take us out of the shadows and into the future.

What, if anything, do men contribute to women's way of knowing? Mill
can only say that they give them "width and largeness," but this seems
of little consequence, especially if it is women's work within the confines
of the family and household that is so essential as a "school" for virtue.
On the other hand, educated women can help men put men's far-seeing
theories into practice by sharing their knowledge of the present. Related
to this asymmetrical relationship between men's theoretical foresight and
women's concrete understanding of the present is what Mill calls women's
mobility of thought. Mill is somewhat nervous about admitting the truth
of this prejudice that women tend to move about in their thinking more
than men, "less capable of persisting long in the same continuous effort,
more fitted for dividing their faculties among many things than for travel-
ling in any one path to the highest point which can be reached by it."[59] But
if it is true, he says, it is hardly a disability. It is their peculiar "excellence"
to occupy themselves "with small things" as they go about their business.
Men tend to lapse into mindlessness when not traveling in any one path to
the highest point where they can see into the future; women, on the other
hand, have the capacity to focus on the minute things of ordinary life
and, if need be, think about more than one thing at a time. Not mobility,
it seems, but juggling is what is most distinctive about women's thought.
Once again, Mill seems to have discovered a strong, valuable affinity between the mostly pedestrian tasks of household management and women's
powers of reason. In short, women are responsible for moral and political
education but almost constitutionally unfit for the more theoretical activities on which the "improvement of mankind" depends. Good women
are not surrogate men as they are in Plato and Tocqueville, but their way
of seeing the world, securely based in the household, complements the
higher/male form of speculation. Women are responsible for maintaining
the household as a "school" for the virtues while men apply their special
visual faculties to more abstract political problems with the help of women.

If liberal democracy is to live up to its promise of liberty *and* equality,
women and minorities have to be heard as well as seen within the public

[58] Ibid., p. 306.
[59] Ibid., p. 306.

domain. This recognition of the voices of the other in liberal theory has taken the form of a renewed interest in dialogue. Building on their comfortable relationship with Socratic dialogue, male liberal theorists have recommended dialogue as a path for political education and a vehicle for making political as well as moral judgments along that path. One female liberal theorist who has made an effort to bring the feminist concern for the anguished voice of the other to bear *within* the politics of policymaking is Martha Minow.

Minow describes her approach to difference as a "social relations approach," indebted to an assortment of pragmatists and feminists.[60] She is concerned with the way equality has been construed under the law according to "normal," mostly male standards. It is natural, for example, to exclude women from hazardous jobs within the workplace; it is not natural, up until very recently, to see the workplace as a space constructed according to the needs of healthy males. It is natural to treat pregnancy leave as a medical problem for women; it is not natural to see it as part of the shared process of raising a family. Minow asks us to question how these social structures have been erected, in whose interests they operate, and not what relevant differences between persons would or would not justify unequal treatment within these structures. The status quo, she argues, is not natural and uncoerced, despite what the laws in liberal democratic societies assume.

Minow does not reject the concept of equal protection, but she would prefer to have judges base their rulings on their reading of the social relations that constitute the cases before them rather than on essentialist notions of natural differences or even a conventional notion of individual rights that permits affirmative action when necessary. Judgment then becomes a tricky business, and Minow is well aware of this. How does a judge decide, for example, when a Native American tribe is still a tribe? Does the judge consult the historical self-understanding of tribal members no matter what demographers say about the assimilation and size of the tribe? Minow does not want to abandon the search for judicially enforceable rights, but she believes that judges can play an educative role here. By attending to the voices of the other, judges can show the powerful how what seems natural to them is really a product of their own power to name and control. "Learning to take the perspective of another is an opening wedge for an alternative to traditional legal treatments of difference."[61] By encouraging citizens to see the connections between self and other rather than simply ruling on the basis of whose individual rights are

---

[60] Martha Minow, *Making All the Difference: Inclusion, Exclusion, and American Law* (Ithaca: Cornell University Press, 1990).

[61] Ibid., p. 379.

at stake, judges can be a force for political education. Judges cannot ignore individual rights any more than they can ignore the bounds of legitimacy defined by the doctrine of separation of powers. But these are not bright lines, and judgments based on a concern for the other may help resolve the underlying political conflicts of which equal protection litigation is only a symptom. In the closing pages, Minow emphasizes the dialogical purpose of this theory of adjudication: "This resolution is not a solution but a shift in assumptions. From here, what we need to do is work, in specific contexts, on the problems of difference. There is no ultimate resting place but instead an opportunity for dialogue, conversation, continuing processes of mutual boundary setting, and efforts to manage colliding perspectives on reality. It is not enough to imagine the perspective of the other; we must also try to share deliberations with the other persons." [62] Legal judgments can be propaedeutics for wider social dialogues in even the hardest cases in which the collision between competing "perspectives on reality" is politically divisive. Minow cites as an example Justice John Stevens's minority opinion in the *Cleburne* case mentioned in the introduction: "I cannot believe that a rational member of this disadvantaged class could ever approve of the discriminatory application of the city's ordinance in this case." [63] By almost taking the perspective of the other, Stevens indicates the kind of internal dialogue he thinks it is appropriate to have in making a judgment on the value of independent living for retarded adults.

If the purpose of Minow's social relations approach is to reveal the connections between dominant and subordinate groups, however, then she must say more about these connections than simply that they are power laden. What are the resources dominant groups use to impose their views of difference on women and other minorities? How do these dominant groups manage to forget, if they do, the constructed nature of this reality and come to believe it is natural? We need more than simply an assertion that this is what has happened. Otherwise it is not clear how taking the perspective of the other, if we accept Minow's claim that this is what Justice Stevens is trying to do, will disclose the power relations that exist and replace them with more egalitarian relations.

Minow is aware of this problem. "Merely borrowing theories and applying them to law may result in an exchange of abstractions rather than a grounded reconsideration of law's treatment of difference." [64] Her answer to the problem, however, is to suggest that feminist movements, as diverse as they have been, can be tapped and a coherent theoretical analysis

[62] Ibid., p. 383.
[63] Ibid., p. 114.
[64] Ibid., pp. 192–93.

of power constructed from them. Minow runs through a lawyer's survey of feminist psychology, literary theory, and history, concluding that a feminist theory of equality under the law must recognize the situated, relational quality of all selves, including those who must judge others. "The act of judgment depends on and simultaneously forges a relationship."[65] But once again the argument trails off. How does the situated, relational power of judging operate? What are its limits and resources? Indeed, what are its goals beyond a vague vision of greater empathy and connectedness? Minow is suggesting that to see how things fit together as a whole we must be able to move back and forth between the perspectives of self and other. Judges must look through the eyes of the other as well as at their own mirror images. This may be attractive to lawyers who pride themselves on being able to argue both sides of a case; it is not much consolation to others who are still dependent on the judgments of experts. Minow lends a sympathetic ear to the voices of women, children, and handicapped persons who have been defined as other against dominant standards of normality, but it is the sympathy of a reasonable, exemplary judge, not a fellow citizen.

Not all feminist theorists have fallen back onto a sight-based theory in order to come to terms with difference.[66] Catharine A. MacKinnon, writing on the same problem of equality, explicitly calls attention to the visual biases of liberal legal doctrines as well as more left-wing critiques that refuse to put the abuse and oppression of women at the center of sex equality. "Liberalism, purporting to discover gender, has discovered male and female in the mirror of nature; the left has discovered masculine and feminine in the mirror of society. The approach from the standpoint of the subordination of women to men, by contrast, criticizes and claims the specific situation of women's enforced inferiority and devaluation, pointing a way out of the infinity of reflections in law-and-society's hall of mirrors where sex equality law remains otherwise trapped."[67] The male bias in the law in liberal society goes beyond the narrow doctrine of equal protection (which holds that the state cannot treat women either like men or differently from men without good reason) to include rape laws that minimize the extent of violence against women, abortion laws that isolate reproductive rights at the point of conception, and pornography laws that protect the free speech of pimps. MacKinnon is arguing that seeing things from the perspective of the other in order to balance the socially constructed

[65] Ibid., p. 219.
[66] For example, Iris Marion Young, *Justice and the Politics of Difference* (Princeton: Princeton University Press, 1990), and Carole Pateman, *The Sexual Contract* (Stanford: Stanford University Press, 1988).
[67] Catharine A. MacKinnon, *Toward a Feminist Theory of the State* (Cambridge: Harvard University Press, 1989), pp. 243–44.

differences of masculine and feminine is no better than a crude reversion to natural differences. In either case women will continue to be oppressed by an omniscient overseer who believes it is too costly to give up his control over women's bodies.

According to MacKinnon, the existing liberal rights of privacy, free speech, and equal protection are not merely incomplete protections for women: they are hostile to sex equality. "Abstract rights authorize the male experience of the world. Substantive rights for women would not. Their authority would be the currently unthinkable: nondominant authority, the authority of excluded truth, the voice of silence."[68] One response to this sweeping claim is to ask how silent women's voices have already been within the law. Many feminists, certainly Minow, would disagree with MacKinnon and cite MacKinnon's own work as evidence. The concept of sexual harassment MacKinnon developed demonstrates that this second voice is sometimes audible, even if its full practical implications are still unclear.[69] Another response, however, is to accept MacKinnon's skepticism and ask how democratic political dialogues between citizens critical of consumerism and clientism are to be fostered, if not through greater insight alone.

[68] Ibid., pp. 248–49.
[69] Katharine T. Bartlett, "Feminist Legal Methods," *Harvard Law Review* 103 (February 1990): 872–77.

# CHAPTER EIGHT

# Emerson Reconsidered

Emersonian democratic theory is not the special preserve of political theorists or philosophers working only within the confines of academic journals. It belongs to public intellectuals who also work in popular media where they can make common sense of the neocorporatist images and voices that liberal theory uncritically accents. This task is difficult for intellectuals who bruise easily, and so Emersonian democratic theorists must have thick skins: "Never mind the ridicule, never mind the defeat; up again, old heart!—it seems to say,—there is victory yet for all justice; and the true romance which the world exists to realize will be the transformation of genius into practical power."[1]

Until very recently Emerson has been severely criticized as an antidemocrat and not much of a political theorist. Wilson Carey McWilliams excoriates Emerson for his individualism, privatism, and romantic mystification of fraternity. Emerson, he argues, had no patience with politics, no sense of moral responsibility to others, and no confidence in the political judgments of ordinary citizens when it came to executing their programs. Politics was a superficial business, and real human community would dawn despite it. On McWilliams's reading, an Emersonian political education is a contradiction in terms: "Believing that only education could change men's 'hearts,' Emerson saw education as something separate from politics."[2]

Despite his aversion to politics and a seemingly callous attitude toward

---

[1] Ralph Waldo Emerson, "Experience," in *Essays: Second Series,* in *The Complete Works of Ralph Waldo Emerson,* 2d ed., ed. Joel Myerson (New York: AMS Press, 1979), 3:85–86. (Hereafter cited as *CW.*)

[2] Wilson Carey McWilliams, *The Idea of Fraternity in America* (Berkeley and Los Angeles: University of California Press, 1973), p. 287.

the poor, Emerson's views on power and the need for public intellectuals to transform their genius into practical power suggest how democratic theory can operate as a critical form of political education. Perhaps this is what Dewey had in mind when he praised Emerson as "the Philosopher of Democracy" and mused that "when democracy has articulated itself, it will have no difficulty in finding itself already proposed in Emerson."[3] But Emerson only suggests and proposes, he does not develop the idea of democratic theory as a political education in power. This chapter pulls together Emerson's thoughts on power and then, in a very preliminary way, explores what they might mean for the relation between democratic politics and the liberal values of tolerance and reasonableness in discussion.

## Power's Laws

Emerson was preoccupied with power,[4] especially as it was embodied in trade and nature. Against these forms of power he advocated the powers of the scholar, the poet, and the representative man, figures who would stand between the demos and the world of commodities and unformed nature to interpret and translate. It is this reforming, form-giving intermediate role of the intellectual that Emerson sometimes reluctantly recommends, sometimes champions, and sometimes bemoans. Conventional political institutions and laws, he believed, could not perform these bridging functions. Like a written constitution, they are paper thin. What is needed most of all is character: a new way of seeing nature and trade, of speaking one's mind, of making the ordinary a source of inspiration, of seeing "the miraculous in the common,"[5] and of connecting the pieces within the arc of human experience.

But power is the subject of politics, and this posed a problem for Emerson, since he was generally, as McWilliams says, repelled by politics and political rhetoric. "Every actual State is corrupt," he argued,[6] and political rhetoric, epitomized in the speeches of Daniel Webster, is easily placed in the service of false idols.[7] "A public oration is an escapade . . . a gag,

---

[3] John Dewey, *Characters and Events: Popular Essays in Social and Political Philosophy,* vol. 1 (New York: Henry Holt, 1929), p. 76.

[4] Michael Lopez, "Emerson's Rhetoric of War," *Prospects: An Annual of American Cultural Studies* 12 (1987): 294, and from a Nietzschean perspective, George J. Stack, *Nietzsche and Emerson: An Elective Affinity* (Athens: Ohio University Press, 1992), pp. 138–75.

[5] Ralph Waldo Emerson, *Nature,* in *CW,* 1:74.

[6] Ralph Waldo Emerson, "Politics," in *Essays: Second Series,* in *CW,* 3:208.

[7] Ralph Waldo Emerson, "The Fugitive Slave Law," in *CW,* 11:219–20.

and not a communication, not a speech, not a man."[8] When forced to play the political game, he complained bitterly. When he could step back and assess politics more dispassionately, the best he could say was that it was an "after-work, a poor patching." What should not have been enacted in the first place is, with great effort, best repealed.[9] This strong aversion to politics forced Emerson to approach power from another direction.

Emerson did not advocate acts of resistance by private citizens to chasten state power as Thoreau did, and he did not cherish much hope for the appearance of a Weberian political leader whose ability to stand above routine politics and resist its temptations could restore meaning to political life. Even Napoleon's power, rooted in a character Emerson otherwise praised, proved egotistical and destructive.[10] Emerson's mediating intellectuals occupy that space in political conversations where final answers are especially dangerous and where you begin to lose your own voice when you lose sight of those whom political institutions and laws have failed. The Emersonian public intellectual has to be able to step in just when premature consensus is about to form, when silence is about to be taken for acquiescence, and before finer points on the horizon are either interpreted as objects of little importance or blown out of proportion.

The Emersonian intellectual's ability to make this kind of intervention depends directly on the power to mix the metaphors of seeing and hearing; he, Emerson says—not she—ministers to a tired political vocabulary on the verge of overreacting. The very first sentences of "Self-Reliance" point the way: "I read the other day some verses written by an eminent painter which were original and not conventional. The soul always hears an admonition in such lines, let the subject be what it may."[11] Through reading, a visual encounter, we can grasp the poetic sounds of a painter, and in them we hear the warning: "Believe your own thought." Seeing, hearing, seeing, and then hearing again, all so that we can hear our own thoughts more clearly. "My life," Emerson claims, "is for itself and not for a spectacle."[12] To reclaim "my life," I must form my own voice without denying the urge to see into nature's secrets and search for the hidden treasures trade promises. Emerson's mixed metaphors capture the tension between the visual spectacles of nature and trade and the voice of the public intellectual who speaks so that citizens can think about what they are doing in

[8] Ralph Waldo Emerson, "Spiritual Laws," in *Essays: First Series*, in *CW*, 2:152.
[9] Ralph Waldo Emerson, "Culture," in *The Conduct of Life*, in *CW*, 6:136.
[10] Ralph Waldo Emerson, "Napoleon; or, The Man of the World," in *Representative Men*, in *CW*, 4:257–58.
[11] Ralph Waldo Emerson, "Self-Reliance," in *Essays: First Series*, in *CW*, 2:45.
[12] Ibid., p. 53.

those difficult liminal moments when "words are also actions, and actions are a kind of words." [13]

Synesthetically mixing things up, experimenting with political languages, is Emerson's way of reminding us not to be seduced by the sight of these spectacles or comforted by familiar words. And despite his famous visual imagery in *Nature*,[14] he was not after clairvoyance. "If we live truly, we shall see truly. . . . When a man lives with God, his voice shall be as sweet as the murmur of the brook and the rustle of the corn." [15] Seeing, he seems to be saying, has to be reattached to voice if we are to make our own way in the world, one step at a time.

The Emersonian public intellectual maps the origins of power back into a world of natural signs and charts its course out among wider and wider circles of commercial relations, all the while marking the compensatory laws of power that pull hard across the surface. "We live amid surfaces," he warns us, "and the true art of life is to skate well on them." [16] It is through tracing these "circles" that the intellectual realizes his own "power of self-recovery," [17] and once fortified, is prepared to serve as a public model of self-reliance.

This movement across the senses is not random or careless. Emerson sought to moderate the visual pull of natural spectacles and awesome machinery by instructing his readers in a new political art, the art of listening to ourselves as we look on in awe. Power initially must be seen, but once seen its seductiveness and the false confidence it inspires must be controlled. J. Glenn Gray, in *The Warriors*, has described the relation between seeing and the spectacle of power in war this way: "Sometimes seeing absorbs us utterly; it is as though the human being becomes one great eye. The eye is lustful because it requires the novel, the unusual, the spectacular. It cannot satiate itself on the familiar, the routine, the everyday." [18] The spectacle of power promises a certain kind of ecstasy or state of being outside the self, a sublime self-transcendence in which spectators come to believe they have merged with the spectacle. Emerson could have agreed with this, but perhaps because he did not witness the spectacles that so chilled Gray during World War II, he refuses to surrender completely to his own lusting eye for "swarthy juices." [19]

---

[13] Ralph Waldo Emerson, "The Poet," in *Essays: Second Series*, in *CW*, 3:8.

[14] Emerson, *Nature*, pp. 8–10.

[15] Emerson, "Self-Reliance," p. 68.

[16] Emerson, "Experience," p. 59.

[17] Ralph Waldo Emerson, "Circles," in *Essays: First Series*, in *CW*, 2:309.

[18] J. Glenn Gray, *The Warriors: Reflections on Men in Battle* (New York: Harper Torchbooks, 1970), p. 29.

[19] Ralph Waldo Emerson, "Power," in *The Conduct of Life*, in *CW*, 6:71.

What seemed almost inevitable to Emerson—"We aim at a petty end quite aside from the public good, but our act arranges itself by irresistible magnetism in a line with the poles of the world"[20]—has become increasingly difficult for intellectuals in this century. Emerson's early efforts were through the church, but he found this was not the place for his kind of public work. In public talks and short essays he found a medium more suited to his own "genius," that is, his own conception of a public intellectual wary of the public (and its public ways of speaking) but unable to turn away and thus forsake the individuals who make it up. Emerson's public intellectual must be able to feel the silent world of power constituted by nature and trade and then translate it into a language the people can hear and respond to so that they are not awestruck. The Emersonian public intellectual "is one who raises himself from private considerations and breathes and lives on public and illustrious thoughts."[21]

Self-reliance, according to Emerson, does not ultimately have to merge into egoism as Tocqueville thought it would.[22] It is the constitution in everyman that is waiting to be written; it is a way of breaking free from the mainstream vocabularies of society and the confines of philosophical consistency. It is the way we recover "life" as "our dictionary."[23] Self-reliance therefore is not a passive, antipolitical stance. It is an active way of taking nature and the commodities that trade threatens us with and then generating enough trust in ourselves to mold them with an eye on one another, that is, with "new eyes."[24] Emerson's "Self-Reliance" therefore is not a glorification of the individual, but rather an alternative political posture for citizens buckling under the weight of social conformity and handcuffed by abstract modes of thought. It is a way for them to tap into the power of nature, like Antaeus, by blending their natural senses of sight and sound in a new yet still common language—the language, Emerson argues, of fresh self-reflective experience. "Man is the broken giant, and in all his weakness both his body and his mind are invigorated by habits of conversation with nature."[25] His power will always be "hooped in by necessity,"[26] but it will be—at least it can be—his own power.

Emerson does not analyze political institutions because they are only the temporary outcroppings of political character. "The law," he wrote, is

[20] Ralph Waldo Emerson, "Compensation," in *Essays: First Series*, in *CW*, 2:110.

[21] Ralph Waldo Emerson, *The American Scholar*, in *CW*, 1:101.

[22] Alexis de Tocqueville, *Democracy in America*, trans. George Lawrence, ed. J. P. Mayer (Garden City, N.Y.: Anchor Books, 1969), vol. 2, pt. 2, chap. 2, p. 506.

[23] Emerson, *American Scholar*, p. 98.

[24] Emerson, *Nature*, p. 75.

[25] Ralph Waldo Emerson, "History," in *Essays: First Series*, in *CW*, 2:31.

[26] Ralph Waldo Emerson, "Fate," in *The Conduct of Life*, in *CW*, 6:19.

only a memorandum."[27] Power is not reducible to acts of state: it is a product of the character that citizens share to make sense of and shape nature and trade. Now let me suggest two ways Emerson interprets these great symbols of power in order to build more self-reliant democratic citizens.

First, Emerson interprets nature, trade, and their interconnections from the perspective of the frescoist—both painter and sculptor—whose words themselves are absorbed into the objects of his work. With a painter's eye he blends foreground and background, creating new colors with a new texture. Plaster and paint fold together into an emergent sculpture of nature blooming and engines driving. As the sculptor of this display of power, the theorist must move across great distances, seeing only small sections at a time, periodically losing sight of the whole and losing himself in the details.

Second, Emerson uses poetic language to transform nature and trade, not with the ambidextrous skills of a frescoist, but in the way a conductor alerts, guides, and coordinates the interpretations of individual musicians. Here power can be likened to a participant in a conversation, orchestrating other voices at the same time as he tries to make room for himself. As much as the power of the conductor stands above the orchestra, his is still not an overpowering voice. In fact it is momentary and sharp, catching the eye and releasing the voice of the other in a split second. The conductor remains stationary, never backing off and then rushing forward to capture a detail as the frescoist does, and thus never running the risk of losing himself in the spectacle of power. Instead, he seeks to affect nature and trade more subtly by changing their phrasing. Unlike the frescoist, who blends a new texture out of the old, the orchestral public intellectual highlights the text.

Emerson's writings on power in these two senses gain their originality from the way the approaches are combined to capture the streaming, driving, awe-inspiring look of power and its possible discipline. The forces of nature and trade—if rewritten, Emerson suggests, like Haydn's oratorios—can combine sound with color and motion in a stable form.[28] Nature, in fact, is the source of language's greatest powers, analogy and metaphor. The power of self-reliance is "new" but still "in nature." Even trade, the source of vulgarity and barbarism, constitutes a world of action that "is the raw material out of which the intellect moulds her splendid products." And the "manufacture goes forward at all hours."[29] When, Emerson seems to promise us, language, nature, and trade are combined in this symphonic way, the spectacle of power can be re-formed on a human scale.

[27] Emerson, "Politics," p. 200.

[28] Emerson, *Nature*, pp. 43–44.

[29] Emerson, *American Scholar*, pp. 95–96.

This means that for Emerson nature and trade do not stand over and against the individual. Language has its roots in natural simplicity, and the path language carves out from actions to thought is analogous to the manufacturing process. Language enables us to make the world of nature and trade our own because it shares certain features with them. "The world, — this shadow of the soul, or *other me*, — lies wide around."[30]

At times, of course, Emerson emphasizes the power of the "eternal One" or the "Over-Soul" as the creative force behind this "other me." But he also offers a less mysterious account of nature's highest power. "In groups where debate is earnest, and especially on high questions, the company become aware that the thought rises to an equal level in all bosoms, that all have a spiritual property in what was said, as well as the sayer. . . . It arches over them like a temple, this unity of thought in which every heart beats with a nobler sense of power and duty, and thinks and acts with unusual solemnity. All are conscious of attaining to a higher self-possession. It shines for all."[31] It is in conversations like these that "tacit references" are made to something that is not social, but impersonal. Call it "God," Emerson says. We might also call it the tacit knowledge the participants share that makes for mutual respect and a willingness to keep political debate and discussion going. The emphasis in "The Over-Soul" is on man's need to "greatly listen to himself, withdrawing himself from all the accents of other men's devotion."[32] But the idea of the oversoul as a third, tacit conversational voice is not a throwaway comment. In "History" Emerson says that to realize any power on a human scale, man must recognize that "power consists in the multitude of his affinities, in the fact that his life is intertwined with the whole chain of organic and inorganic being." Even the most self-reliant man "is a bundle of relations, a knot of roots, whose flower and fruitage is the world. . . . He cannot live without the world."[33]

It is often the case, however, that Emerson's aversion to this other me made up of the multitude of affinities gets the better of him, and he retreats from the social world. Then nature's "magazine of power"[34] can be found by listening only to ourselves, making "daylight shine through" us in our "silent moments."[35] Even more forcefully in "Experience": "In this our talking America we are ruined by our good nature and listening on all sides" (p. 82). But despite these moments, he still maintains that power "abides in no man and in no woman, but for a moment speaks from

[30] Ibid., p. 95.
[31] Ralph Waldo Emerson, "The Over-Soul," in *Essays: First Series*, in *CW*, 2:277.
[32] Ibid., p. 294.
[33] Emerson, "History," p. 36.
[34] Emerson, *Nature*, p. 35.
[35] Emerson, "Spiritual Laws," p. 161.

this one, and for another moment from that one" (p. 58). It is this part of nature, possibly, that is the most "unhandsome" to Emerson, the part most likely to slip through our fingers and refuse to let us draw our own circle around it. "Our relations to each other are oblique and casual" (p. 50): it is hard to take their measure and contain them. But to repeat, it is impossible to avoid them entirely. It is only in the echoes of our own voices, coming back to us in the voices of others, that we can catch a glimpse of how we look to them and how we stand with regard to them. This is the thin surface Emerson says we must learn to skate on.

One final comment on the difference between nature and trade. Nature, left to itself, even with all its spectacle, appears relatively benign to Emerson. Trade and its modern product, the commodity, are never entirely on their own and thus are always suspect. Their power, consequently, is more corrupting. They crowd into the foreground. "The invasion of nature by Trade with its Money, its Credit, its Steam, its Railroad, threatens to upset the balance of man, and establish a new Universal Monarchy more tyrannical than Babylon or Rome." [36]

The tyranny that angers Emerson, however, is not the exploitation of workers. "Wealth," he believed, "brings with it its own checks and balances." Political institutions should respect "the only safe rule . . . the self-adjusting meter of demand and supply." They should not "meddle." [37] Emerson argued that there was a more universal tyranny. Whereas natural simplicity can cleanse language, the power of trade can corrupt our language, and through this corruption deny us access to a nature we can make our own and to our "affinities." "Secondary desires—the desires of riches, of pleasures, of power, and of praise," dominate our character under the influence of trade. Because of them we speak in a "paper currency." As "new imagery ceases to be created, and old words are perverted to stand for things which are not," our language loses its natural simplicity. Our analogies and metaphors are bargained for, cheapened, and sold. They are not our own. Power politics is one source of these "secondary desires," but trade is the major source.[38]

Emerson gives us the symptoms of this corruption of character and language, but their origins in trade are not dissected. Instead he turns to the task of reconstructing the role of those who might remedy this situation, who can see nature for what it is and put trade back in its place as a set of human affinities tied together by the products of human genius. To this

---

[36] Quoted in Carolyn Porter, *Seeing and Being: The Plight of the Participant Observer in Emerson, James, Adams, and Faulkner* (Middletown: Wesleyan University Press, 1981), p. 59.

[37] Ralph Waldo Emerson, "Wealth," in *The Conduct of Life*, in *CW*, 6:105.

[38] Emerson, *Nature*, pp. 29–30.

end he invites us to rethink the duties of an "American Scholar," one who can "pierce this rotten diction and fasten words again to visible things."[39]

What does Emerson mean when he says that the intellectual, after years of silent apprenticeship, will be able to raise "himself from private considerations" so that he "breathes and lives on public and illustrious thoughts"?[40] Stanley Cavell has argued that this is an example of Emerson's use of "transfiguration and conversion" as methods of "aversive thinking." The term *illustrious* condenses the illustrative quality of the scholar's work as a representative figure and its status as a form of thinking that attains to something like Kantian universality. The scholar's work illustrates what all thinkers are capable of attaining. It illustrates the illustriousness of the moral law common to them all. On Cavell's interpretation, what is "public" is what is common to humanity as members of a kingdom of ends. Each individual as an end in himself carries in his soul the constitution of this moral domain. Each private life, lived according to Kantian duties of respect, is like an "illustrious monarchy."[41] It is the only alternative we have to "the base estimate of the market of what constitutes a manly success."[42]

Although supported by other passages,[43] this Kantian reading of Emerson understates Emerson's ambivalent attitude toward politics and public life here and now, not in a kingdom of ends. His public intellectual often may see himself as an illustrious/illustrative member of a potential moral community of dutiful noumenal selves. But Emerson is also uncomfortable with simply occupying this high ground and calling down to his fellow citizens to keep their eyes on the ultimate prize. Perhaps this is what Judith Shklar means by the "inhibitions of democracy" that work on Emerson.[44] "Where do we find ourselves?" he asks in "Experience." The answer is hardly transcendental: "We wake and find ourselves on a stair; there are stairs below us, which we seem to have ascended; there are stairs above us, many a one, which go upward and out of sight."[45] If the kingdom of ends is "out of sight," what do the next steps leading in its direction look like? What doors do the intellectual's "keys of power" open?[46]

At the core of the intellectual's public role for Emerson is the task of

[39] Ibid., p. 30.

[40] Emerson, *American Scholar*, p. 101.

[41] Stanley Cavell, *Conditions Handsome and Unhandsome: The Constitution of Emersonian Perfectionism* (Chicago: University of Chicago Press, 1990), pp. 44–45.

[42] Emerson, "Compensation," p. 95.

[43] Emerson, "Over-Soul," pp. 295–97.

[44] Judith N. Shklar, "Emerson and the Inhibitions of Democracy," *Political Theory* 18 (November 1990): 601–14.

[45] Emerson, "Experience," p. 45.

[46] Emerson, *Nature*, p. 32.

creating common forms—forms that can be held in common. If public life is to be anything more than simply a "jailyard of individual relations," the intellectual must enable citizens, in midstride, to publicly affirm their "common wealth." "The breadth of the problem," Emerson acknowledges, "is great, for the poet is representative." He shares the weaknesses as well as the strengths of us all. "He stands among partial men for the complete man, and apprises us not of his wealth, but of the common wealth."[47]

The wealth that all "partial" men hold in common is their ability to use the language of commerce against the reifying power of trade and politics by endowing it with its own nearly natural simplicity. "The poet is the person in whom these powers are in balance, the man without impediment, who sees and handles that which others dream of, traverses the whole scale of experience, and is representative of man, in virtue of being the largest power to receive and to impart."[48]

For this reason, Emerson argues, writers must learn their trade in the "public square. The people, and not the college, is the writer's home." And while he confesses that society is to him "vulgar" and people in public conversations tend to be attracted to their own kind, he also concludes that society is still the "natural element" in which "our [principles] are to be applied."[49] The most "exquisite" minds may need some insulation from society, but for intellectuals committed to educating the public, whose words and actions are indistinguishable and who stand among "partial" men to make them more complete, the "public square" is their natural habitat. So situated, the poet has the power to make the "symbols" we inhabit, our "tools, words, and things," alive again. To do this he must take pleasure in the pleasures of "common influences" and give them "a power which makes their old use forgotten, and puts eyes and a tongue into every dumb and inanimate object."[50] Then he will have created the "affinities" between "partial" persons that reconstitute them as self-reliant individuals.

When the writer and poet, according to Emerson, enter the "public square" to learn their trade and build a "common wealth," political education becomes their primary concern. Does the new language that puts eyes and a tongue into every dumb and inanimate object give the demos greater purchase on the powers of nature and trade, greater control over the sources of their own power? In other words, what kind of insight into power do Emerson's self-reliant citizens acquire? Whose voices do they hear?

[47] Emerson, "Poet," p. 25.
[48] Ibid., p. 6.
[49] Ralph Waldo Emerson, "Society and Solitude," in *CW*, 7:11, 16.
[50] Emerson, "Poet," pp. 20–29.

The answer is not to be found in Emerson's explicit interpretations of "Power" and "Wealth" in *The Conduct of Life*. These essays tend to be narrow and predictable. Instead, I would emphasize the two earlier essays on action, "Compensation" and "Circles," in *Essays: First Series*. It is in these two essays that Emerson re-forms power as a public intellectual in order to put eyes and a tongue into "partial" men. It is in these two essays that he ties his own style of interpretation to the words and actions of citizens.

"Compensation" is the beginning, the "smallest arc of this circle" of power (p. 96). Emerson moves back and forth between shifting visions of the whole and detailed constructions of its parts—from floor to scaffolding and then back down again. Human actions, on this rendering, are awesome spectacles that reveal a deeper layer of meaning: they are also products of the tones that color our own voices and that we can hear only when we see the reactions they elicit in others. Human actions, in Emerson's own words, like all of nature, are composed of opposites. They constitute a "polarity" from near and far, we might say. Hot and cold, ebb and flow: "An inevitable dualism bisects nature, so that each thing is a half, and suggests another thing to make it whole." This dualism extends to human nature as well, and to political and social relations. We must pay dearly for the finer things. Mild laws encourage vigilantism; harsh laws, light sentences. "If the government is a terrific democracy, the pressure is resisted by an over-charge in the citizen, and life glows with a fiercer flame" (p. 100).

In these passages Emerson anticipates a similar argument by Simone Weil in her essay "The *Iliad*, Poem of Might." There Weil also argues for something akin to a natural retribution. The powerful, because they feel no resistance, have no time to deliberate and consider the consequences of their actions. They inevitably overstep and overreach, finally becoming the victims of their own might.[51] Emerson calls this the "ancient doctrine of Nemesis, who keeps watch in the universe and lets no offense go unchastised."[52] But his argument does not rest on a phenomenology of violence like Weil's. It is not the grotesque effortlessness of the powerful as they destroy their enemies that ultimately brings down the powerful. In Emerson, the balance of justice is restored by the "portrait" of ourselves that we paint through our words in the eye of the other.[53]

When we have done someone an injustice we speak fearfully, and the fear that we will be called to account soon makes us hated for what we did. "There is hate in him and fear in me."[54] It is not so much that we are gov-

[51] Simone Weil, "The *Iliad*, Poem of Might," in *The Simone Weil Reader*, ed. George A. Panichas (New York: David McKay, 1977), p. 163.

[52] Emerson, "Compensation," p. 107.

[53] Ibid., p. 110.

[54] Ibid., p. 111.

erned and then judged by an external, universal standard as Hector was after he slew Patroclus. For Emerson, "a man cannot speak but he judges himself."[55] We condemn ourselves in our own words—not explicitly, but in our tone and phrasing. Similarly, "There is confession in the glances of our eyes, in our smiles, in salutations, and the grasp of hands." There is no avoiding it; a "man passes for that he is worth."[56] When we sow fear in the hearts of others, we seal our own fate. Fear is not, as Hobbes thought, the basis for social cooperation, but "an instructor of great sagacity and the herald of all revolutions."[57] The justice that fear heralds, according to Emerson, is the intuitive justice of retribution, not the far-off Hobbesian promise of a future life of peace and material comfort.

A citizen schooled in the laws of compensation, then, could read his own confessions more quickly and rewrite them before "vice glasses his eye."[58] He would be less confident that he possessed the ring of Gyges or that fear was the best way to guarantee social cooperation. In short, the Emersonian citizen would read the images he projects just as he would read nature and the products of his labor. The simpler the language he can use to represent his treatment of his fellow citizens, the more likely that he will remain in control of his own "portrait" and its effects on others. The more tangled he becomes in his own gestures, the more uncertain he is of his own interpretations, the more fearful he makes others and the less they hold in common.

At the beginning of "Circles" Emerson alerts us that he will be addressing a second dimension of action—not its compensatory "polarity" but its instability. Every action has a tendency to be superseded by a greater action; every object is impermanent (p. 302). Actions are sounds that gradually fade, not images that endure. The cause of this impermanence, Emerson suggests, or at least what activates this change, is perspective. We would call it our frame of reference. The most permanent structure in the eyes of one person becomes only a way station on the road to another's destination. "An orchard, good tillage, good grounds, seem a fixture, like a gold mine, or a river, to a citizen; but to a large farmer, not much more fixed than the state of the crop" (p. 303). What Schumpeter called the process of "creative destruction," Emerson seems to view as continuing enclosure.

What drives this process? It is, Emerson claims, something rooted deep in the human soul. It is not the simple search for more general truths, but a distrust of approbation. The drive to overpower nature and the world we have constructed out of it springs from intellectual insecurity. "We thirst

[55] Ibid., p. 110.
[56] Emerson, "Spiritual Laws," p. 159.
[57] Emerson, "Compensation," p. 111.
[58] Emerson, "Spiritual Laws," p. 159.

for approbation, yet cannot forgive the approver. The sweet of nature is love; yet if I have a friend I am tormented by my imperfections" (p. 307). And as our circles of friends are redrawn so that we do not have to confront the fearsome thought that they might see through us, we rationalize our actions by underlining the others' shortcomings. A wider circle is needed to avoid their imagined deficiencies, and we soon forget that it was our own deficiency, our own fear of disapproval, that forced us outward.

This repeated redrawing of our world—Emerson calls it "swift circumscription" (p. 311)—is exhausting. Approbation and distrust again follow one another in rapid succession until the only escape is silence. Not the silence of the hermit, but the silence of the poet who can step out of his own field of vision for a moment and look back over the course of this swift circumscription. Then he can describe a new circle from this "platform" that gives us some practical, temporary purchase on our common lives (pp. 310–11).

We are, he tells us, like the impermanent world, but we need not let this impermanence get to us. "There is no virtue which is final; all are initial." By this Emerson means that viewed from the perspective of the other, one's prudence or one's sense of justice may appear off-center, extreme, or insensitive. Which debts must be paid first? There is no final answer. The best we can do is "experiment" and "unsettle all things." If accused of talking in circles, Emerson says: "No facts are to me sacred; none are profane; I simply experiment, an endless seeker with no Past at my back" (p. 318). Once we understand our own character as a product of experimentation and provisional enclosure, we can bear up much better under the constant reshuffling. It is not so much that the poet steps outside the concentric circles of approbation and distrust as that he is able to see how they extend across his own character, remaking it as they remake the contours of nature and trade. This is the only home a citizen can have on a surface that is not "fixed, but sliding" (p. 314). Poise is the political value the Emersonian law of circularity teaches, just as the law of compensation teaches self-awareness and the value of experience and plainspokenness in politics. The poise citizens need is not the Sophoclean moral virtue of balancing on the "razor's edge of fate" or the bending with the wind and current that Martha Nussbaum has singled out for praise.[59] It is the poise you need to keep your feet from flying out from under you as you skate across sliding surfaces. It requires an eye for the grain and an ability to lean into the turn. It is what skaters call getting on your edges. It is a dynamic, not a static, balance, which enables citizens to mitigate the effects of their own insecurity.

[59] Martha Nussbaum, *The Fragility of Goodness* (New York: Cambridge University Press, 1986).

Emersonian political education is not didactic civic education: it is not to be found in the prescribed duties of civics texts. "What we do not call education is more precious than that which we call so."[60] Nor is it the pious proclamation of ideals of moral excellence and individual rights. For Emerson, political education is found in the reconstruction of words and actions governed by the laws of compensation and swift circumscription. He offers his readers a way of reading themselves in their surroundings as they meet head-on the challenges that the powers of nature, trade, and language itself create. To the extent that democracy depends on experience and poise so that citizens can hear themselves as well as one another, Emersonian self-reliance can be an important political asset for democratic citizens. In a world in which actions are compensatory and their effects unpermanent poise is no small achievement.

## Emerson Today

To illustrate how this Emersonian democratic character can be transposed into today's neocorporatist context, I begin with two very different cases. The first is a case described by Lucie E. White, a legal aid attorney representing a welfare mother at a fair hearing.[61] The story White tells is about recognizing the complexity of dialogue, the interplay of consumerism and clientism, and the arrogance of expert authority. It illustrates the Emersonian law of compensation and its relevance for democratic political education.

As White tells the story, Mrs. G, a black mother of two, is appealing a ruling that she must return part of her benefits from Aid to Families with Dependent Children because of additional income she received from an insurance company after an automobile accident. White reports that, as her attorney, she advised Mrs. G of two possible lines of defense. She could blame the caseworker, a black woman, for telling her to keep the insurance money, or she could request that an exception be made to the "lump sum rule" on the grounds that the one-time insurance payment was used for necessities such as personal health care items and school shoes for Mrs. G's daughters.

White then describes what she heard Mrs. G say in response to White's own questions at the fair hearing, after they had rehearsed Mrs. G's testi-

---

[60] Emerson, "Spiritual Laws," p. 133.

[61] Lucie E. White, "Subordination, Rhetorical Skills, and Sunday Shoes: Notes on the Hearing of Mrs. G," in *At the Boundaries of Law*, ed. Martha Albertson Fineman and Nancy Sweet Thomadsen (New York: Routledge, 1991), pp. 40–58.

mony. To White's total surprise, we are told, Mrs. G balked. She "stammered" when White asked her about showing the check to the caseworker before cashing it and then repeatedly said she could not remember for sure even though she had earlier described these events to White quite clearly. When she then tried to enlist Mrs. G in the second line of defense, White says, the same thing happened. Mrs. G described the necessities she had purchased with the insurance money. When asked directly why she had to buy new shoes, she looked back at White with an unreadable expression. Then, according to White, Mrs. G stated in a voice that "sounded different—stronger, more composed" that the new shoes were for church. The girls already had school shoes.[62]

In her account of the experience, White congratulates Mrs. G for standing up for her own conception of personal dignity and for showing solidarity with the caseworker, another black woman. But Mrs. G is not the only one who finds a voice of her own in this drama. The attorney demonstrates through this candid account of her own narrow construction of the alternatives open to Mrs. G just how deaf she was to the sound of her own professional voice. White thought she was making perfectly good sense to Mrs. G. The arguments were presented simply; the choice seemed clear. She thought she saw agreement in Mrs. G's eyes. But under questioning, Mrs. G was looking back at her with "an expression I couldn't read." It was the stammering, the seemingly evasive tone of voice, and then the cautious pride that finally made Mrs. G's position clear and made attorney White aware of how she must have sounded to her client: confident that they had exhausted all the reasonable lines of defense. In her retelling of the case, White has found another voice of her own by hearing how she sounded to Mrs. G. It took Mrs. G's emotional strength to resist the pressures she was under before White could hear what she herself sounded like as an expert.

In Emersonian terms, White's matter-of-fact statement of the legal strategies open to Mrs. G elicits a modest but firm compensatory response: professional expertise provokes a competing moral imperative. This in turn leads White to attend to her own assumptions and rephrase her arguments for a wider audience in print. Her own political education becomes the starting point for a conversation among professionals in what Ellison's invisible man called "black and white."

White's political education in this case may be exceptional, but it reveals what kinds of citizens professionals and their clients are capable of becoming. Both White and Mrs. G learn how to listen to the administrative rules governing liability, eligibility, and coverage that often conspire to silence the voice of the other. White hears how Mrs. G understands these

<hr>

62 Ibid., p. 45.

rules: for those on the margins, it is not always worth sacrificing personal dignity and solidarity for a temporary grant of eligibility. Mrs. G's seeming unreasonableness turns out to be quite reasonable given the strength of her religious convictions and her love for her daughters. White's newfound modesty is complemented by a new sensitivity to the voice of the other and, equally important, to her own voice as well. It is this political education, at close quarters, to which Emerson alerts us, despite his own coldheartedness.

The story of Mrs. G, then, illustrates how the stiff political voices within some quarters of the policymaking process can be rewoven so that both professionals and clients can escape this tunnel of rules and regulations. In the simulated classroom of Mrs. G's fair hearing, where Weberian matter-of-factness has been the dominant tone, the boundaries of self and other are redrawn; one political voice gives rise to another. In this case we can feel how compensation moves the professional in response to the quiet strength of her client. Beyond professional policymaking spaces like these, however, where the narcissistic imagery of the mall prevails, Emerson's law of circularity, "swift circumscription," gives us more purchase. The imagery of consumerism does not respect quiet strength: it quickly overwhelms it with cynicism and facile irony. What is the task of an Emersonian democratic political education in the world of malls, mirrors, and videotapes? What character strengths do citizens need to keep track of themselves and keep in touch with one another under this bright light? What contribution, if any, can public intellectuals make to democratic political education in this context?

The example I have chosen to respond to these questions is the intimate spectacle I began with, the Iran-contra affair. It is less compact and finished than the story of Mrs. G. It is also, as I suggested at the beginning, striking for the way it combines, almost simultaneously, the intimacy of clientism and the spectacle of consumerism. For both these reasons it poses a much greater challenge to democratic theory.

Understood from an Emersonian perspective, the Iran-contra affair teaches us just how difficult it is to come to terms with power when public discourse revolves around the reflections of trustworthy and sinister faces. But the plot is not as linear and the lessons are not as clear for either consumers of public policies or public intellectuals. In this case the law of swift circumscription applies, and power does not move back and forth in compensatory cycles. It expands, fades, and then reappears, driven by insecurity and self-aggrandizement, creating treacherous surfaces on which democratic political dialogue must find some foothold. This, of course, has not happened yet. Under an Emersonian light, the Iran-contra affair gives us a sharper picture of the obstacles that democratic political education now faces.

The main events in the Iran-contra affairs, as Theodore Draper has correctly called them,[63] are tangled but no longer opaque. Who actually did what is no longer much disputed.[64] And even who knew what and when they knew it seems to be settled. What is interesting about this episode in United States foreign policymaking is the way it has moved out from its epicenter and in the process strengthened rather than weakened the national security state—the engine of Manichean rhetoric that has driven this part of the politics of policymaking. Americans appear to be more anxious to trust in the images of national security since the Iran-contra affairs, and this trust reached its zenith in the Persian Gulf War. The Iran-contra affairs made spectacular images more, not less effective as the medium of policymaking.

The sale of military arms to Iran, contrary to stated United States policy, and the supply of weapons to the insurgent contra forces in Nicaragua, in violation of United States laws, are the two points from which a series of overlapping and conflicting investigations, hearings, and trials have emanated. It is important to see the Iran-contra affairs in their totality, however. It is not just the sale of arms and the clandestine shipment of supplies, the shredded paper trail, and the profiteering that are important. Iran-contra began before these two projects got under way and continued literally until the closing days of the Bush presidency, when several key figures were granted presidential pardons.

For my purposes what is most important is the way the unstable process of "circumscription" surrounding the main events made the later Persian Gulf War both possible and more likely. It made the Gulf War possible because the Iran-contra affairs broadcast a new set of images for foreign policymaking, designed to reestablish the national security state in light of the damage inflicted on it as a political ideology immediately after the Vietnam War.

Second, the Iran-contra affairs made the Gulf War more likely because they were only a muddling step in this direction. They depended on too many ambiguous images. There was Colonel Oliver North, but there was also CIA director William Casey. There was Khomeini, but there was also Israeli influence. And there were all the denials, counterdenials, and claims of "plausible deniability," which is neither a denial nor an admission but simply an evasion in the name of policymaking for its own sake. The plot thickened, patience grew short, and the ambiguous images, instead of being emblematic of national security interests and threats, began to slip

[63] Theodore Draper, *A Very Thin Line: The Iran-Contra Affairs* (New York: Hill and Wang, 1991).

[64] Lawrence E. Walsh, *Final Report of the Independent Counsel for Iran/Contra Matters,* 3 vols. (Washington, D.C.: Government Printing Office, August 4–December 3, 1993).

through the grasp of image makers and handlers. They were not, in Emerson's sense, "handsome" truths. The Gulf War, in contrast, seemed clean, at least as it was depicted in the media. It was fought between the latest forces of good and evil. It was staged and videotaped for mass consumption. The Gulf War finished what Iran-contra started: the resurrection of national security policymaking.

National security as the organizing ideal of United States foreign policymaking originated in the late 1940s with the Korean War and a global system of alliances and international agencies. "The central innovation of the 1947 National Security Act," better known at the time as the "Unification Act," writes Harold Koh,

> was its recognition that the management of this complex structure of alliances and agencies required a national security system centered in the executive branch. The act therefore sought to place American governmental decisions regarding warmaking, intelligence, covert operations, military sales, and military aid under the executive's unified and coordinated control. As originally structured by the act, the national security system had two key features. First the system was designed to be personally managed by a strong plebiscitary president with support of a bureaucratic institutional presidency. Second, the system was intended to operate not just in times of declared war, but also during a "false peace." Thus, the system was meant to be flexible enough not only to meet the pressing demands of the cold war, but to cope with new and unknown challenges that were yet to come: for example, overt undeclared wars, such as the Korean conflict, and overt creeping wars, such as the Vietnam War, that start and build before anyone is fully aware.[65]

This ideal of national security, of course, has been used to rationalize a variety of adventures and excesses, but the relevant feature is the conscious decision to couple plebiscitary appeal and bureaucratic support. The "commander in chief" would have to be able to appeal directly to the people and at the same time be able to count on a unified executive bureaucracy to produce and implement policy.

Initially, what smoothed the way for popular consumption of this ideal was the Cold War imagery of rollback and containment. These metaphors were soon combined under Eisenhower with a "domino theory" of international conflict. These images, however, conjuring up the epidemic spread of communism and the seemingly inevitable fall of its victims, lost their bite as Southeast Asia resisted United States forces in the late 1960s. To reverse this and reestablish the ideal of national security, policymakers

[65] Harold Hongju Koh, *The National Security Constitution: Sharing Power after the Iran-Contra Affair* (New Haven: Yale University Press, 1990), p. 102.

introduced a new metaphor: the Vietnam syndrome. By the late 1970s, after the "loss" of Southeast Asia and the Iranian hostage crisis, a new diagnosis based on this psychological metaphor was offered. The spread of communism was not due to its epidemic proportions or to simple Newtonian mechanics. The "free world" itself was at fault: its leader, the United States, suffered from a weakness of will. The United States couldn't pull the trigger. When Ronald Reagan, in the language of Hollywood, regularly told the Soviet Union, the Nicaraguans, and Congress, "Go ahead, make my day," he was demonstrating just how tough a gunslinger he was. Americans were treated to a new image: this Rambo was not going to back down, and the plebiscitary support for national security shot back up, at least for the moment.[66]

After the disastrous Lebanon war and the bombing of an American marine base in Beirut, the imagistic reconstruction of national security in the 1980s focused more exclusively on Central America. An alleged communist dictatorship in Nicaragua and the leftist guerrillas in El Salvador were next in line. But despite the bravado, the picture was still murky. Soviet arms shipments to Daniel Ortega and alleged guerrilla atrocities in El Salvador were often overshadowed by memories of Anastasio Somoza, ghastly acts of Salvadoran "death squads," and heroic stories of peasant resistance. At the same time, the Iran-Iraq war and the economic need for stability in the Middle East made the continued demonizing of Khomeini more risky. Out of this chaos came the Iran-contra affairs—a magic formula concocted by the supposedly supportive national security bureaucracy to renew the national security ideal. Rid Central America of communism and restore United States hegemony in the Middle East.

Hubris and self-deception characterized this joint venture from the start. Interrupted briefly by the crusade against Manuel Noriega, it defined United States foreign policy through the last half of the 1980s and dominated domestic politics even more than the neoconservative social agenda. It failed, however, to cure the Vietnam syndrome. To say that the Iran-contra affairs unraveled is to miss the critical Emersonian dynamic. Iran-contra was not an unwinding string of illicit arrangements but a process of self-enclosure with one circle of power giving rise and then giving way to the next. Let me briefly trace these circles.

The boundaries of power that enclosed the National Security Council and its staff were first redrawn when Casey, North, and Richard Secord

---

66 "Boy, I'm glad I saw *Rambo* last night. Now I know what to do next time." Ronald Reagan, testing his microphone before a press conference following the release of thirty-nine United States hostages in Beirut, *New York Times*, July 1, 1985. Also, Richard Slotkin, *Gunfighter Nation: The Myth of the Frontier in Twentieth-Century America* (New York: Atheneum, 1992), pp. 649-52.

created their own private company, the Enterprise, and its satellite funding sources in order to hide CIA involvement and circumvent Congress. Then the capture of one of their operatives by the Sandinistas broke this second circle of power. The result was the creation of a more public body, the Tower Commission, narrowly charged to exonerate the president and call attention to the need for bureaucratic reorganization. Under scrutiny by the press, the feebleness of this response and the narrow, incomplete nature of its investigation made a wider, more public congressional inquiry unavoidable. The investigations and televised hearings of the select House and Senate committee overshadowed the findings of the Tower Commission and precipitated even wider-ranging investigations and commentaries by journalists and filmmakers. Bill Moyers's 1987 PBS documentary, "The Secret Government," punctuated with MTV images and protest songs, retold the story of the national security state and in a judicial tone raised "the constitutional question": If national security can justify the suppression of individual rights and democracy in other countries, will it soon be used to threaten the rights of American citizens as well? But Moyers's lament was lost in the very medium he tried to exploit. As much as he tried to caricature North, Moyers was no match for him.

Oliver North's performances during this period, whether they were broadcast "live" or spliced into critical documentaries, epitomize the Emersonian dynamic of circumscription. More than anything else, North projected an image that broke open the official circles of power and redrew the boundaries of public display. He appealed directly to the individual consumer of American foreign policy, and in doing so he set the pace of the hearings and the scope of the questions. At the same time North anticipated the next circle of power, the criminal investigation directed by Special Prosecutor Lawrence Walsh.

North did not have to do this alone. Anxious to seize a political opportunity, members of the select committee granted limited immunity to witnesses testifying before them who correctly anticipated that they would be the target of Walsh's investigation. Not only were they able to intentionally taint future testimony in court, thereby creating grounds for successful appeals, but they also fed and capitalized on the political appetites and insecurities of the members of the select committee who were caught between the fear of a public backlash if they looked as if they were going after a popular president in a replay of the Watergate hearings and their own lust for the political spotlight. Unsure how to handle their witnesses—witnesses all too willing to tell all for the sake of criminal immunity—the members were easily put on the defensive by the likes of North and his lawyer.

The dynamics of immunity, while legally complex, offer a fascinating study in the details of "swift circumscription" and the impermanence of the power of the Office of the Independent Counsel and the trial court. Congress's grant of immunity to North, for example, did not require that he first give private immunized testimony to the select committee. This left the committee both unprepared and unable to impeach his public testimony when it contradicted private testimony.[67] Even though the OIC made strenuous efforts to shield itself from North's public testimony, North's lawyer called Robert McFarlane, who conveniently admitted that he had been deeply affected by North's immunized public testimony.[68] North's convictions were subsequently overturned on appeal as a result, and the same thing happened in the case against John Poindexter.[69] These successful appeals were made possible by the defendants' abilities to widen the circle of power. The OIC had sought to shield itself from all immunized testimony given to Congress about North's and Poindexter's actions. But the OIC had not anticipated that the introduction of testimony by defense witnesses mentioning how *they* had been affected by the immunized testimony they heard would taint the prosecution.

In short, the power of the national security bureaucracy gave way to the power of a special commission, which in turn triggered Congress's jealous power of oversight. This power was dampened and distorted by the power of the Office of the Independent Counsel, appointed jointly by Congress and the Justice Department, whose own power was then undercut by appeals courts and a series of presidential pardons. In the world of imagistic power, there is no outer circle, no final closure.

As we look at the Iran-contra affairs as a sequence of expanding circles of power in desperate search for an effective expression of national security, they also form a set of shifting surfaces whose fault lines and tremors make it difficult to keep one's balance as a consumer of public policy. The competing definitions of the problem offered by the Tower Commission, the Democratic and Republican congressional committee reports, criminal indictments, and pardons could not be rearranged using the ambiguous images of Oliver North and John Poindexter, Ortega and Khomeini. On the contrary, the imagery seemed to exacerbate the conflicts between these competing circles of power. Plebiscitary and bureaucratic support for the ideal of national security in the midst of these clashes could not repair the foreign policymaking process.

To give national security a higher resolution, the ambiguous imagery and the competing, overlapping circles of power that had emanated from

67 Walsh, *Final Report*, 1:33.
68 Ibid., p. 122.
69 Ibid., p. 136.

the epicenters of the Iran-contra affairs had to be scrapped. That meant that the Vietnam syndrome had to be resuscitated and a new campaign, less ambiguous and more plebiscitary, had to be waged against it. From the beginning, the Gulf War was staged to simultaneously reestablish the need for a national security state and extinguish the Vietnam syndrome. For mass consumer appeal it is unmatched. Dubbed the Nintendo war, in it television producers and the military worked symbiotically with one another, despite the latter's objections to the new press rules, to heighten public interest and manufacture public support for a clean victory over aggression.[70] At the same time, the script for this video was written by military experts who explicitly described just how much better the national security system was working now than in the Vietnam era.

Take the case of Colonel Harry Summers Jr. In 1984 Summers published *On Strategy*, a loyalist critique of the Vietnam War.[71] According to Summers, in language that eerily prefigured the Gulf War, the doctrines of nuclear deterrence, limited warfare, and counterinsurgency had intimidated the professional military, while dovish theories of just war deprived the United States, and especially the military, of the public support needed to win the war. The war, he claimed, was an act of aggression from North Vietnam, and these false doctrines so obscured this basic fact that it became impossible to win. The United States won the battles it did fight in Southeast Asia, Summers argued, but it was not fighting the right battles in the right ways.

To avoid the debilitating doctrines and moral theories that subverted United States policy during the Vietnam War, Summers suggests, wars should be fought according to a doctrine of middle-intensity warfare, regulated by a principle of national security and world order and prosecuted according to Clausewitzean rules of strategy. Unlike the low-intensity doctrine of the early 1980s that got the United States involved with untrustworthy surrogates and minor client states in small brushfires,[72] the doctrine of "mid-intensity conflict" brings massive military force to bear in regions of the world that are necessary for United States national security. Military force should not be used misguidedly to build social and political institutions; it should be used to "make the enemy sue for peace." It should be backed by strong domestic support; it should be conducted without unnecessary prying and carping by the media; and it should be done under a single command. Overcoming the Vietnam syndrome re-

---

[70] Bruce Cumings, *War and Television* (New York: Verso, 1992), pp. 103–28.

[71] Harry G. Summers Jr., *On Strategy: A Critical Analysis of the Vietnam War* (New York: Dell, 1984).

[72] See Michael T. Klare and Peter Kornbluh, eds., *Low Intensity Warfare: Counterinsurgency, Proinsurgency, and Antiterrorism in the Eighties* (New York: Pantheon, 1988).

quired the application of these rules of engagement, popular support, and a military with the moral character to stand up to civilian bureaucrats and academic intellectuals. When Summers appeared on television during the Gulf War as a network commentator, he declared the Gulf War a success on precisely these grounds.[73] The "remarkable trinity," he announced, had been restored. And the *Wall Street Journal* agreed: "Victory in the Gulf War Exorcises the Demons of the Vietnam Years."[74]

The Gulf War was successfully coded in images designed to promote this Manichean moral realism. General Norman Schwarzkopf replaced Colonel North; Saddam Hussein replaced Ortega and the Iranians. Unlike the Iran-contra affairs, the unambiguous power of the military seemed to be targeted on a demonic enemy with laserlike precision. There were no enterprising soldiers of fortune to excite the press and disturb public opinion, no whitewashes, no televised hearings, no special prosecutors, and effectively no congressional dissent. Plebiscitary and bureaucratic support for the national security state, despite the fall of communism in the Soviet Union and Eastern Europe, was for the moment, at least, restored.

If this Emersonian reading of imagistic foreign policymaking is accurate, what does it suggest about the role of the public intellectual and the task of political education? In a world in which the violence of war has become antiseptically reduced to a video game and the shifting surfaces of power have been at least temporarily stabilized, is there a place for Emerson's naturalism? In other words, how do we come to terms with power when it is electronically managed and no longer ripples through our lives in waves of "swift circumscription"? Emerson's lens enables us to focus on extended events like the Iran-contra affairs in which there is some natural texture, even if it is the texture of quasi-judicial hearings, but if the future turns out to resemble the Gulf War, an Emersonian public intellectual may have a more difficult time. It is too early to tell.

My Emersonian interpretations of the voices of expert authority in the case of Mrs. G and the images of the policymaking process in the case of the Iran-contra affairs both rely on synesthetic metaphors to help us keep our balance as we traverse the shifting surfaces of power. This, I have suggested, seems to be an effective way of fostering a democratic political education within limits. The Gulf War seems to defy this kind of rewording.

For example, consider the bombing of Iraqi soldiers along with Palestinians and other civilians as they fled Kuwait City. The images of this "turkey shoot," as some United States military personnel described it, were carefully managed and sanitized in order to maintain a moral differ-

---

[73] See his sequel, Harry G. Summers Jr., *Strategy II: A Critical Analysis of the Gulf War* (New York: Dell, 1992).
[74] Ben Wattenberg, *Wall Street Journal*, March 1, 1991.

ence between Iraqi atrocities and Allied liberation.[75] These images were not motivated by Emersonian anxiety or intellectual insecurity. The laws of compensation and circularity do not apply easily. How one begins to put these images together in order to initiate democratic discussion is a question that takes us beyond Emerson's natural language of power—if not into Baudrillard's "hyperreality," then at least into a world so slick that it is free of any lasting memories.[76]

Earlier I argued that a theory of democratic political education can draw on the insights of past political theorists like Thucydides, Aristotle, and Dewey who have called our attention to the historical dimension of power, the way language—spoken and written—shifts and buckles under its own weight, and the importance of a self-critical stance toward our own voices and visual habits. Emerson, I believe, combines these insights in a language that strives to be free of technical jargon. He gives his readers a way of coming to terms with some of the dominant forms of power by emphasizing the importance of poise to political character. This is not a precious or genteel manner. Poise describes one way to listen closely and keep one's balance in the unpredictable rush of events in a modern democracy.

## Democratic Character and Moral Virtue

Throughout I have stressed the contrast between the political character that liberal theory as political education has fostered in clients, consumers, and experts and the political character a democratic theory of power would cultivate. Emerson plays a key role on both sides. Now, in closing, I want to suggest one possible point of intersection between Emersonian democratic character and the liberal moral virtues of tolerance and reasonableness in discussion. Just as Emersonian democratic theory may have severe limitations when confronted with the frictionless surfaces of the Gulf War, liberal theory still has something to tell us about the moral virtues that clientism and consumerism have rendered impotent.

Political character refers to the skills, knowledge, habits, and dispositions that citizens bring to their encounter with power. Consumers and

[75] Asa Aksoy and Kevin Robbins, "Exterminating Angels: Morality, Violence and Technology in the Gulf War," in *Triumph of the Image: The Media's War in the Persian Gulf—A Global Perspective*, ed. Hamid Mowlana, George Gerbner, and Herbert I. Schiller (Boulder, Colo.: Westview, 1992), p. 209.

[76] For a detailed account of the broadcasting of the war, see Douglas Kellner, *The Persian Gulf TV War* (Boulder, Colo.: Westview, 1992). On Baudrillard's interpretation, see Christopher Norris, *Uncritical Theory: Postmodernism, Intellectuals, and the Gulf War* (Amherst: University of Massachusetts Press, 1992).

clients have the political character that makes trust in expert authority sustainable. They can bear up under the risks they face as consumers and the dependence they share with other clients of professional service providers. This is not a matter of either Hobbesian calculation or Lockean Stoicism. The political character of clients and consumers is an active Millian and Rawlsian response to the dual imperatives of progressive individuality and political stability. Political clients and consumers must know how to look for the promise of progress and heed the domesticated voices of those above and below them within a neocorporatist political economy.

Emersonian democratic citizens have the ability and disposition to listen more self-critically to their own harsh voices as they echo through the voices of others, to keep their balance as they engage in frustrating and even frightening political dialogue, and to remain aware of their limited power to fashion provisional solutions to political problems. They know how to compose themselves for democratic politics. These strengths of character, I have argued, are to be preferred to the accommodating dispositions of clients and the narrow-minded skills of consumers.

Liberal moral virtues are not the same as democratic character. Toleration, according to Rawls, marks the "historical origin of political liberalism."[77] As a moral virtue tolerance is especially demanding, because it requires acceptance of practices or beliefs that liberals consider morally wrong. This extends to even the most intolerant minorities, right up to the point where the actions of the intolerant systematically threaten the liberties of others. The liberal arguments for tolerating even the intolerant include prudential caution and the Millian belief that it is hard to anticipate the contributions unpopular minorities may make to human progress. Toleration can also be justified on the Kantian grounds of respect for individual autonomy.[78] Rawls also is tempted to say that in a just society toleration may persuade the intolerant to be more tolerant out of gratitude.[79] His more considered opinion is that toleration is owed to those who are capable of reasonableness in discussion within a reasonably pluralistic society, and conversely, reasonableness in discussion includes, among other things, being tolerant of those who hold reasonable morally comprehensive doctrines to which we object.

Because with the help of others they may be able to achieve goals they could not otherwise reach either alone or in opposition, liberals should be

77 John Rawls, *Political Liberalism* (New York: Columbia University Press, 1993), p. xxiv.

78 Susan Mendus, *Justifying Toleration: Conceptual and Historical Perspectives* (Cambridge: Cambridge University Press, 1988).

79 John Rawls, *A Theory of Justice* (Cambridge: Harvard University Press, 1971), pp. 219, 474.

reasonable in discussion. They should be able to make concessions, search for areas of agreement, and avoid unreasonable demands that will drive others away prematurely. Not only may this serve their long-term interests, it may reveal new areas of agreement and new goals they were not aware of.[80]

Second, reasonableness requires that liberals be willing to play the role of the loyal opposition. The views of minorities can be voiced in a variety of ways within a political system based on majority rule, but political minorities still remain at a distinct disadvantage regardless of mitigating devices like proportional representation. Therefore liberals, because they all are likely at one time or another, on one issue or another, to be in the minority, should learn how to contest the views of the majority without contesting its right to have the greater say. Knowing the limits of contestation is an important element of reasonableness in discussion. Contesting the majority's will too sharply may create deeper divisions than existing political institutions can cope with.

In a mixed, neocorporatist society, these moral virtues of tolerance and reasonableness in discussion are likely to be exploited cynically by some and then regarded skeptically by others. As intolerant groups exploit others' commitment to toleration, the practical value of tolerance as moral excellence declines. Unholy alliances between civil libertarians and intolerant sects only depreciate tolerance. Reasonableness in discussion suffers the same fate. For clients and consumers, reasonableness too often is a smoke screen for self-serving bargains. Be reasonable, women and minorities are told, while the remedies they have lobbied for are being implemented one step at a time "with all deliberate speed."[81] As moral virtues, tolerance and reasonableness are unexceptionable. Without the composure to act on these virtues, however, we quickly become cynical about them.

Can Emersonian democratic character avoid this cynicism? Mari J. Matsuda's reflection on her own professional voice illustrates how tolerance and reasonableness may be reconstructed and revived within an Emersonian orientation toward power. Like Lucie White's discussion of the case of Mrs. G, Matsuda shows how expert authorities can be deaf to the power of their own voices, the unreasonableness of their own assumptions, and their own intolerance of other accents. The result, in place of cynicism, is a new interpretation of these moral virtues based on political experience.

[80] See Martin Benjamin, *Splitting the Difference: Compromise and Integrity in Ethics and Politics* (Lawrence: University Press of Kansas, 1990).
[81] *Brown v. Board of Education*, 349 U.S. 294 (1955).

Everyone, Matsuda reminds us, has an accent. There is no separating you and your accent, and "someone who tells you they [*sic*] don't like the way you speak is quite likely telling you that they don't like you."[82] This hostility toward different accents, however, is not easily corrected within liberal society. In theory, when accent discrimination can be linked to discrimination based on national origins it is prohibited by law in the United States. In practice, when an employer argues that a foreign accent becomes an impediment to communication and therefore to job performance, the discrimination is not unlawful. It is the status of the language in question, however, not the clarity of the speech or the status of the job or profession, that often determines whether the listener can understand what is being said. Doctors and teachers may suffer from this kind of discrimination as much as street-level bureaucrats and radio announcers. "Low-status accents will sound foreign and unintelligible. High-status accents will sound clear and competent."[83]

Liberal toleration and reasonableness in discussion require that accent discrimination not be a cover for more invidious discrimination based on race, ethnicity, or national origin. But liberal toleration and reasonableness in discussion also require that speech, especially the speech of someone responsible for communicating with the public, must be generally intelligible. Matsuda questions the liberal assumption that the right of students, patients, and consumers of public services to intelligible communication overrides the right to equal treatment regardless of accent. The value of accommodating foreign accents—that is, the importance of learning how to understand low-status, seemingly unintelligible accents—she believes is greater than the value of uninterrupted service. Why?

One answer might be that accommodating foreign accents, like accommodating disabled students in so-called regular classrooms, places everyone on a more equal footing. But Matsuda suggests that this argument is too abstract. It ignores the experience of individuals who are, of necessity, always speaking with an accent. It perpetuates the myth of the accentless person as the best source of intelligible speech.

It took a student's voice to help me understand what hurt and enraged me about accent cases. After giving a formal presentation of my ideas on accent and Title VII to a group of Asian American students and faculty at a California University, I answered several questions. The questions were posed in formal "school" voices as were my answers—carefully phrased legal language

---

[82] Mari J. Matsuda, "Voices of America: Accent, Antidiscrimination Law and Jurisprudence for the Last Reconstruction," *Yale Law Journal* 100 (1991): 1329.

[83] Ibid., p. 1355.

in "acrolectal" accents. Suddenly a woman who had been silent during the entire exchange began to speak softly, without first raising her hand, without using her school voice. She was an Asian American student born and raised in Hawaii. She said quietly, "I don't see how they can come to our place and tell us we can't talk the way we talk," and she began to cry. As she spoke, I began to cry as well, and for the first time I realized that inside this law professor who argues doctrine and rationale was a person deeply wounded by the notion that people like me, people I grew up with, my parents, my aunts and uncles, are somehow unworthy because of the way we talk.[84]

A matter-of-fact Weberian teacher, taught to value the Socratic method, is tone-deaf to the power of expert authority. She can see the bright lines of Millian progress and hear the domesticated voices of Rawlsian citizens, but until she has been reminded of the experiences of "people like me, people I grew up with," she cannot hear her own voice with its peculiar acrolectal accent. Toleration and reasonableness in discussion depend on hearing accents more distinctly, not on pretending you can teach or force people to speak without them at all.

Reading Matsuda reminded me of a similar experience of my own. I was a graduate teaching assistant in 1975 leading a discussion section in an introductory course on American politics. Our text for the day was James L. Sundquist's *Dynamics of the Party System*, a study done for the Brookings Institution and published in 1973. Sundquist examines the prospects for a realignment of the American party system as a result of racial conflict, conflict over the Vietnam War, and conflicts over other related social issues such as abortion and crime. He concludes that if there is to be a "critical realignment," it will only be as a result of demands made by "blacks and their liberal allies." This is not something he appears to favor. "If the blacks," he argues, "heighten and focus their demands, if they unite behind them and present them with militance and determination, it is not impossible that they could bring the country to a new intensity of racial polarization."[85]

Trying to stay within the framework of Sundquist's argument, I labeled this the "black problem." Just as there was an antiwar problem and a "law and order" problem, I said, black militancy posed a problem, at least a potential one, for the stability of the party system. Soon after I said this, the one black student in the class politely but very gravely asked me what I meant by the "black problem." I immediately felt uncomfortable, realizing that as I had been characterizing the "black problem" I had been espe-

---

[84] Ibid., p. 1391.

[85] James L. Sundquist, *Dynamics of the Party System: Alignment and Realignment of Political Parties in the United States* (Washington, D.C.: Brookings Institution, 1973), p. 366.

cially aware of his presence in the class, hesitating just a bit and glancing quickly in his direction. I said I was just trying to summarize Sundquist's views, and that I did not think blacks were the real problem at all. Racism against blacks was the real problem. He did not respond to my explanation, even with a nod, and the class went on.

It was only many years later, reflecting on the opening lines of W. E. B. Du Bois's *The Souls of Black Folk*, that I realized how I had sounded to this student. "How does it feel to be a problem?" That is the question implicit in many otherwise well-meaning questions whites have put to blacks in the United States. "To the real question," Du Bois tells us, he answers "seldom a word."[86] I had used this young man, the only black student in the class, to represent the "black problem." He was there for the rest of us to see—a specimen of the potential cause of party realignment. When he asked me what I meant by the "black problem," he certainly already knew what I would say. The purpose of his question, I suspect, and his silence, was to let me hear what I said to him by repeating the "black problem" in his own voice. I had heard only my school voice when I tried to rephrase Sundquist's hypothesis. I had not heard the "real question": What is it like to be a person labeled a problem and then ignored as if it hadn't really happened to you?

Experiences like the one Matsuda describes and this one of my own may not be that common. Without a prior understanding of the way accents can be carriers of intolerance, Matsuda might well have responded unsympathetically to the student's comment. She would have heard it, no matter how quietly expressed, as an emotional outburst. Instead, she heard it as an echo of one of her own voices that belonged within a discussion of the harm done by seemingly reasonable discrimination against foreign accents. I did not hear the echo of my own voice until much later, after reading Du Bois.

These two cases illustrate only one possible intersection between the liberal moral virtues of toleration and reasonableness and Emersonian democratic political character, one that occurs within the confines of the classroom. In these cases toleration means listening hard precisely when the voice of the other sounds unreasonable and challenges our authority. Multiplying these points of intersection within other contexts is something public intellectuals can work on. They can prepare us to hear unspoken questions as Du Bois does and to read the silences of those who have been present to us only as problems. They can teach those of us who speak in schooled voices how to read the emotions in our own arguments.

---

[86] W. E. B. Du Bois, *The Souls of Black Folk*, in *Writings*, ed. Nathan Huggins (New York: Library of America, 1986), p. 363.

Emersonian democratic theory as political education would teach this kind of poise to those who possess "unhandsome" power so that they can hear "new yet unapproachable" voices.[87] It would teach us to listen to the students Matsuda and I have described without becoming defensive. It would teach us to recognize our own sideward glances and hesitations. It would be an education in power that sets aside faith in Hobbes's "prospective glasses" designed to look beyond the present circumstances.

According to Emerson, "We have learned that we do not see directly but mediately, and that we have no means of correcting these colored and distorting lenses. . . ."[88] "Power," Emerson reminds us, "keeps quite another road than the turnpikes of choice and will; namely the subterranean and invisible tunnels and channels of life."[89] Toleration and reasonableness are much harder to master within these subterranean and invisible tunnels and channels. There are no right and wrong turn signals on this road, no clearly marked interchanges.

Like the inhabitants of the Crystal City Underground, democratic citizens who accept responsibility for the power they generate and exercise cannot see very far around the next bend. It is as members of a company of travelers, who speak in different accents and are carving out the same channel, that democratic citizens need one another's willing cooperation, including the cooperation of the democratic theorist. This metaphor of political passage, just like competitive games, is open to abuse. The Emersonian democratic theorist must be able to articulate what it means to hold on to those whose voices sound alien and who might fall behind if the desire to see what lies ahead were given free rein.

[87] Emerson, "Experience," p. 72.
[88] Ibid., p. 75.
[89] Ibid., p. 67.

# Index